AIRPORTS ON-HOLD

TOWARDS RESILIENT INFRASTRUCTURES

Sara Favargiotti

ACKNOWLEDGMENTS

This book is the result of my PhD research titled "Airports On-hold. Towards Resilient Infrastructures" investigates the transitory condition as challenge for obsolete infrastructures, with particular attention to airfields. It also serves to update the investigation of the relation between small and medium airports and landscape in specific territories.

The research has been grown through several research experiences in different Universities. Thanks to the Office for Urbanization at Harvard Graduate School of Design, the University IUAV of Venice, the University of Genoa, the Universidad Autónoma de Barcelona, and the Leibniz Universität Hannover for hosting me during these years. These experiences have significantly improved my work and knowledge and they allowed me to meet such incredible and generous people.

Thanks to all professors of the Villard d'Honnecourt Doctoral Programme for the advices and the critiques. A special thanks to Mosè Ricci for guiding me during the doctoral years and beyond, always encouraging me and teaching me. Thanks to Charles Waldheim for sharing with me the passion for airports, involving me in an inspiring and challenging project. Thanks to Laura Cipriani, Sonja Dümpelmann, Alberto Ferlenga, Francesc Muñoz, Christian Salewski, and Johanna Schlaack for the inspiring conversations and the interest expressed on this work.

A special thanks to my family, Graziella and Carlo, Davide and Livia for having supported me during this travel. Thanks to Jeannette, Mathilde, Alessandra, Anna, Giorgia friends and reliable colleagues. Thanks to Barbara for the precious support with the translation. Thanks to all the LISt Lab team for their efforts and contributions. Thanks to all those who have sustained and encouraged me with advices and suggestions. Thanks to Andrea for all those travels we will do together.
Good journey!

CONTENTS

7   PREFACE | BOARDING

8   FOREWORD | An Interview with Charles Waldheim

14   INTRODUCTION | TAKE OFF

22   **1. A VIEW FROM ABOVE**
25   **1.1 Demystifying Infrastructural Myths**
       Peripheral territories
       The infrastructures and the crisis

32   **1.2 *La RE- Époque***
       Infrastructure Recycle beyond Urban Transformation
       Resilient Infrastructure towards Adaptive Landscapes

38   **1.3 From Glamour to Low-Cost Experience**
       Dis-comfort

48   **2. AIRPORT ON-HOLD**
50   **2.1 Airport, City and Territory**
       Big hub, regional, low-cost, on-hold airports

60   **2.2 Airport Life Cycle**
       On-hold state

68   **2.3 Mapping Airports On-hold**
       European contexts: Italy and Spain

80 **3. PLANNING OBSOLESCENCE**
Tendencies

84 **3.1 Technology**

87 **3.2 Landscape**

91 **3.3 Recycle**

102 **4. RESILIENT LANDSCAPE RESERVES**
A place to live instead of a place to leave!

105 **4.1 Airport Second Life**

107 **4.2 Devices for Airports On-hold: 4 tools**

110 **4.3 Experimentations: 3 cases**

138 **5. POSITIONS**
Significance in the European framework
International Research Platforms

150 **Conversations with**   Alberto Ferlenga
Laura Cipriani
Francesc Muñoz
Christian Salewski
Sonja Dümpelmann

176 **AFTERWORD | An Interview with Mosè Ricci**

184 **BIBLIOGRAPHY**

PREFACE

On the way to Lleida-Alguaire Airport
October 2011

In this remote part of inland Catalonia, I see around me vast stretches of cropland, small villages and flocks of sheep. With me are thirty young, curious architects - certainly not local - that roam fascinated by the vastness of this space. They have reached this place as I did, coming from different parts of Spain and utilizing various means. Getting closer, I enter into the main building. It could be a conference room, but catering has already organized a service so perfect that it could pass as a restaurant: I can imagine official lunches or even parties organized here, or perhaps a wedding. Actually, with its high tower, soaring towards infinity, amid the immensity of the surrounding fields, it seems like a church: a cathedral in the desert. Suddenly, I see a huge dark-grey mark in the landscape. And the sound of a single-engine airplane, humming overhead, reorders my thoughts: I'm in an airport. After three days I see the first airplane landing. But everything began few days before...
It's 6.10 in the morning and I'm already in a long queue at Gate D11. An "animated" trip is waiting for me. My compact and reliable trolley pulled by one hand, the ID document and the boarding pass—printed the day beforeready to be exhibited in the other hand, have allowed me to quickly pass the procedures for the security control. Despite it being very early in the morning and placed well ahead in the process, I find myself in a queue with hundreds of combative people, ready to run and to lay claim to a seat between row 03 - because the first three rows are always reserved for business class - and row 16, preferably the large seat next to the emergency exit—even if it's always only assigned to the "appropriate" people—and to guarantee the right to store their own luggage in the space above (and below) their seats. Finally, I find a seat and, shortly after, the plane takes off. The flight is very short, only an hour and forty minutes accompanied by the sequence of: crew welcoming, explanation of the emergency regulations, captain's greeting, control of tables, window covers, and belts position for take-off, description of food, snacks and drinks, garbage removal, duty free purchase options of cigarettes, perfumes, toys, scratch-cards, shuttle-bus tickets and... *"Gracias por viajar con nosotros, estamos llegando a en el Aeropuerto El Prat. Bienvenidos en Barcelona."* After the flight, there are "only" a couple of hours to wait for a local bus followed by another two hours to reach Lleida (in Catalan) or Lerida (in Castilian). Then, I hail a taxi and in half an hour I reach my destination: the Lleida-Alguaire Airport. I have one question that keeps coming to mind: why not land directly at this airport?

FOREWORD
AN INTERVIEW WITH CHARLES WALDHEIM

Charles Waldheim is a North American architect and urbanist. Waldheim's research examines the relations between landscape, ecology, and contemporary urbanism. He is author, editor, or co-editor of numerous books on these subjects, and his writing has been published and translated internationally. Waldheim is John E. Irving Professor at Harvard University's Graduate School of Design where he directs the School's Office for Urbanization. Waldheim is recipient of the Rome Prize Fellowship from the American Academy in Rome; the Visiting Scholar Research Fellowship at the Study Centre of the Canadian Centre for Architecture; the Cullinan Chair at Rice University; and the Sanders Fellowship at the University of Michigan. The interview has been carried at the Graduate School of Design, Harvard University, on November 12, 2013, on the occasion of the conference "Airport Landscape: Urban Ecologies in the Aerial Age" and it has been edited in July 2016.

This account situates the emergence of landscape as a medium of urbanism in a variety of sites. Most often the sites associated with rethinking the urban through landscape are found at the limits to a more strictly architectonic order for the shape of the city. Most often these are sites where a traditional understanding of the city as an extrapolation of architectural models and metaphors is no longer viable given the prevalence of larger forces or flows. These include ruptures or breaks in the architectonic logic of traditional urban form as compelled by ecological, infrastructural, or economic change. Landscape has been found relevant for sites in which a strictly architectural order of the city has been rendered obsolete or inadequate through social, technological, or environmental change. The discourse and practices of landscape urbanism have been found particularly useful for thinking through large infrastructural arrays such as ports and transportation corridors. Airports, in particular, have been central to the discourse and practice of landscape urbanism as sites whose scale, infrastructural connectivity, and environmental impacts outstrip a strictly architectonic model of city making.

From: "Introduction: From Figure to Field." Charles Waldheim, *Landscape as Urbanism: a general theory* (Princeton, New Jersey: Princeton University Press, 2016): 3.

SF | Why are you interested in studying airports?
CW | The Harvard GSD has this interest in Landscape Urbanism or Ecological Urbanism and in those discourses the airport is a very central case study from the beginning of the projects. This is because the other disciplines—architecture, urban design and planning—have not really developed a coherent approach to airports and so if you are interested in ecological performance and urban form then Landscape Urbanism or Ecological Urbanism provides a way of thinking about the city that integrates ecological function. People advocating for traditional or neo-traditional urban form, generally speaking overwhelmingly believe that if you put back a traditional urban model, you can get back something that's been lost socially or environmentally. The school's position is to try to be more progressive than that in terms of design, incorporating ecological function into the design of cities. It's an on-going project. The airport is a very good case study for me because it's very difficult

to argue for a traditionalist position about an airport. It's very difficult to make it look old. It's very difficult to try to put it back into the old structure of the city. Furthermore, it has a combination of specific characteristics. It has a centrality because airports tend to be planned very far away from cities but they become the center of the American cities, geographically. Airports have this horizontality where most of the space is really empty space that is engineered for margin of error or accident. And at the same time, it is among the most economically productive sites in the city that they serve. It is also among the most environmentally problematic. That combination of centrality, invisibility, environmental contamination and economic ability, makes them a very good case for us because it's a place where we can play offense, in a way..

SF | Which paradigms are imagined by research on *Airport Landscape*?
CW | Landscape Urbanism is very much interested in projects, not in plans. We don't really make any claims about larger territorial or national planning. In our culture we don't really have any planning mechanisms beyond the individual airport. The Federal Aviation Authority does require permits and environmental protection, State by State, more than a planning mechanism. What I've found is that describing an airport as a landscape is already an important conceptual break through. Just claiming it as a landscape gives us a kind of coherence, and a way of approaching it that if you simply did engineering or if you simple did architecture, it would lack. It allows for a more coherent framework and most often it is a mechanism that also allows us to plan for the ecological function of the site over time. It also allows us to think about what's outside the airport and what's on the airport in relationship to each other because you're thinking in a landscape way as opposed to thinking about buildings, land use or ownership. And the other thing that it does is it allows you to consider the planning of the airport, the life of the airport and then its decommissioning as one long life cycle.
The best Airport Afterlives cases studies that are built tend to be from Germany or Scandinavia. Among Operating Airports, Schiphol Airport, Oslo Airport and Munich Airport are good examples. For instance, Schiphol is an important node in Europe but for the designer the idea that it is constantly being updating allows a landscape architect to plan over time something more ecological rather than simply something architectural. There are several others in Europe that are very good examples of "operating" or "afterlives". In North America we have many more examples of decommissioned airports that are being converted. It is an international process also. But we are very much focused on being site-by-site, project-by-project. We don't really have any political or territorial agenda about planning at a larger scale.

SF | What is the specificity of an airport's renewal?
CW | We have this economic restructuring in the last thirty years which means we have a lot of brownfields, a lot of former industrial sites. In one way the abandoned airport is another brownfield. While we have the general category

of brownfield, we have more specifically at the airport a site that is typically too large and too peripheral and too contaminated to be redeveloped. In many places where you have brownfields, you either have shrinkage and you have no ability to rebuild or you have places that are rebuilding but the scale of the industry is such that you can usually or often convert that into some other form of use. The airport, because is so much larger and because it is typically so much further outside the city, resists that often. Sometimes it can be converted into housing, most often into suburban housing. Those examples also we are critiquing, because we really feel that converting an airport into more suburbs is not really much of an improvement. Rather we are looking at examples where landscape is used to remediate, to clean, but over long periods of time and in which landscape ecology strategies can be used to clean the air, the water and the ground over some time. That is different than the typical brownfield site. There are some parallels between larger brownfield sites that don't have the development pressure around them. What's unique about the airport is that most typically they are public, in a way that most brownfields are not public. In our culture, the ownership of the brownfield ends up being very important and because the airports are mostly public, they can more easily be converted than many brownfields can.

SF | How is recycling included in Landscape Urbanism or Ecological Urbanism?
CW | Recycling is one of the central claims of Landscape Urbanism. We can use ecological processes to clean, remediate and rebuild places like abandoned airports. Ten years ago we had a theory, now we can see projects around the world that are built. Examples are the High Line or Fresh Kills Park in New York, Millennium Park in Chicago, or the waterfront in Toronto. Increasingly, landscape architects are engaging in city structure. Ten years ago most of what we were doing could be described as large parks and it was. What has changed in the last ten years is that now landscape architects like Adriaan Geuze, James Corner, Michael Van Valkenburgh, and Chris Reed are designing parts of cities through landscape. They are taking a kind of work away from urban designers: landscape architects are in a better position to correlate ecological process to urban form. When you look at the examples of the conversion of former airport sites, generally speaking, there are three typologies. The first type, most often in western Europe, is where the airport is completely renovated and replaced with some combination of public park and housing and a new city form, like in Reykjavik or Berlin. The second typology is where the airport is partially converted and then other parts are simply left. Finally, the third type is the places that are simply abandoned to natural processes. One thing that I'm clearer about now is the scale of the airports and the intensity of construction, because the amount of material to have a 2km long runway that's a meter and an half deep is immense. The intensity of resources that it would take to remove that are so great that more often these projects tend toward keeping traces of things. And in part, it's a question of design, heritage and

memory. It is also a question of simple investments and materials. I think often there is something about the simple scale and material fact of the airport that resists being changed because the resources that we have, even in North America, are very modest. In those cases that's why landscape urbanism took them up because the first problem was not to demolish the airport, the first problem was how do you bring back some biological activity that over fifty years can demolish the airport through natural processes. That's a different kind of problem than simply demolishing it. Recycling is a good metaphor for that. But immediately it means de-engineering the airfield because the airfield has been engineered to move the water away as quickly as possible, to not allow any biology at all to happen and typically the landscape architects has to reverse that. So they do this by de-engineering the site: clogging up the drains, moving the topography a bit. Because they can't afford to demolish the entire runway and at the same moment, there's not nearly enough demand for housing or new development to take the entire site. But they're using natural processes to change the site over longer periods of time. And they do this by curating or seeding natural ecologies. In many ways, the airport is even in its operations defined by its ecologies: it is trying to manage water, birds and animals. And because it's a very large territory it ends up trying to manage very large territories. Many of them are interested in low carbon, green, sustainable practices and others are returning to wildlife management practices. And so that allows us to see them as similar to the problems of the old abandoned airport. They are different, obviously, but they are related in the sense that the landscape architect has an advantage in both cases. Obviously, most of them are still dominated by engineering but in the better examples they have landscape architects who are in charge and can steer a little bit and do something slightly more progressive.

INTRODUCTION

Schipol Airport
Amsterdam | The Netherlands
Photo by Sara Favargiotti | 2014

> I've long suspected that people are only truly happy and aware of a real purpose to their lives when they hand over their tickets at the check-in.

J. G. Ballard, *Airports: The Cities of the Future*, 1997

TAKE OFF

TAKE OFF

Field of research

Since the late 1990s, the development of physical infrastructure networks immediately accelerated the changes of urban structure, thus changing landscape, city and territorial interpretations. The history of modern infrastructures coincides with the need to respond quickly to the necessity of connecting different places and territories within countries influenced by a complex geography, and to remove them from physical isolation and marginalization.[1] This has generated one of the main myths of the last century, that infrastructures bring development. According to this idea, cities competed with each other through major airports and major stations. The role of architecture for large infrastructure was to build the image of urban competitiveness. The effects of these processes on urban and territorial development have been enormous. They have lead to an overestimation and overproduction of airports across the European and North American territories, often becoming burdens on local communities and economies. This has significantly compromised the financial stability of several cities and regions particularly in Europe. During the height of the construction boom, authorities rushed to take advantage of opportunities to plan new airports. Many of the newest regional and secondary airports did not see a single passenger through their terminals. Empty waiting rooms, check-in areas with more employees than passengers and fire-fighters waiting for planes that never arrive are a few of the elements that characterize their landscape. In many cases, political motivations and economic interests guided the investment decisions, rather than real need. These underused and speculative airports are all examples of the waste of public money on mega-infrastructure that covers the European landscape. This book is built on these assumptions, noting that at the beginning of 21st Century, the infrastructural myth is no longer valid. The global economic crisis has had a profound effect on local and regional communities, accelerating globalization and at the same time, increasing vulnerability to external shocks. The crisis, however, offers the opportunity for a transition to efficient structures and to a more sustainable development of economic resources, land use and energy efficiency. Very often, economic decline foresees urban regeneration. In this framework, the airport infrastructure becomes one of the main topics: focusing landscape-urban-infrastructure-related issues in a context of development is different from doing it in a state of constant slowdown or in deadlock.

"Cathedrals in the desert, ghost airports, white elephants" are just few of the name used to define all those airports that have been recently built and never or partially used. It is evident that the risk of closure is very high for the majority of these structures. Airports are the epitome of the widespread obsolete infrastructural condition in Europe as well as all in North America. In fact, the analysis of their regions shows how territories became filled with obsolete, decommissioned and abandoned airfields that never reached their full potential or lost their central role. They have completely or partially lost their function and brought about negative consequences for their surrounding contexts, becoming structures that have higher maintenance costs than benefits for their territories. What are the possible futures for these recently produced infrastructures that are already in decline? The process for the closure and the consequential transformation of an underutilized airfield in not obvious, and it might take several years before choosing to definitely deactivate an airport. Very often, in fact, airport owners don't see the option of demolishing the infrastructure as the most convenient alternative. Some destinies may be opened and can generate unexpected uses and, in the meanwhile, airports can be kept as reserves with gradual transformations. This phase is a transitional condition in which airports are holding possible patterns that might potentially activate a new life cycle. For airports on-hold, the cycle is not over yet, but it is rather a phase of transition to realign the cyclical nature of airfields by diversifying the operations and preparing the field for a future transformation. In that sense, it is not uncommon that an underutilize airport remains in a limbo for some time, valuating possible alternatives scenarios.

The book explores this transitory condition, defined as "on-hold," as challenge for the transformation of obsolete airfields. On-hold refers to a phase of transition, implying an embryo of activation, an embryo of life that can be activated or re-activated. The renewal of on-hold infrastructures can become a significant landscape and architectural "figure" in contemporary contexts, improving the quality of urban environments. If infrastructure does not bring about development, dealing with the life cycles of existing infrastructures can improve the settlement context, from an architectural and urban design point of view. Rethinking urban infrastructure, architecture and landscape, is seen as an opportunity to create new relationships between the city, the environment, landscape and ecology.[2] "Airports On-hold. Towards Resilient Infrastructures" aims to update the investigation of the relation between small and medium airports and the landscape in specific areas, outlining several strategies for the conversion of on-hold airports. A sensitive evaluation of the sustainability of the interventions for landscapes, cities and territories is necessary so that the on-hold airports do not become problematic black holes, but rather, they enhance the potentialities of the airfields itself as a catalytic agent and a generator of new productive landscapes.

Hypothesis

What do huge flocks of sheep, hundreds of rabbits, business parks, metropolitan parks, leisure parks, high-tech parks have in common with airports? These are the most frequent visitors to airports recently constructed. These are the new ways of inhabiting an airport and connecting it to its context. In fact, having so many airport infrastructures has caused a premature obsolescence of many of them. Many airports were abandoned becoming a problem for cities in terms of space and cost. This creates among other consequences many brownfields. The dilemma is urgent. However, airports are challenging case studies because they are very difficult to try to put back into the old structure of the city. The combination of centrality, emptiness, environmental contamination and economic capability makes a good case for study from a landscape perspective. How should our disciplines deal with these complex landscape and urban elements? How can a new landscape and urban design approach rethink and recalibrate obsolete airfields through ecological, social and cultural valuations?

Many abandoned airports have already been redeveloped as a new part of the city. Orange County Great Park (Irvine, California), Crissy Field (San Francisco), Maurice Rose Airfield (Frankfurt, Germany), Tempelhofer Park (Berlin, Germany) are few of the numerous projects that show the reconversion of an existing airfield into an new part of the city: a re-naturalized park providing new economic and social activities. Generally, the growing population, the high demand for new dwellings or their physically centrality in the city simplify their reconversion in new urban developments, natural parks or productive fields. Even the proliferation of low-cost companies started to promote the revitalization of secondary airports. However, what happens when the airport destiny is not yet clear or when the resources are not sufficient to generate similar processes?

The current forms of policy development and land management are showing their limitations and the necessity that architectural, urban and landscape projects deal with on-hold airport infrastructures, generating new life cycles. To view the airport as something that can be reloaded means to consider its rhythms, its life cycle, and its metamorphoses.[3] Contrary to recycled airports, for airports on-hold the life cycle is not yet finished. It refers to a phase of transition or a changing condition. This condition allows a potential combination of functions and could also open up the possibility of a return to aviation as a future step. In that sense, the indeterminate state of these airports could be transformed into an opportunity. The book aims to offers the documented registration of this phenomenon in progress. Some destinies may be opened, and sometimes the on-hold state generates unexpected uses. Therefore, questioning the nature of airport infrastructure becomes a key consideration in the approach to this research topic. The book explores how airport infrastructure can function as catalytic agents and activators of contexts owing to their dimension and relationship with the territory. This interpretation of the airport landscape allows us to understand the crucial step that many small and medium airports are currently facing: they conceive the airport not only as transport infrastructure but also as a key element for the development of territories according to new paradigms.

Objectives and structure

Airports On-hold presents the transformation of obsolete airfields as new productive landscapes. It explores the challenges for the conversion of abandoned, decommissioned and on-hold airports thought the exploration of their life cycles. The theme of a new life cycle for infrastructure is increasingly central in landscape urbanism and urban design. Many airfields will become obsolete, many will serve other functions, and many will begin a new cycle of life generating new trade within cities, landscapes and territories. Therefore the book aims to

On the way to Lleida-Alguaire Airport
Catalonia, Spain | 2011
Photo by Sara Favargiotti

transfer the concept of resilience into infrastructures within the landscape design disciplines: the capacity of airfields to express new meanings over time, beyond their original function. These interpretations of the airport landscape conceive the airfield not only as transport infrastructure but also as natural reserves for city developments or as spaces for landscape reclamation. Accordingly, airfields may become new urban resources, improving the quality of urban life and becoming a place to live instead of a place to leave. The work is divided into five chapters. The first and the third propose infrastructural and airport topics from a cultural perspective, confronting past and future tendencies. While the second and the fourth chapters are devoted to a deepening of discussions of real contexts and case studies, by proposing devices for the renewal of on-hold airports. The last chapter reports the conversations that I have carried out with researchers (academics and practitioners) involved in the field of airport landscape in the last ten years between North America and Europe.

The first chapter, "A View from Above," discusses the dynamics of building new infrastructures, their impact on urbanization and landscape and the theme of urban recycling. A retrospective view presents the relevance of the topic since the Modern Age, comparing different approaches in contemporary societies and landscapes.

The second chapter, "Airport On-Hold," explores the definition of the on-hold condition as an embryo of activation. It is supported by an in-depth investigation into the European context, analyzing and mapping two specific territories: Italy and Spain. These Mediterranean countries have strongly believed in the myth of infrastructure as carrier of development. Even though the contexts are different, the dynamics have been the same: the excessive over-construction has left two countries full of derelict airport infrastructures. Specifically, this chapter describes the problems and opportunities of on-hold airport infrastructures, from the urban and landscape point of view, through the analysis of the European airports condition.

This analysis is supported by and integrated with the exploration of international projects on a global scale, developed in the third chapter "Planning Obsolescence." The possibilities for the renewal of newly built airports have been explored to reevaluate their uses, potentialities and performances that add value to the landscape and urban area. Accordingly, it becomes interesting to shift the perspective on obsolete airfields from "a planned obsolescence" to "planning for obsolescence." This chapter investigates projects and processes for the transformation of obsolete, abandoned, and underutilized airfields. The trend is moving away from the modern attitude of domination and submission of territories, particularly with infrastructure, that characterized previous decades. Contemporary approaches follow an attitude of understanding and balance with the legacy that has been inherited, as atonement for the excesses of the past. Airports are specifically manifesting an earlier obsolescence that brings a complexity of problems not solely related to mobility and transport systems. In this context, it is possible to outline some tendencies that have characterized recent decades and may continue in the future: technology that bring in a personalization of the transports, landscape that reclaim and compensate for what has been destroyed, recycle as paradigm to renew abandoned places looking for new meaning.

Chapter four, "Resilient Landscape Reserves," assesses the relationships and synergies activated with the surrounding contexts through new uses and potentialities hosted by new airport landscapes. It chapter explores how the theme of generating a new life cycle is a particularly significant issue for the airport that we have built over the years in exuberant form. The airports can become points of territorial aggregation with multiple functions: environmental, tourism and services. Three European countries (Finland, Greece and Italy) have been investigated as case studies to experiment on their on-hold airports a set of renewal strategies through the activation of airports' second life.

Chapter five, "Positions," reports the conversations carried out between 2013 and 2015 with academic and practitioners involved on landscapes, cities and infrastructures in a broad sense. The connection with other research platforms engaged in the study of airfields in the last ten years supported the creation of an international research network of experts that allows the sharing of cultural experiences and the different research approaches. Travelling from Europe to United

States, I have interviewed some of the most relevant academics and practitioners that have investigated the relationships between landscapes, cities and airports. They contribute to highlight the network of research platforms involved in the topic of airport landscape across different scales and fields of interest. The conversations focus on the past and on-going projects of each platforms that deal with landscape, infrastructures and urban transformations to outline the interpretation of landscape in the contemporary age.

---

[1] Referred to the essay of Pino Scaglione, "Osmotic Infrastructure. From Highway to Eco-boulevard". In: Ricci M., *New Paradigms*, List, Trento, 2012, p. 207.
[2] According to Charles Waldheim and Sonja Dümpelmann, although airports have come to occupy pivotal positions in the economy, ecology and geography of the cities they serve, the design disciplines have not given them much attention. In recent years the economic centrality, environmental impacts and cultural relevance of airports have provided landscape architecture with new opportunities. While the modern airport can be read as an engineering project or architectural object, its manifold social, cultural and environmental implications raise *a number of* significant questions for the design disciplines. Source: Waldheim C., Dümpelmann S., (eds.), *Airport Landscape. Urban Ecologies in the Aerial Age*, Pamphlets, Harvard Graduate School of Design, Cambridge, Massachusetts, 2013.
[3] Pierre Bélanger highlights how new urban pressures are requiring a thorough rethinking, re-strategizing and reinvestment. Bélanger P., "Redefining Infrastructure". In: Mostafavi M., Doherty G. (eds.), *Ecological Urbanism*, Lars Müller Publishers, 2010, pp. 332-349.

CHAPTER 1

Flying above Germany
Photo by Sara Favargiotti | 2015

"

But to-day it is a question of the airplane eye, of the mind with which the Bird's Eye View has endowed us; of that eye which now looks with alarm at the places where we live, the cities where it is our lot to be.

Le Corbusier, *Aircrafts*, 1935

"

A VIEW FROM ABOVE

1. A VIEW FROM ABOVE

Roads, railways, harbors and airports brought significant innovations but also shaped cities and changed people's way of life. The railroad first opened the continents to bring food and materials in order to build the great industrial cities of the nineteenth century. Then, the steamer allowed manufacturers to expand around the globe. The car started the decentralization of the territories with the development of the sprawled suburbs. And then the airplane, together with growing economic prosperity, created a new phenomenon: mass tourism. Above all, airports redefined territories and people's life styles. These processes have been described in 1976 by Turner as "the fourth technological revolution" that has changed the social geography of the world since the end of the 1800s.[1] They shown how infrastructures are destined to be overcome over a short time. This is influenced also by the way we conceive and use infrastructures and airports in particular. More travellers require more routes, which in turn necessitate more airports. However, over the past quarter of century, European countries with the most significant growth in air travel are those where the air traffic is less concentrated in larger airports.[2] Small and medium airports have become a fertile ground for the development of low-cost carriers all over Europe. This spurred a growth in Italian air travellers at an average greater than other European countries. However, also in North America, a country dimensioned for the plane, airline networks had become its efficient nervous system.[3]

Infrastructures deal with accessibility, urban configuration and territorial transformation. The history of modern infrastructure coincides with the need to respond, with priority, to the necessity of connecting different places and territories. Through the construction of new infrastructure, marginal areas became less peripheral and more connected to the geographic, economic and territorial centralities as commonly recognized. But things are changing. The persistence of a crisis—that changes the nature, the speed and the priorities of phenomena—requires new forms of analysis and sustainable alternatives. New urban paradigms—like recycling and resilience—are leading to a greater sensitivity with respect to change and persistence of new contexts. In this framework, infrastructure becomes one of the main topics in local as well as international urban and landscape debates but with a different approach compared to the past. It is one thing to talk about infrastructure issues from a context of development, and quite another thing to talk about them as been in a state of constant slowdown or perhaps even a stable situation.

Talking about aviation implies to consider the meaning and purpose of infrastructure from cultural and performance perspectives. The flying experience has rapidly changed. At the beginning, airplanes have been built for élites, transforming quickly by their popularity into vehicles for mass transportation: from an élite carriage to a low-cost bus. We have passed from "air vessels" to exchanging machines. Many procedures, security controls and waiting times have transformed the sublime experience of air travel into a "battle" of procedures, often accompanied with a nostalgic view back to the Golden Age of Flying.[4] More recently we also could have seen new attitudes and new unusual occupants in airports. According to J.G. Ballard, transience, alienation and discontinuity are all airport hallmarks. At an airport such as Heathrow, the indeterminate flicker of flight numbers trembling on an annunciation screen defines the individual. Airports have become a new kind of discontinuous city, whose vast populations, measured by annual passenger flow, are entirely transient, purposeful and, for the most part, happy.[5] People access airports through a series of rules and codes: they enter a world of discontinuity and prohibition with several boundaries and obstacles to overcome.[6] After entering the door, people became passengers. Their liberty is achieved after getting rid of their baggage and obtaining a boarding pass. This requires the individual to merely wait for the course of events to unfold. Personal nationalities are virtually abolished because nationality becomes far less important than where we are going.

1.1 DEMYSTIFYING INFRASTRUCTURAL MYTHS

The twenty-five year period, coinciding with the rise of postmodernism in architecture, had seen a massive funding of urban infrastructure. This was not entirely coincidental.[7] The development of physical infrastructure networks immediately accelerated the changing of urban structure, thus changing landscape, city and territorial interpretation. Infrastructure networks, high-speed transport and migration flows have redefined the relationship between space and time as well as changing Europeans' habits and human relationships. It is also true that the most significant transformations in the organization of the territory are caused by changes in the economic organization and in lifestyles. In fact, one of the dominant drivers behind urban processes is infrastructure. Investments in infrastructures for individual cars, pedestrians, aviation and for public transport lead to greater requirements for accessibility and thus to unimagined economic potentials. As Stan Allen claims "infrastructure works to construct the site itself. [...] Infrastructure prepares the ground for future building and creates the conditions for future events. [...] Infrastructure's medium is geography."[8] In fact, infrastructures have significantly changed the relationship between city and landscape. All over the world, during the Modern Age, infrastructure networks and new transport systems have developed countries, improving local economies and starting to connect places far away in the world. After the Second World War, roads and highways were constructed to assert the emancipation of the nation and influence an economic boom away from poverty. Through the construction of new infrastructures, marginal areas became less peripheral and more connected to the commonly recognized centralities (geographically, economically, and territorially).

Italian modern infrastructures' history coincides with the need to connect different places and territories of a country influenced by a complex geography, and to enhance their condition, characterized by isolation and marginalization. This generated one of the main myths of the last century: that infrastructure brings development. The role of infrastructures was to build the image of urban competitiveness in the last thirty years. Cities competed with each other through major airports and

*Heathrow Airport | Terminal 5
Photo by BAA*

major stations. At the beginning of twenty-first century this system entered into crisis. The global economic crisis and the acceleration of globalization processes have had effects even on local communities and regions. Even if the construction of new infrastructures has moved money, the economy, and the market, once construction was completed many infrastructures remained isolated, proving that the best strategy would perhaps have been not to build them at all. During the last quarter of century, the number of unfinished or unused infrastructures has grown exponentially. Hence the paradox: the infrastructures often become the main problem and a huge cost for local administrations. The infrastructure, without real and widespread processes of economic support, and without coherent strategies and territorial projects, don't generate any development.[9] From these conditions comes one of the questions of this investigation: what are possible futures for these recent infrastructures already in decline?

Peripheral territories

The phenomena of urban sprawl, the loss of center, the role of infrastructure and the fusion between city and country are widely studied territorial and urban transformation phenomena, starting from the 1960s. When the city "invades" everything, does it still make sense to talk about periphery? Economists consider what is peripheral as a consequence of multiple factors: accessibility, intensity of transport flows and gross domestic product per capita (GDP). According to this interpretation, the areas least accessible are the most peripheral. At the same time, the territories with fewer regular flows (transport of persons or goods) are the areas where there is more poverty. Peripheral territories exist: these are a recognized and widespread reality. The definition of "peripheral" commonly comes from a Eurocentric vision of the world. Defining what is peripheral in Europe is a very difficult and ambiguous issue. The first objective is therefore to reorient the point of view, from the national to the local scale, by combining information provided by the indexes to establish parameters that define what is peripheral in relation to each local territory. Periphery is a condition less related to a physical condition or to distance but more related to the economic condition of territories, being peripheral is an ambiguous condition and it is continuously mutable. The *peripherality* in the European territories today is perhaps more a social issue than a geographical question. It depends on the development processes that are not necessarily related to the intensity of physical connections and material flows of people or things. There are peripheral areas in the heart of large metropolitan areas and it is possible to identify important centralities in remote areas. Furthermore, some territories that are economically well developed have limited their accessibility and connections: an enclave territory is an affirmation of local identity. For example the Alto Adige or the surrounding areas of Cuneo are the richest and most developed regions of the Italian territory but their accessibility is limited. Also some Greek islands, those less affected by the crisis, are classified as economically peripheral areas in the European Union only because they don't have a high development of infrastructures and they are far from the main flows of traffic. To clarify this concept, the research proposes a comparison between the three stakeholder nations - Finland, Italy and Greece - involved in the targeted analysis described in *Chapter 4*. The peripheral context of a region in Central Finland is very different due to the heterogeneous contexts (geographic, economic, social) from an Italian or Greek region.[10]

Economic theory also states that accessibility is one of several relevant location factors. During the last century, in the European urban settlements, the speed of connections have fortified some territories and marginalized others. These processes have directly involved the cities transformation and have affected the image of the public space. These new urban realities have established the postmodern idea of change: production does not create by itself the essential conditions for the economic growth of a territory, but connections are the major factors. This belief establishes a direct relationship between the future of local communities and the myth of infrastructure development. It has steered major European financial policies toward territorial cohesion and major investments in the physical shape of settlement expansion with the idea of *mega-infrastructured* territories. This vision of growth is essentially founded on three axiomatic principles.[11] The first is deterministic: infrastructure produces economic development in peripheral areas. The second is complementary to the first and states that economic development cannot exist without new infrastructure. The third axiom implies that infrastructure networks establish and give value to a new kind of landscape that holds speed and permanence together: cathedrals and shopping centers, the metropolis and the sprawling town, the traces of history and the uncertain, magma-like shapes of dispersion and change. Today, none of these axioms seem functional. The world perspective has been changed by the *mondialisation* that is referred to, on one hand, as the globalization that corresponds to the extension around the world of the liberal market, technology, information and communication networks, and on the other, as the planetary consciousness, which is ecological and restless.[12] Furthermore, the persistence of a global crisis changes the nature of the phenomena, its speed and priority - affecting local communities - and the acceleration of globalization at the regional level, as well as increasing vulnerability to "external shocks". In some cases, prosperity, stability and sustainability of cities and regions are also endangered. The economic crisis and a higher ecological sensibility clearly show the saturation of new landscapes and the incoherence in increasing the physical infrastructure network. This new socio-economic era requires new forms of analysis and sustainable alternatives within a context of greater sensitivity with respect to change and the persistency of the present time. In a way, the crisis creates the opportunity for a transition to efficient structures and for a more sustainable development of economic resources, land and energy.

The infrastructures and the crisis

In the last quarter of century, infrastructure development has been closely associated with impacts on urban phenomena. Their development processes help to determinate the end of the compact city and the beginning of the sprawling city. This is a city without limits, where continuous expansion has brought a high consumption of land and has forced the connection of many points in a network. Hence, road networks have the spread in the territory, increasing exponentially the individual use of cars. This well-known and widely studied urban model produced extensive suburbs, marginality, precarious economic development, and heavy pollution but has already been deeply investigated. More pragmatically, accessibility has generally been accepted as a major feature of economic attractiveness for cities and regions. With growing globalization, accessibility has changed dramatically. Whereas for many centuries it had been fundamental to ensure connections with large cities or neighboring regions, now it is imperative to be connected to the whole world, which is why airports are playing an increasingly important role. To have a regional airport is an important asset and may be the decisive factor for attracting investors or retaining talent in a region. However, in many cases, having a regional airport or a big infrastructure is often a political requirement rather than a real need for accessibility, highlighting the fact that many areas have unused or poor operative infrastructures. In many cases, policy makers don't see a real convenience to improve technical and physical characteristics of infrastructures. Approached in this way, infrastructures dramatically burden the regional economy. Other areas are economically developed but are not equipped with *mega-infrastructures*. These conditions reveal how accessibility, economic development and peripheral issues are transversal to each other but can also develop in parallel. In fact, new social and economic conditions are redefining these issues. It is clear that European peripheral regions encounter many difficulties to keep up or develop their competitiveness in this era of declining resources and generally poor economic development.

In contemporary territories and landscapes—with significant impacts in North America and Europe—there is a widespread reality of underused infrastructures that have never reached their full potential or have lost their central role. They have partially or completely lost their usefulness and brought negative economic consequences to their surrounding contexts. In Italy, for example, there are many abandoned railway lines: these lines are closed to traffic, unfinished or variations of the main route.[13] There are many stations and tollbooths abandoned or only partially used, including some that were very recently built. There are 112 airports open to traffic. Furthermore there are hundreds of airfields and heliports suitable for landing. Only 31 of these airports are classified as commercial airports and very few have regular flight traffic. It is not possible to list all the abandoned or underused roads. [14] Going back to the original question, does physical infrastructure (roads, railways and airports) really lead to the development of peripheral territories? According to the scene set out above, the answer may be "no" or at the very least "not always."

The modes of transport are saturated and a shift of perspective is required:[15] one of contemporary dilemma is how to use the infrastructure that we already have, as opposed to building new ones. How can architecture play a role in recycling these existing forms? From this perspective, the research of Mirko Guaralda on abandoned infrastructures is significant,[16] as well as the icon-projects of the High-Line in New York as well as the Trento Tunnel in Trentino where abandoned infrastructures became an extraordinary public space for culture, leisure and representation of local identity. The focus on soft and slow infrastructures, underlines how today, in Europe, the myth of the construction of *mega-infrastructures* is in crisis.[17]

In 1984, Michel Foucault claimed that architects are not the engineers or technicians of the three great variables: territory, communication and speed.[18] Instead, Stan Allen noted that territory, communication, and speed are properly infrastructural problems, and architecture as a discipline has developed specific technical means to deal effectively with these variables. This affirmation was clearly understood in the past.[19] Today, however, it has again become a priority in the urban approach. Pierre Bélanger highlights that underlying this legacy is a major network of post-war infrastructures - airports, harbors, roads, sewers, bridges, dikes, dams, power corridors, terminals and treatment plants - that are now suffering major decay from lack of repair and maintenance.[20] Emerging from current economic exigencies and ecological imperatives, the main motive is to understand how the collective requirement for infrastructure—the basic system of essential services that support a city, a region or a nation—emerged from public necessity in crisis and conflict during the nineteenth and twentieth centuries, and how new urban pressures are requiring a thorough rethinking, re-strategizing and reinvestment. "And while architects are relatively powerless to provoke the changes necessary to generate renewed investment in infrastructure, they can begin to redirect their own imaginative and technical efforts toward the questions of infrastructure."[21] A new urbanity has been gradually defined by new environmental and landscape qualities with a higher respect and consideration of local territories and identities. New temporal regimes have been identified by new work life and social attitudes. The scarcity of non-renewable energy, economic change and new lifestyles enhanced a more conscientious ecological awareness. This generated a complex change in the way of thinking and living the territory, the landscape and the city. Contemporary cities, facing difficult decisions about scarce resources and investments, strive for urban and ecological efficiency.

Hauptbahnhof Berlin | 2015
Photo by Sara Favargiotti

Infrastructure Recycle

Adaptive Landscapes

Obsolete Heritage

Place of Memory

*The High-Line and
Trento Tunnels
Photos by Sara Favargiotti*

Productive Landscape

Wild Nature and Cultivated Areas

1.2 LA RE- ÉPOQUE

Rehabilitate, rebuild, recalibrate, reclaim, reconnect, recover, recycle, redistribute, reform, refurbish, regenerate, reinvent, remake, remediate, renovate, reorganize, repair, restore and reuse are some of the most significant RE- key words used in research projects during the last decade.[22] It seems to be a time of reflection and reuse of what has already been produced. The concept of recycle has been present in architecture, city and landscape since ancient time but the conditions for which it is proposed have changed. According to Mosè Ricci, "architecture and the city have always recycled themselves. Examples like Split, Marcello Theater in Rome or the Dome in Syracuse are just a few of the most obvious manifestos of recycling. It's not a question of restoration: the idea of conservation tends to embalm the image of architectural or urban space by attributing value to the unchangeable."[23] In fact, recycle differs from operations of restore and reuse. Reuse refers to operations at the medium scale and is based on reprogramming the uses rather than on refurbishing the building or infrastructure. Whereas, recycle breaths new life into structures, which will reincarnate in a different body. Recycle is a process that transforms the original material by adding proprieties not related to the original use. Recycle works on existing structures and territories from open perspectives and covers issues with wide contents such as hybridization and integration, aiming to confront the old and new through the merging of mixed uses, epochs, attitudes and technical solutions. In the beginning of the twenty-first century, the term recycle seems to have come into vogue.[24] Indeed, several superimposed crisis—financial, political and environmental—brought a higher sensibility to climate and social changes and even a change of paradigms in the dynamics of urban transformation. Design projects and theory turned towards environmental, efficiency, cost or energy saving factors. An increasing number of design projects aim to recycle existing buildings in particular contexts, with specific attention to social and ecological issues. In fact, "two disguises have been applied to the architect in recent decades: firstly, that of destroyer of the past and secondly, that of interpreter of history, and now he has become an ecologist."[25] But recycle also allows for a range of imaginative and metaphorical associations, moving towards an attitude of understanding and balance with the legacy that has been inherited.

The idea of recycling the existent to design cities is growing in importance in certain European towns due to social problems connected with the conditions of certain suburbs, but also as urban tool for institutions to regulate the land use. During the 2006 Venice Architecture Biennale, the German pavilion exhibited the Convertible City. Modes of Densification and Dissolving Boundaries, which presented architectural interventions on existing buildings and the idea of a city that grows on itself.[26] The German research claims that the city must be re-stabilized and regenerated to mirror its lively and complex society. The economic context changes the social and cultural framework but it also brings into the foreground specific conditions in the construction of cities and territories, put aside for a long time, but that may return to importance. This moment does not seem to be a time for great innovation. It's rather a time of reflection, reuse and recycling what has been already produced. The exhibition Vacant NL for the 2010 Venice Architecture Biennale showed thousands of buildings that remained unoccupied in The Netherlands.[27] The installation aimed to highlight the potential of temporarily vacant government space for use by creative enterprises. The existing buildings were considered to be matter which could be transformed and through which the idea of the city could be renewed. This was also one of the main aims of the exhibition RE-CYCLE. Strategies for Architecture, City and Planet held at the MAXXI Museum in Rome.[28] The topic of recycling was addressed through a transversal and interdisciplinary approach: it was not viewed simply in its better-known role of re-using discarded materials, but as a strategy in a wider sense. Again, at the Venice Architecture Biennale, the German Pavilion highlighted the changing urban transformation processes and recovery of existing buildings. In 2012, the German contribution Reduce/Reuse/Recycle. Architecture as Resource claimed a successful shift in value from waste to reusable material.[29] The three terms—reuse, reduce, recycle—describe a waste hierarchy that gives the highest priority to the most efficient strategies of minimization: avoidance comes first, followed by direct reuse and, finally, recycling which changes the properties of the material. This same logic may be applied in setting up a new value system to address existing buildings: the fewer changes that are made and the less energy used, the better the process.[30]

Swimming pool at Zeche Zollverein | 2014
Photo by Aviller71 @flickr

In just a few years, recycle became a clever word used internationally in multiple projects and academic research debate. It arises from two main themes: the progressive abandoning of buildings in the post-production city and the new ecological urban dimension. In fact, "the trend is moving away from the modern attitude of domination and submission which characterized previous decades towards a mechanism of atonement for the excesses of the past"[31] with an attitude of understanding and reclaiming what we have hyper-produced. In contrast to other urban and architectural theories, recycling is not a formal or spatial approach. It works with the specificity of each context and improves their potentialities. In fact, recycling means the reuse of waste materials, which have lost value or meaning. It is a practice that helps to reduce waste, to limit its presence, to reduce disposal costs and to limit production of new waste. Recycle means, in other words, to create new value and new meaning. "Another cycle is another life. [...] Recycling is the ecological action that pushes into the future by transforming the existing waste in the prominent features and producing the city's culture, the beauty and the urban quality."[32] It is also evident that recycle offers different possibilities of action. According to Francesc Muñoz recycle could also mean new activities that reinforce (enhance) the main infrastructural use and not necessarily as the simple replacement (substitute) of the original use. [33] However, recycle's main purpose is to work on the sense of things, on their meaning, on their memory. In that sense, recycle offers different possibilities of action. Although it depends on each case, generally the more immediate idea of recycling is to take out what is there and put in something else. But Muñoz approach adds value to the complexity of the recycle process because there might be several alternatives instead of one single project.

Infrastructure Recycle beyond Urban Transformation

The recycle process in Italy is linked to the need for recovery of the obsolete heritage, the land preservation through the reduction of land use, the redevelopment of abandoned areas and, in particular, of obsolete infrastructures in an economic environment of reduced resources. Infrastructure gives life to cities. Infrastructure sustain cites.[34] But what happens when an infrastructure ends its life cycle, becoming obsolete? They become an incredible burden for cities and local or regional administrations. As previously described, building new infrastructure today, in this moment of crisis, does not appear to be the most sustainable strategy considering that sustainability is an aim in relation to social and territorial changes. The recycling of obsolete infrastructure in order to optimize their potential becomes the most sustainable and desirable solution. Furthermore recent projects highlight the challenges in re-thinking not only the abandoned and unused infrastructure in search of a new identity, but also recycling all those infrastructures that are already active but poorly operating and unproductive. Currently, the identification of strategies to recycle existing obsolete buildings and infrastructure rather than the construction of new ones is also spreading into urban design practices. The experimentation with different approaches, that are defined case by case, offer a network of paths in the landscape rather than presenting one-way routes that strongly limit the way of living in the territory.[35] Focusing on infrastructure, recycle infrastructure is an emerging attitude in the reactivation of obsolete urban infrastructures. Two manifesto projects of the recycle

View north on the HIgh Line from West 17th Street | 1934 Photographer unknown

process are the High Line in New York and the Trento Tunnels in Trento. The projects are experiments in the reinvention of infrastructure's significance and identity, the mending of a tear in the urban fabric. In fact, these recycled infrastructures reinterpret surfaces, buildings, and fragments of former transport infrastructures, converting them into public places with pedestrian and cultural uses.

The High Line is a new 1.5-mile long public park built on an abandoned elevated railway stretching from the Meatpacking District to the Hudson Rail Yards in Manhattan.[36] In 1980 the last trains ran on the High Line. For almost twenty years a group of property owners lobbied for demolition of the entire structure until 1999 when *Friends of the High Line* was founded by Joshua David and Robert Hammond, residents of the High Line neighborhood, to advocate for the High Line's preservation, transformation and reuse as public open space. In 2002, the City of New York advocated for a recycle project with the Federal Surface Transportation Board for rail-banking, making it City policy to preserve and reuse the High Line. The project began in 2006, with the first phase opening in 2009 and the second phase opening in 2012. The third and final phase will open in the fall of 2014. The High Line Park is meant to offer an urban promenade, a bucolic space floating nine meters in the air with Hudson River views. Inspired by this post-industrial ruin, the new park interprets its inheritance, translating the biodiversity in a string of site-specific urban microclimates along the stretch of railway that includes sunny, shady, wet, dry, windy and sheltered spaces.[37] Yet it retained many elements of its past, such as the rails that have been restored in the park to cultivate wild grasses or allocate sliding benches. Much of the designers' work has been devoted to seeking a balance between preserving "the romance of the ruin" and creating a fresh green corridor for pedestrians, through a strategy of agri-tecture: part agriculture and part architecture. The project wants to teach that gardens can be born in an asphalt crib generating a peaceful place to escape from the frenetic energy of the city streets. The park generates alternating moments of varied character to be discovered: wild nature next to cultivated areas, intimate areas and social spaces. The High Line process has spurred real estate development in the neighborhoods that lie along the line. [38] Condominiums, hotels and office buildings designed by international architectural firms like Jean Nouvel, Annabelle Selldorf, Renzo Piano, and Della Valle Bernheimer are growing along the park's span. This project "reveals the extent that

The Trento Tunnels have remain active from 1974 to 2007

recycling projects can be attractive and glamorous as well as contagious. In other words, they are capable of generating effects of emulation and reproduction inducing requalification and new economies on the side."[39] In 2014 was opened the final section of the High Line. Within this missing piece it has become a platform for watching the city's change, including the project of High Line itself as one of the great urban transformation phenomena of 21st century.

In 2010, the symposium entitled *Next Stop on the High Line: The Trento Tunnel Project* presented the Trento Tunnels as an experiment in the recovery of an abandoned industrial site, in the reinvention of the history museum, and in the animation of historical archives.[40] The tunnels were built in 1974 splitting the ancient neighborhood of Piedicastello in two and during their first life they had an average estimated daily traffic of 30,000 vehicles. Abandoned in 2007, in less than one year the two former highway tunnels were converted into a history exhibition gallery. The Trento Tunnels were reopened on August 19th, 2008 with a celebration for the public. Their second life has become. More than 3,000 people attended the inauguration. Like Diller and Scofidio's NYC High Line, the Trento Tunnels reinvent a fragment of transportation infrastructure, converting it from vehicular traffic to pedestrian use. Also, like the High Line, they accompany this shift from passengers to perambulators with a program of city gardens. Unlike their High Line counterpart, however, the Trento Tunnel gardens serve as geo-spatial boundary markers.[41] In fact, the Tunnels frame this shift with city gardens that transfigure the tunnels into symbols of a region that serves as a conduit between the Mediterranean South and the Germanic North. More than a museum, it is a space for memory in which is possible to reinterpret the sense of place. "To enter them is to travel in time through the twentieth century. To see the light at their end is to espy the seam where a territory's past meets its future."[42] The project aims at urban reclamation: it merges recycling, restoration and renewal. "When the twin tunnels in Trento were replaced by a new passage further west, so as to avoid bisecting an old nucleus of the town, the sudden appearance of empty passages through the mountain took on a calamitous presence. Remedying a planning mistake that dates back to a period of public infatuation with automotive travel left a gash in the landscape. What to do with a monumental piece of obsolete infrastructure? Instead of pretending that the tunnels were now useless, consigning them to some ignoble purpose such as municipal storage for cumbersome equipment, the provincial government and the historical museum of Trentino sought to return them to the community as a site of its own history and as theatre for its sense of self. At the time of this curatorial decision, the eye of an architect proved to be decisive, for the new destination of the tunnels changed their nature even before a single shovelful of earth was moved."[43]

Resilient Infrastructure towards Adaptive Landscapes

In the last ten years, it is increasingly evident how the ecosystems function, "ecological thinking across the scales of inquiry and application has moved toward a more organic model of open-endedness, flexibility, resilience and adaptation, and away from a mechanistic model of stability and control. In other words, ecosystems are now understood to be open systems that behave in ways that are self-organizing and that are, to some extent, unpredictable. In effect, change is built into living systems; they are characterized in part by uncertainty and dynamism."[44] To face that, many cities have been considered and redeveloped as resilient systems, able to absorb external negative shocks and return to a state of equilibrium Taking into account future risks and uncertainties, resilience relies on redundancy. The term resilience, associated with the planning disciplines and territorial governance, has gained increasing importance over last ten years, with reference to features of sustainable development, the prevention of environmental risks, as well as the adaptive capacity of territories. Unlike mechanical resilience—which refers to the capacity of elastic return to the physical original structure—resilience is the capacity to return to the initial condition by re-generating a new balance within the ecological and territorial systems.[45] Moreover, resilience becomes an aim to be achieved in order to re-integrate urban elements into the dynamics of the city and to give them multiple functions and meanings. It reflects an approach coming from landscape and ecology fields that can support urbanization defining the place for public transport, organizing urban development, managing the energy production, constructing and reorganizing open public space in the city. While landscape and open space can work as an urban infrastructure, giving new meanings and uses to existing settlements, new ecologies can be designed and programmed in order to improve urban environmental performances. Shifting from traditional planning dictates of growth and development, ecology, sustainability and sensibility to landscape, emerge as the paradigms on which to found resilient and sustainable urban transformations. From these come the redefinition of urban elements imagining them as latent public spaces, relational engines and ecological devices and outlining specific resilient strategies for a development integrating new urban models, social needs and risk prevention strategies.

The concept of ecological resilience comes from the indeterminate nature of the future, the structural weaknesses of the human ecosystems and the poor adaptability to ecological stresses. The numerous examples of infrastructures' transformation into urban ecological devices, their conversion into public parks, the reclamation of the dismissed areas and tracks, suggest that, once again, the future of worldwide patterns has to be oriented towards a new interpretation of urban elements. Therefore the exploration of fostering new life cycles is a particularly significant issue for the obsolete urban elements. If a building, an infrastructure or an open space is no longer used (or needed), it is possible for a renewal and rethinking through adaptation and resilience. Transposing the concept of resilience to infrastructures refers to the capacity of a structure to express diverse meanings over time, beyond its original function or use. In that sense, the exploration of fostering new life cycles is a particularly significant issue for the airport but it can be transferred to other types of infrastructure. If an infrastructure is no longer used (or needed), the challenge is to rethink the structure through its resilience, in order to activate a process of renewal of its own physical and functional condition. Resilience is therefore a function of sustainability, which requires a thorough review of the organizational and management models upon which urban coexistence relies. "All ecosystems are constantly evolving, often in ways that are discontinuous and uneven. While some ecosystems are perceived to be stable, this is not strict stability in a mathematical sense; this is simply our human, time-limited perception of stasis."[46] But resilient infrastructure is also something that we can plan to produce a long term strategy that ensures social homeostasis through a shared governance, in order to generate the conditions for better efficiency as we move in the direction of creating a low carbon civilization—through new technologies for a collaborative management of land, energy resources and mobility. Resilient infrastructure represents a system capable of renewing its balance within the changing surroundings, able to adapt to the stresses arising from climate change and tasked with finding solutions for some of the social, economic and environmental crisis that characterizes our era.

1.3 FROM GLAMOUR TO LOW-COST EXPERIENCE

Flying is a physical and cultural experience. It has characterized our culture and it has been influenced by society since the beginning of aviation. At the same time, the evolution of the airplane accelerated not only the speed of travel but also the speed of human transformation. This has had an influence on airports. In fact, airports have been transformed and have grown (or closed) according to new procedures, new passenger typologies, new airplanes, new security measure and the facilities required during the last decades. In the Golden Age of air travel, flying was a magical and marvelous experience. It was an experience of attitude and style. Flying itself was exciting. Since the beginning of aviation, airlines realized that they needed to keep passengers happy and encourage them to return to flying. From the male crewmembers of the late 1920s, to the female flight attendants of the 1930s, the airline staff attempted to make passengers more comfortable, offering them water and a meal, reassuring nervous passengers and helping people get around the plane. They also carried baggage, took passenger tickets, checked for gasoline leaks, and tidied up the cabin after a flight. The Golden Age of Flying was also an era of sumptuous design. The flying experience also involved the visual look of the cabin, the stewardess's uniform, right down to the silverware. If the airplane was the home of the new human, its details were prototypes for a new kind of house on the ground.[47] Passengers made plane reservations by telephone: it was a new experience for former rail travellers, who usually bought tickets in person. The air passenger would phone the airline office, which in the early 1930s was often at the airport since airports were very close to larger cities. As the historian Guillaume de Syon explained, the tradition at the time was that people would use their in-flight time to write to people they knew on the ground, describing their experience of flight.[48] And these were experiences lived by few elites. In fact, in the early 50s there was only one class of travel. Fares were expensive and passengers were either very wealthy or claiming the trip on expense account

Air travel exploded in 1950s with the introduction of the passenger jets: the Golden Age of Flying had begun. Airplane trips weren't just a means of getting to vacation: they were a vacation in themselves. Passengers dressed in their finest to fly. They lined up for group photos before boarding. Riding an airplane made them feel like a movie star because it pretty much took the salary of a movie star to do so. Plane travel was glamorous, on time and exciting. In the 1950s and 1960s, before flight became cheap with the rise of the jumbo jet or later low-cost carriers, there were many real luxuries and comforts that were catered to. There was plenty of legroom, nary a security hassle and planeload of excitement when people could buy a ticket to defy gravity and arrive in new cities in hours instead of days. For one thing, airline security simply did not exist during the Golden Age of Flying. Compared to today, when airlines recommend getting to the airport three hours ahead of time to make sure you catch your flight, the recommendation of most Golden Age airlines seems positively quaint: people were guaranteed to make their flight even if they showed up just 30 minutes before. However, one of the first major differences between the Golden Age of Flying and contemporary aviation is that it was significantly more expensive and dangerous. Statistically, there were more plane crashes, flight accidents and less sophisticated flying technology. . By the end of the 50s, there were four classes of travel: deluxe, first class, tourist class and economy class. Free food for tourist and economy passengers had become common in the 60s. However, even in the 60s, to fly meant to be part of the jet set. The 1963 film The VIPs tells the story of a group of wealthy people stranded at Heathrow by bad weather.[49] Flying still had an image of glamour, excitement and style. Things definitely changed at the end of the 1960s when commercial jets airlines were proliferating and super sonic travel promised to shape the future of air travel. The evolution of the aviation system accelerated not only the speed of travel but also the speed of human transformation. In fact, the arrival of the ballistic logic of jet travel reconfigured both passenger and world. "[...] Since the advent of the jet, a new threshold has been crossed: it is a projectile, a perforator and not a glider."[50] Jets were more reliable, faster and safer than the piston-engine planes they replaced, and they could carry more people. Their safety was improved and technology increased their means. One negative effect of this change was that the experience of flying was already losing some of its appeal. Queues, crowding, delays whilst waiting for luggage and luggage damage, all became problems. The airlines themselves had been wrestling for years with the problem of transporting increasingly large numbers of people.

Dis-comfort

In 1969, the Boeing 747 started its airline service, opening up international travel to the masses. At that time, safety and control measures became more restricted. However, even in 1970s, passengers could board planes without an ID of any sort. Passengers could arrive at the airport thirty minutes before the flight and well-wishers could walk right up to the gate where people boarded by stairs, not jet bridges. Passenger screenings wouldn't become mandatory until 1973. Furthermore, from 1980s the aviation market was opened to new interstate airlines and jet carriers that flew wherever they wanted, whenever they wanted, and at whatever prices they wanted. With deregulation, airlines started to compete on the basis of service and not on the basis of price. The liberalization of air transport had an enormous impact on the mobility of people and businesses, reducing flight costs significantly and bringing economic development and tourism to otherwise remote areas. This development was permitted by a policy that allowed the market to reduce entry barriers and to develop a new competition between airports (large and small) and airlines. Paradoxically, it was this lack of rigid planning that allowed the industry to take advantage of unpredictable growth potentials, which allowed for the sudden development of the low-cost market.[51] The decrease in prices was one of the main reasons that the low-cost model became so successful, starting a process of travel "democratization:" from an experience for elites, to a mass phenomenon. The air transport service became a basic necessity and a full-fledged commodity.[52] This democratization is derived from two elements: disposal of free time and financial resources. Flying low-cost is no longer an exclusive means for a highly selected society, but it is a vehicle for a transversal, multicultural and plural society. Anyone can fly with low cost airlines: tourists, city-users, air-commuters, business travellers, students, families, and regular immigrants.[53] Today people go on low-cost flights in the same way as they take a bus. The air mobility has changed from a high-class and glamorous model of transportation of the twentieth century, to a low-cost practice. Flights have become the proximity bus of the twenty-first century. The low-cost traveller is the nomad of the third millennium.

In order to get lower tariffs, people trade-in several comforts for performance. Thus, in less than fifty years we moved from the idea of flying as a "comfort experience" to the experience of "wild mobility". Comfort is a clever idea. The modernization process of society is based on, among others aspects, a continuous process of adding and creating comfort. But there comes a point when you have added so much comfort that it generates *dis*-comfort. Making a comparison with cars, almost everyone has a car so almost everyone is driving on the highways and that causes us to drive slower due to traffic congestion. Therefore, the comfort in driving decreases. Something similar has happened with flying. For decades we found ways to add comfort to the air experience, making flight accessible to more and more people. Now there are so many people flying that we have long queues, excessive security controls and a lot of waiting time. All of these factors generate dis-comfort. The space of low-cost flows is no longer a practice for a select few, but has turned into a place of everyday life, as well plane travel becoming an everyday practice. This has influenced the concept of the airport, changing the activities and practices that can take place within it. The collective imagination changed: the paradigms of the city-airport are contradicted. From a non-place of modernity,[54] the airport has become a place of everyday life; as well as air travel being a practice of everyday life, since a growing population of fliers visit these places monthly, weekly and sometimes daily. With the new bus of the sky, people can even travel from airport to airport, just to do some shopping and return home.[55] In recent years, small and regional European airports have benefited from the low-cost model. There are two basic advantages of low cost airlines: firstly, they have fostered competition and price reductions; secondly, they have driven the development of secondary airports, with many of these being underused for long periods of time. The low-cost airlines have created competitiveness among traditional network carriers, allowing them to achieve lower operating costs. This has generated an incremental growth in air traffic. At the same time, it brought significant consequences in the airport's structures and then in passenger's attitudes: a new culture of flight has become widespread.

*Landed in 1950s
United Air Lines
Photo by
1950sUnlimited | Flickr*

*Boarding in 2007
Ryanair*

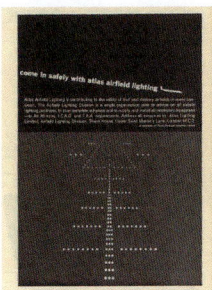   

Airlines Posters from 1910 to 1990
Source: www.vintageadbrowser.com/airlines-and-aircraft

CHAPTER 1. A VIEW FROM ABOVE

[1] Louis Turner and John Ash, *The Golden Hordes: International Tourism and Pleasure Periphery*, St. Martin's Press, New York, 1976, p.11.
[2] Stefano Paleari, Renato Redondi, "Piccoli aeroporti perché non sono troppi". In: *LaRepubblica.it*, December 6, 2010.
[3] See Le Corbusier, Précisions, *On the Present State of Architecture and City Planning*, Edith Schreiber Aujame, trans. (Cambridge, MA: The MIT Press, 1991; originally published in French as *Précisions sur un état present de l'architecture et de l'urbanisme*, Paris: 1930), 215-219.
[4] In 1923 Le Corbusier described in his most famous book *Vers une Architecture* the airplane as a product of high selection, "a new fauna [...] that handles the overseas transports of people and letters. [...] What are its laws? Precise, dramatic, rigorous: economy." At that time, it was a necessary transformation for a globalized and hyper-mobile society. The post-human was an animal that flew and the airport network was its efficient nervous system, 'its web covering the globe.' It was the beginning of the 'heroic era of aviation.' Le Corbusier saw this collapse of traditional space and time as nothing less than the emergence of a new kind of human. But it is not just that space had collapsed with the introduction of rapid air travel; time had expanded. Source: Beatriz Colomina, "Towards a Posthuman Architect." In: Design of the *In/Human International Symposium*, Akademie Schloss Solitude, November 19-21, 2009.
[5] J. G. Ballard, "Airports: The Cities of the Future." In: *Blueprint: Architecture, Design and Contemporary Culture*, issue: 142, September 1997, p. 26.
[6] See Marc Augé, *Nonluoghi. Introduzione a un'antropologia della surmodernità*, Elèuthera, Milano, 2009, pp. 12-13.

1.1 Demystifying Infrastructural Myths

[7] See Stan Allen, "Infrastructural Urbanism". In: *Points and Lines: Diagrams and Projects for the City*, Princeton Architectural Press, New York, 1999.
[8] *Ibid.*, p. 54
[9] See Pino Scaglione, "A22 From Infrastructure of Connect to the Osmotic Infrastructure of the Platform Trans-European MOMO (Modena-Monaco)". In: Pino Scaglione and Mosè Ricci (eds.), *A22 New Ecologies for Osmotic Infrastructures*, LISt Lab Barcellona/Trento, 2015, p. 107.
[10] See the Final Report of *Airports as Drivers of Economic Success in Peripheral Regions*, ADES-ESPON 2013 Programme, financed in part by the European Regional Development Fund INVESTING IN YOUR FUTURE, 2013.
[11] See Mosè Ricci "Osmotic Infrastructure". In: Ricci M., *New Paradigms*, List, Trento, 2012, pp. 213-217.
[12] It is referred to the definition of *mondialisation* interpreted by Marc Augé in *Nonluoghi. Introduzione a un'antropologia della surmodernità*, Elèuthera, Milano, 2009; originally published in French as *Non-lieux. Introduction à une anthropologie de la surmodernité*, Le Seuil, Paris, 1992.
[13] The 2011 *Ferrovie Abbandonate* report (available at the website: www.ferrovieabbandonate.it) rdocumented that out of a total of 22,846 km of Italian railway lines (www.rfi.it), about 500 km of railway tracks were unfinished and almost 6000 km were abandoned.
[14] In August 2015, the Council of Ministers approved a draft decree on the identification of the airports of national interest. The decree defines the airport systems of national interest taking into account the size and type of traffic, land and location, and the strategic role of the airports as well as the relevance in the TEN European projects. The preliminary scheme was outlined in the *Notice of Address for the definition the National Plan for Airport Development* (*Atto di indirizzo per la definizione del Piano Nazionale per lo Sviluppo Aeroportuale*), Ministry of Infrastructure and Transport, January 29, 2013, Rome.
[15] See Jesse H. Ausubel and Cesare Marchetti, "The Evolution of Transport". In: *The Industrial Physicist*, 2001, p. 22.
[16] See Mirko Guaralda, *Le Infrastrutture Viarie Dismesse o Declassate ed il Progetto di*

Paesaggio, Libreria CLUP Soc. Coop., Segrate, Milano, 2006.

[17] The 2011 European Transportation White Paper but already the European Commission's White Paper in 2001 indicates that it is absolutely necessary to interrupt the connection between increased mobility and economic growth. See the *WHITE PAPER Roadmap to a Single European Transport Area – Towards a competitive and resource efficient transport system*, COM (2001) 144 final, and the *WHITE PAPER European transport policy for 2010: time to decide*, COM (2001) 370. Reviewed in 2006 by the Council Commission Communication and the European Parliament.

[18] Answering to the question "So architects are not necessarily the master of space that they once where, or believe themselves to be." In: Foucault M. (author), and Rabinow P. (ed.), "Space Knowledge and Power." In: *The Foucault Reader*, Vintage Books, New York, 2010, (Original: 1984), p. 244.

[19] Stan Allen states that while it is hard to argue Foucault's point as an assessment of the current condition, it deserves to be pointed out that historically this has not been the case. Land surveying, territorial organization, local ecologies, road construction, shipbuilding, hydraulics, fortification, bridge building, war machines, and networks of communication and transportation were all part of the traditional competence of the architect before the rise of disciplinary specialization. See Stan Allen, "Infrastructural Urbanism." In: *Points and Lines: Diagrams and Projects for the City*, Princeton Architectural Press, New York, 1999, p. 52

[20] See Pierre Bélanger, "Redefining Infrastructure." In: Mohsen Mostafavi and Gareth Doherty (eds.), *Ecological Urbanism*, Lars Müller Publishers, 2010, pp. 332-349.

[21] Stan Allen, "Infrastructural Urbanism." In: *Points and Lines: Diagrams and Projects for the City*, Princeton Architectural Press, New York, 1999, p. 51.

1.2 La RE- Époque

[22] Javier Mozaz defines these operations as Re-processes whose aim is to intervene on the world that is already built. Javier Mozas, "Remediate, Reuse, Recycle. Re-processes as atonement." In: *Reclaim. Remediate, Reuse, Recycle*, a+t architecture publishers, issue 39-40, 2012, p.25.

[23] See Mosè Ricci, "New Paradigms: Reducing Reusing Recycling the City (and the Landscapes)." In: Pippo Ciorra and Sara Marini (eds.), *Recycle. Strategies for Architecture, City and Planet*, Electa, Milano, 2011, p. 73.

[24] According to Marco Petroni "[…] recycling is a philosophy, not just another way of building things. Ciorra's philosophically-oriented overview makes reuse and recycling central to a topical debate on the latest trends in architecture." Marco Petroni, "Re-Cycle at Maxxi". In: *Abitare*, December 5, 2011.

[25] Javier Mozas, "Remediate, Reuse, Recycle. Re-processes as atonement." In: *Reclaim. Remediate, Reuse, Recycle*, a+t architecture publishers, issue 39-40, 2012, p.15.

[26] The 10th International Architecture Exhibition at the 2006 Venice Biennale of Architecture, was titled "Cities, Architecture and Society". It lasted from September 12 to November 7 and was directed by Richard Burdett.

[27] Rietveld Landscape curated the Dutch Pavillion at 2010 Venice Architecture Biennale. The 12th International Architecture Exhibition at the 2010 Venice Biennale of Architecture, was titled "People Meet in Architecture." It lasted from August 29 to November 22 and was directed by Kazuyo Sejima.

[28] The exhibition was curated by Pippo Ciorra with Mosè Ricci, Paola Viganò, Sara Marini, Reinier De Graaf, Jean Philippe Vassal. It lasted from December 1, 2011 to May 20, 2012.

[29] It refers to the German Pavilion in the 13th International Architecture Exhibition. The 2012 Venice Architecture Biennale was titled "Common Ground." It lasted from August 29th to November 25th and was directed by David Chipperfield.

[30] See Rosenfield, Karissa. "Venice Biennale 2012: Reduce/Reuse/Recycle / German Pavilion". In: ArchDaily, August 27, 2012.

[31] Javier Mozas, "Remediate, Reuse, Recycle. Re-processes as Atonement." In: *Reclaim. Remediate, Reuse, Recycle*, a+t architecture publishers, issue 39-40, 2012, p.15.

[32] Mosè Ricci, "New Paradigms: Reducing Reusing Recycling in the City (and the Landscapes)." In: Pippo Ciorra and Sara Marini (eds.), *Recycle. Strategies for Architecture,*

City and Planet, Electa, Milano, 201, p.73.

[33] For more information see the "Conversation with Francesc Muñoz" carried out at the Universidad Autònoma de Barcelona on August 19, 2013, in *Chapter 5* of this book.

[34] Referred to the conference of Michael Jakob, "Urban Infrastructure" in *Séminaire théorique 9*, Geneve, December 2012.

[35] Mirko Guaralda, *Le infrastrutture viarie dismesse o declassate ed il progetto di paesaggio*. Libreria CLUP Soc. Coop., Segrate, Milano, 2006.

[36] The High Line green promenade was designed by James Corner Field Operations as landscape architects with Diller Scofidio + Renfro, Piet Oudolf and Buro Happold, together with Friends of the High Line. It was approved in 2002 and work was begun in 2006. It is owned by the City of New York, and maintained and operated by the *Friends of the High Line*.

[37] Pippo Ciorra and Sara Marini (eds.), *Recycle. Strategies for Architecture, City and Planet*, Electa, Milano, 2011, p. 74.

[38] Gregor, Alison, "As a Park Runs Above, Deals Stir Below". In: *The New York Times*, August 10, 2010.

[39] Mosè Ricci, "New Paradigms: Reducing Reusing Recycling in the City (and the Landscapes)". In: Pippo Ciorra and Sara Marini (eds.), *Recycle. Strategies for Architecture, City and Planet*, Electa, Milano, 2011, p.76.

[40] The Trento Tunnels project started in 2008 carried out by a multidisciplinary team made up of Studio Terragni Architetti (CUNY), Stanford Humanities Lab (Stanford), FilmWork (Trento), and Gruppe Gut (Bolzano), under the aegis of Fondazione Museo Storico del Trentino and the regional authorities.

[41] See Studio Terragni Architetti, "The Trento Tunnels Cultural Space". In: *Phaidon Atlas*.

[42] Pippo Ciorra and Sara Marini (eds.), *Recycle. Strategies for Architecture, City and Planet*, Electa, Milano, 2011, p. 28.

[43] Kurt W. Forster. "The light at the end..." In: *Tunnel REvision*, Book of 12th International Architecture Exhibition Venezia, 2010, p. 57.

[44] Chris Reed and Nina-Marie Lister, "Parallel Genealogies." In: Chris Reed and Nina-Marie Lister (eds.), *Projective Ecologies* (Cambridge, MA: Harvard University Graduate School of Design; New York: Actar Publishers, 2014): p.25.

[45] *Resilience* in Physics is the capacity of a material to return to the original form after being deformed. Etymologically it derives from "resilient," from Latin *"resiliens"* which comes from *"resilire"* that literally means "to bounce." The concept of resilience has been used and adopted in several fields. In engineering, resilience is the capacity of a material to absorb energy of elastic deformation. In information technology, resilience is the capacity of a system to adapt to the conditions of use and to resist wear in order to ensure the availability of services. In psychology, resilience is the ability to cope in a positive way to traumatic events and to positively reorganize life by facing the difficulties. In biology and ecology resilience is the capacity of a material—of a community or of an ecological system— to auto-repair after damage and to return to its initial state, after being subjected to a disturbance that has changed the original condition.

[46] Chris Reed, Nina-Marie Lister, "Parallel Genealogies." In: Chris Reed, Nina-Marie Lister (eds.), *Projective Ecologies* (Cambridge, MA: Harvard University Graduate School of Design; New York: Actar Publishers, 2014): p.26.

1.3 From Glamour to Low-Cost Experience

[47] Le Corbusier took specific inspiration from the airplanes that he lived in, paying attention to every little detail of the design. Referred to the book of Le Corbusier, *Verso una architettura*, Longanesi & C., Milano, 2002.

[48] See the article of John Brownlee, "What It Was Really Like To Fly During The Golden Age Of Travel," December 5, 2013.

[49] Fog delays a group of travelers headed for New York. They wait at the V.I.P. lounge of London Airport, each at a moment of crisis in his or her life. The V.I.P.s, 1963, director: Anthony Asquith. In fact, "Jet Set" conjures up an image of well-healed and sophisticated international travellers. Today air travel seems far from glamorous. Yet even as far back as the 50s flying was opening up to ordinary people as well.

[50] See the essay of Beatriz Colomina "Toward a Global Architect". In: *Architect's Journeys*, GSAPP Books, The Graduate School of Architecture, Planning, and Preservation, Columbia University, New York, 6 Edition, 2011, p. 25.
[51] See the article of Stefano Paleari and Renato Redondi, "Piccoli aeroporti perché non sono troppi". In: *LaRepubblica.it*, December 6, 2010.
[52] Laura Cipriani, *Airport urbanism. Aeroporti Low Cost e Nuovi Paesaggi*, Aracne, 2012, p. 12.
[53] *Ibid.*, p. 144.
[54] As described by Marc Augé in his well known book *Nonluoghi. Introduzione a una antropologia della surmodernità*, Elèuthera, Milano, 2009.
[55] It refers to an interview conducted by Laura Cipriani "We arrived this morning. We have been shopping in Bergamo Alta and also in the shopping mall Oriocenter. It is the second time that we flown here to shop". Laura Cipriani, *Airport Urbanism. Aeroporti Low Cost e Nuovi Paesaggi*, Aracne, 2012, p. 52.

CHAPTER 2

Lleida-Alguaire Airport
Catalonia | Spain
Photo by Sara Favargiotti | 2011

Natalie: What?
Rayan: Follow me.
Natalie: I really like my luggage.
Rayan: That's exactly what it is. It's luggage. Do you know how much time you lose by checking in?
Natalie: I don't know. Five, ten minutes?
Rayan: Thirty-five minutes a flight. I travel two hundred seventy days a year. That's a hundred fifty-seven hours. That makes seven days. You willing to throw away an entire week on that?

Rayan Bingham, Natalie Keener, *Up in the Air*, 2009

AIRPORT ON-HOLD

2. AIRPORT ON-HOLD

What do huge flocks of sheep, hundreds of rabbits, business parks, metropolitan parks, leisure parks, high-tech networks and airport networks have in common with airports? These are the most frequent visitors to airports recently constructed in Europe. These are the new ways of inhabiting an airport and connecting it to its context. In fact, many underused and obsolescent airports have never managed to gain their central role, causing them to completely or partially lose their function. Those are airports on-hold. Over the last one hundred years, the world—with significant impacts in North America and Europe—has built thousands of airports. Given the history of rapid growth of air travel but also due to the cities expansions, many airports have become obsolete; many have been abandoned, either because they are too small, in the wrong places, no longer needed by a military use, or for the functional obsolescence of the structures. Only in Europe there are around 500 abandoned airports, in North America more than 1,000.[1] It is a condition widespread in the world. It is a phenomenon that will not slow down soon rather it might be increase, thinking also to hundreds of inner city airports that will not exist in approximately ten years. What to do with these flat, concrete, highly complex sites, often urban spaces, once they are no longer needed for air travel?

Having so many airport infrastructures has caused a premature obsolescence of many of them. Many airports were abandoned becoming a problem for cities in terms of space and cost. It is one thing to talk about abandoned airports but another thing altogether to consider them on-hold airports. "On-hold" is different from similar expressions such as "stand-by" or "in-pause". In English stand-by or in-pause express a more passive meaning. These infrastructures are in a transitory phase in their life, with an indeterminate future. There is the potential to regenerate or reuse, although not necessarily connected to aviation activities that can re-activate these underused infrastructures. It can be the beginning of a new life cycle. The question is therefore: how can they be re-used, re-generating themselves, their central role and the surrounding territory? Airports have often been considered as islands isolated from cites and at the same time hyper-connected to the world but in order to reactivate on-hold airport it becomes relevant to consider airports not only as places in a territory, nearby or far from cities, but also their rhythms and environmental implications.

2.1 AIRPORT, CITY AND TERRITORY

The conflict between airports, their fundamental role in the urban structure, the oppressive impacts that they generate on the surrounding territory, their potential role as attractors and generators in local economies through their strategic connection with their surroundings, gives them an ambivalent, but fundamental, role in contemporary urban development strategies. Airports today, have never been more central to the life in cities, yet they remain relatively peripheral to many discussions in urban design and planning. According to Pearman, the world's architects and planners are increasingly treating the airport not as a separate entity but as just another part of the urban condition.[2] Airports are architectural structures with a high-specific urban function: in most cases they lack a physical and spatial integration with their urban context. The task is then to design effectively for the whole physical, environmental and emotional experience of the airport over a wide area. Operative airport hubs, both small and large, generate iconic images marking their presence in the territory and are used as a centrality in their new urban condition. However, looking at the numbers of airports in Europe, we see a territory completely full: 475 in France, 549 in Germany, 505 in England, 150 in Spain, 112 in Italy.[3] The presence of a multitude of airports, especially of small size, is not an exclusive characteristic of the Italian system. In fact, the percentage of smaller airports in Italy is lower than others major European countries, with a share of 53.3% compared to a European average of 62.0%.[4] Even if the distribution of the Italian population is more fragmented compared to United States or other European countries, Italian aviation traffic reflects the characteristics of the population, with a higher dispersion of potentialities. The geography of Italy adds to this effect: a peninsular territory with mountains and large islands increase fragmentation while also increasing the need for air transportation. From this perspective, airports are fundamental in relation to the physical characteristics of the territory and they overcome the structural deficiencies of other modes of transport, like railways. In many regions, airports are the only way to have a door that connects territories to the other side Italy and Europe. This also has important implications for social and economic development.

Big hub, regional, low-cost, on-hold airports

The airport structure and its dimensions have changed over the last hundred years. During the pioneer phase (1900-1920), after the enthusiasm generated from the first flight of the Wright brothers, the first airfields were large meadows of grass, without a precise direction, to allow aircrafts to land and take off easily. The wide and circular shape developed naturally to avoid wind difficulties. In the post-war period, the evolution of the flying experience corresponded to an improvement in the technical infrastructure of airports. Longer runways and new covering materials were added, but also the organization of the facilities around the terminal area generated a new space for people. This technological evolution brought a growth of demand, transforming the airport into a more complex architectural and territorial structure. At that time, the airport acquired a territorial as well as functional role.[5] With the introduction of new jet airplanes and the increase in passenger demand, airports grew and were more connected, through other infrastructures, to nearby cities. The relationship between airports and cities became inseparable. The Hub and Spoke Era had begun. The existing airport facilities soon became unsuitable in dimension and proximity to the unceasing development of nearby cities. So, obsolete airports were abandoned for a more ideal location: new, bigger airports were built along the major infrastructure in the territory. The airport became a real *city-airport*. During the 1980s, big hubs competed with each other in Europe. The word "hub" refers to a major airport that allows passengers to take flights and to make transfers to national and international destinations. An airport hub is an economic locomotive for the surrounding territory.[6] In fact, large multinational firms choose the cities with the most connected hubs worldwide in order to establish their headquarters. The reduction in time by not having to go to another airport is one of the assets most valued by professionals in the new economy. According to the Japanese economist Kenichi Ohmae without an intercontinental airport, a city will be off the global map of the twenty-first century.[7] Regional airports have been connected to main hubs and served national destinations with fewer passengers per plane but with several flights per week. The presence of a regional airport constituted a positive element for territorial development and for communities. In other cases, however, it was a failure. Competitive airport terminals became relevant for airport development or decline. In particular, in these airports, the localization of new enterprises, service facilities, transport infrastructures, pollution consequences, agricultural land use, natural areas protection and related dynamics have been carefully assessed.

Among these structures, territories have been soon colonized by smaller airports, the majority of those were military airports. In the 1990s, deregulation of the air traffic allowed the emergence of low-cost carriers and the consequential transformation of many secondary airports into Low-cost airports. This process gave a new possibility for aviation to all those airfields that were too small to compete with the big hubs but close enough to cities to gather a consistent amount of passengers. In fact, many airports recalibrated their fundamental function through the integration of air traffic transportation facilities together with activities that regenerate their life and the surrounding territories. Several secondary airports have been incorporated into the low-cost airport network, generating a renewal of both infrastructure and function, and in the growth of activities not limited to air transportation. Reusing small airports became crucial on the local scale because it generated a rapid transformation of land use and of the infrastructure network relative to land transportation: the airport became a landmark in the territory and an important element for local economies. Those airports were the satellites of major hubs, smaller than regional airports and, for that reason, better connected to cities. Satellite airports soon became nodes in a dense, complementary network with many national and short-distance connections. This network also included private airfields and aerodromes. They were no longer only structures for flight operations, but new urban places: the localization of alternative facilities increased the quality of the land and the value of the airport. They established a stronger relationship between the infrastructure and their surrounding territories. At the same time they were creating economic improvements and new uses for the airports. In this context the reuse of secondary airports, projecting the territory in the European mobility network, offers interesting development opportunities. Land use management becomes a fundamental issue since airports operating at the international level attract other functions and activities that are not strictly related to air traffic that also benefit local economies. It is therefore necessary to understand the nature of these transformations in order to manage their development.

This process shows the exponential growth of airports. Given the history of rapid growth of air travel but also due to the cities expansions, many airports have become obsolete; many have been abandoned, either because they are too small, in the wrong places, no longer needed by a military use, or for the functional obsolescence of the structures. However, the process for the closure and the consequential transformation of an underutilized airport in not obvious, and it might take several years before choosing to definitely deactivate an airport. Very often, in fact, airport owners don't see the option of demolishing the infrastructure as the most convenient alternative. Some destinies may be opened and can generate unexpected uses and, in the meanwhile, airports can be kept as reserves with gradual transformations. This phase is a transitional condition in which airports are holding possible patterns that might potentially activate a new life cycle. For airports on-hold, the cycle is not over yet, but it is rather a phase of transition to realign the cyclical nature of airfields by diversifying the operations and preparing the field for a future transformation. In that sense, it is not uncommon that an underutilize airport remains in a limbo for some time, valuating possible alternatives scenarios.

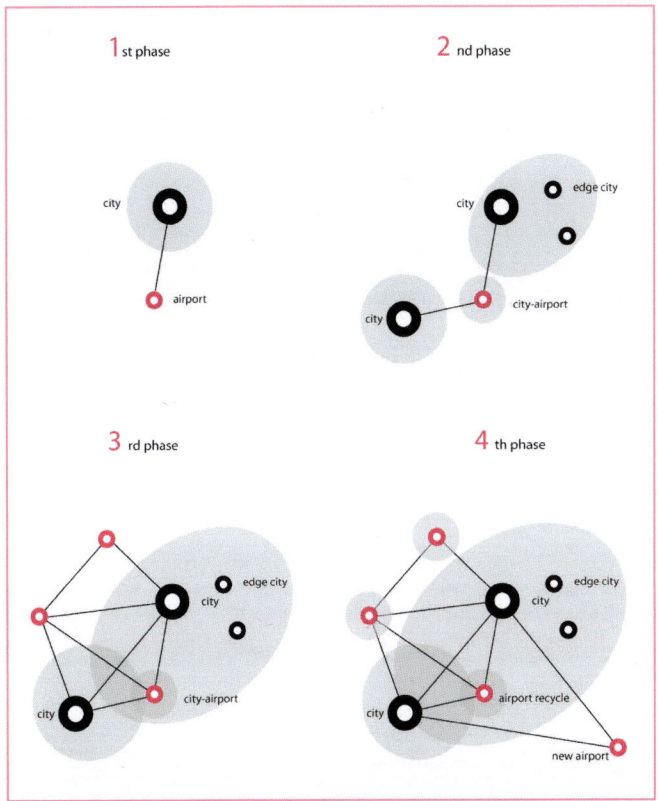

Airport and city development. Diagrams by Laura Cipriani in "Ecological Airport Urbanism", redrawn by Sara Favargiotti | 2013

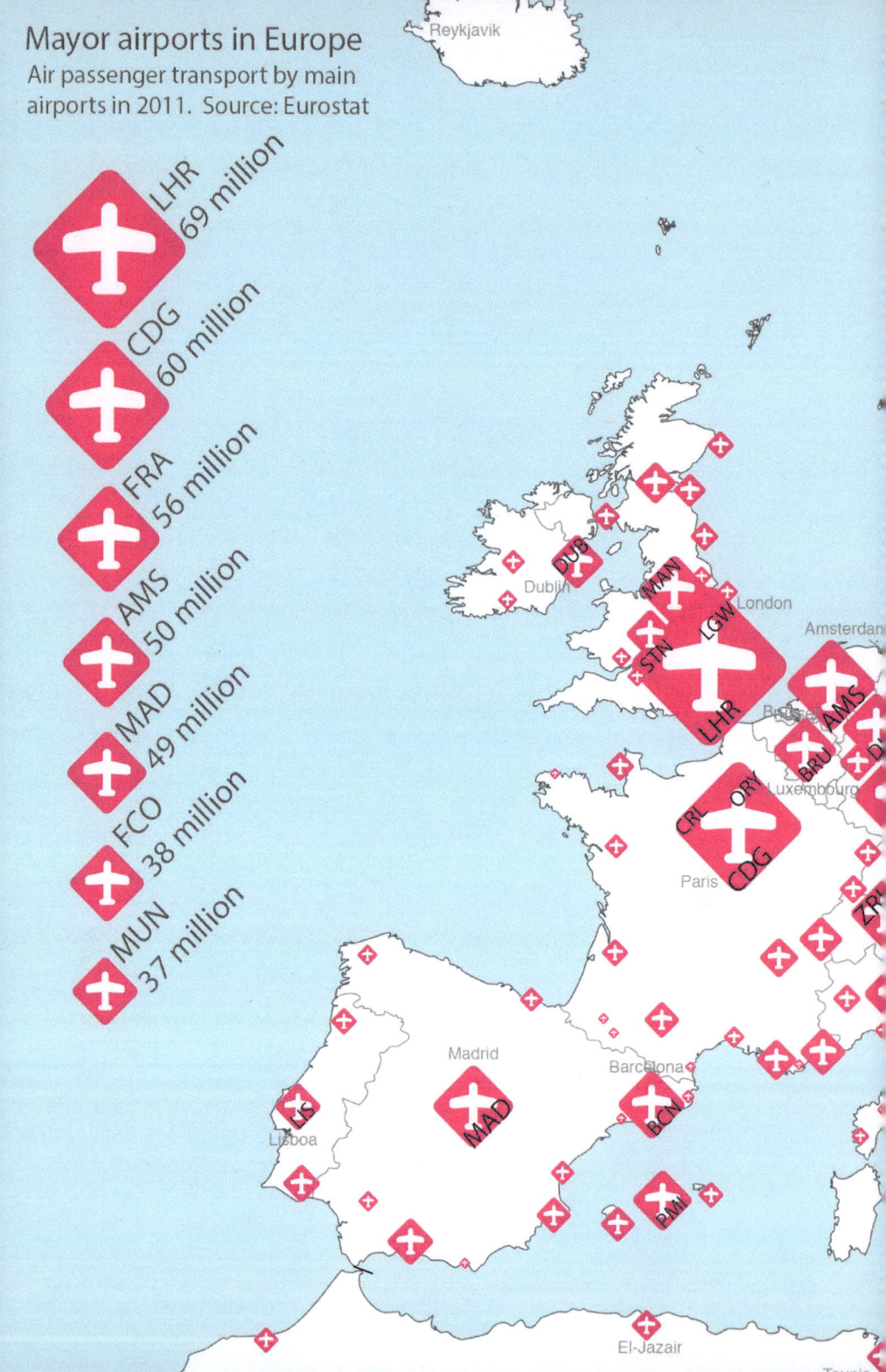

Low Cost Airports in 2013

● Low Cost Carriers

287 Europe
33 France
30 Italy
29 England
24 Germany
23 Spain

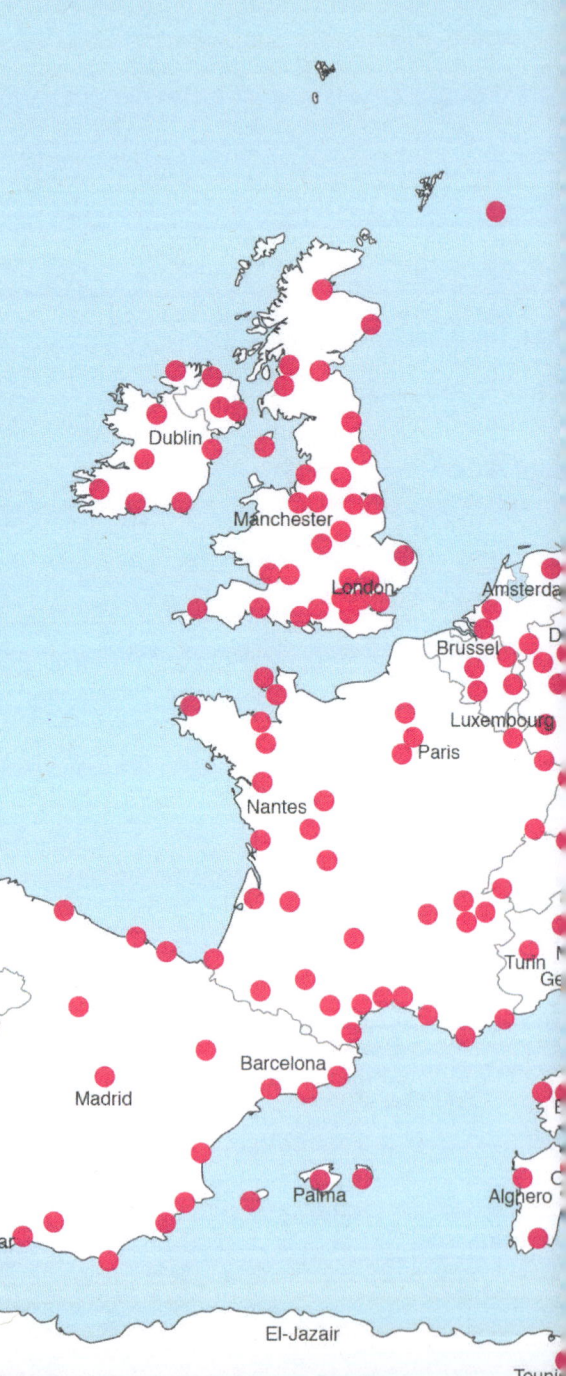

2.2 AIRPORT LIFE CYCLE

Everything is characterized by a life cycle: products, services, and structures. [8] Product Life Cycle (PLC) is a business analysis that attempts to identify a set of common stages in the life of commercial products. In other words the Product Life Cycle is used to map the stages through which a product moves during its lifespan. The stages of a product's life cycle can be classified as follows: Introduction, Growth, Maturity and Decline. Stages of Product Life Cycle can vary in length. In the initial phase, the product sales are the lowest and increase very slowly (low and slow stage). During this period of introduction or development, promotional expenses consume the highest proportion of sales. Once the market has accepted the product, sales begin to rise. This is the Growth stage, this is the most crucial stage that helps the brand establish itself in the market. In the Maturity stage, the market becomes saturated because the house-hold demand is satisfied and distribution channels are full. By now the product is widely accepted and growth slows down. Before long, however, a successful product in this phase will come under pressure from competitors. The producer will have to start spending again in order to defend the product's market position. Sooner or later actual sales begin to fall under the impact of new product competition and changing consumer tastes and preferences (decline stage). A company will no longer be able to fend off the competition, or a change in consumer tastes or lifestyle will render the product redundant and obsolete. The "first" life cycle of the product is ended, giving the opportunity to new "secondary" uses through the recycling of its parts. Not all products reach this final stage. Some continue to grow and others rise and fall. The product life cycle is an important concept in marketing. It includes four stages that a product goes through from when it was first thought of until it is eliminated from the production, with the consequent possibility of activation of new life cycles through the recycle of some elements.

The theme of new life cycle for infrastructure could bring interesting possibilities in urban and landscape design but also urban planning: faced with the uncertainty of the market and of the future, hybrid urban elements and structures could define changeable scenarios of resilience. Mohsen Mostafavi—talking about the Branzi definition of adaptive urbanism—states that for Branzi it is the fluidity of the city and its capacity to be diffuse and "enzymatic" in character that merits acknowledgment. In a series of projects that deliberately blur the boundaries between the disciplines (and are as much indebted to art practices as they are to agriculture and network culture), Branzi has proposed adaptive urbanism based on their symbiotic relationships.[9] Starting from the same assumptions, cities have to gather the capacities to be "reversible, evolving and provisory" as the qualities necessary to respond to the changing needs of society in a state of constant reorganization. "The blurring of boundaries—real and virtual, as well as urban and rural—implies a greater connection and complementarity between the various parts of a given territory."[10] In a way, this could be the opportunity given by resilience to infrastructure renewal. Infrastructures have been built to be a solid element in space and time. Structures that have lasted longer over time, could have achieved higher performances. However, the present conditions and statistical data highlight that the situation is more complicated. As described above, the airport's concept itself seems in crisis. The symbol of Modernity has quickly declined, at least conceptually. Born in the Modern Age to become the evolutionary, fashionable and futuristic way of transport and, in less than one Century, it is in decline. Many airports seem new archaeologies to be rethought rather than

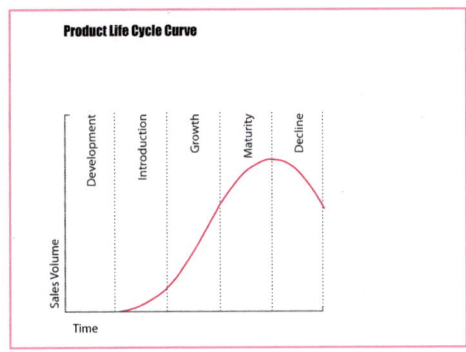

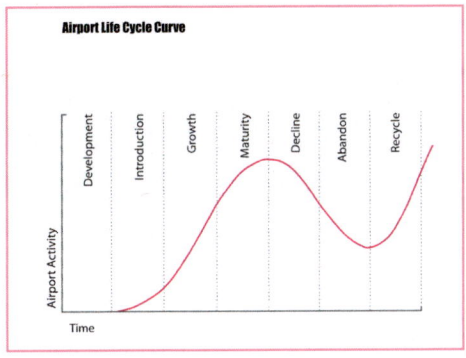

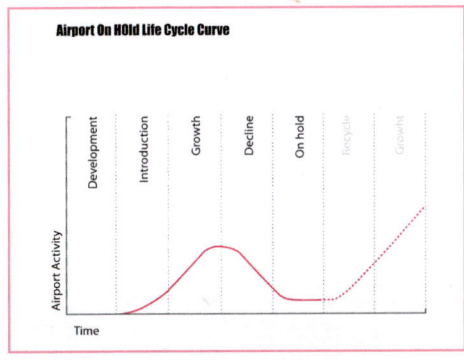

Comparison between product life cycle with airport life cycle and airport on-hold life cycle. Diagrams by Sara Favargiotti | 2013

places of innovation and progress: in a shorter time than other infrastructure, these structures have already been used, dismissed, abandoned and even recycled. A condensed life-cycle. In the same way as a general product, airports have a life cycle: it becomes a fundamental concept in the design of cities and territories. Airports have a development phase of aviation activities and related facilities that bring a growth. After a time of activity and production and reached the "peak" of development, they begin to decline. Becoming obsolete because of a number of problems concerning inadequate physical and technical structures for flights (runways, inadequate spaces for airlines), safety, noise and pollution problems the construction of new airports seems to be more convenient. Thus, new generation airports are built, while the previous become rapidly outdated and obsolete, until when their activities is definitively suspended. After their official closing, airports became abandoned. This generates a decrease in the value of the territory and leaves wide polluted structures in the landscape: ruins of the modern age. For many years, former airports will remain in an indeterminate state: uncertain and also unpredictable futures characterize this long phase. Looking for new alternative uses, airports became increasingly damaged and compromised. Again, processes of reuse and recycle can reactivate the airport areas, generating a renewal of airport areas but also a new phase of growth for the airports and their surrounding contexts. A new life begins. But what happens when this life cycle is not able to reach the "peak" of its development, and the indeterminate airport on-hold state is anticipated at an early phase?

On-hold state

In North America and Europe the majority of airports built in the quarter of century were not necessary at all. These are now costly problems. These territories encounter many difficulties to keep up or develop their competitiveness in this era of declining resources and generally poor economic development. In many cases, policy makers don't find a real benefit to strengthening scheduled flights or improving technical and physical characteristics of their underused airports. Since the beginning of the Landscape Urbanism design process, the airport has been a very central case study for American landscape designers. This is because the other disciplines—architecture, urban studies, planning—have not really developed a coherent approach to those places and landscape designers "are interested in ecological performance and urban form."[11] However, the widespread reality of underuse makes this topic crucial in the contemporary debate. Many airport infrastructures have never managed to reach their full potential or have lost their central role. When this happens, airports drastically burden the regional economy. What are possible futures for these new infrastructures already in decline?

To view the airport as something that can be reloaded means to consider its rhythms, its life cycles, and metamorphoses. It is a constantly changing condition. However, the transition from one cycle to another cycle allows continuous rebirth. The in-between phase is a transitional state in which airports in the on-hold state can potentially generate a new life cycle. "On-hold "is different from similar expressions such as "stand-by" or "in-pause." In English "stand" or "pause" express a more passive meaning. Instead, the preposition "on"[12] implies a pro-activity: it has an embryo of activation. Speaking about on-hold infrastructure is speaking of infrastructures that are still having an embryo of life that can be activated or re-activated. It's one thing to talk about abandoned airports and another thing to consider on-hold airports. In fact, for airports on-hold, the cycle is not over yet. It refers to a phase of transition. In that sense, the indeterminate state of these airports could be transformed into an opportunity. Understanding and interpreting previous design and theoretical research experiences that deal with the airports topic, it could be possible to outline hypothesis for the reactivation of airports on-hold. Experimentations on specific case studies of these operations are described in Chapter 4. Because cities are increasingly difficult to enter, it is smart to approach these spaces as incoming terminals (for airplanes, trains, cars) and, at the same time, as a place that maintains its character as gateway to the city. To use what once was a network, and specifically the airport network, it is possible to forge a closer link with more of the territory. It could become a cultural or productive hub where the transport is almost minimal. However it could also be a mix of productive, cultural, territorial elements that are no longer the proper or official airport activity but a movement of and production of ideas relative to cities and in relationship to each other (network). This defines a set of services related to other things. A cultural terminal that allows entry into the city with a specific relationship to the territory is the scenario that could be developed during the on-hold phase.

The transition time from one cycle ending to another one beginning, could allow for several possibilities in airport evolution. In the majority of cases, temporary and sometimes illegal activities reactivated the airport field and bring attention back to it. Other times aviation can stop for a while and be substituted with alternative activities related to the city.[13] Aviation activity can return again once there is a reactivation of the demand. This will allow for the possibility to re-introduce in the future productive development. There is also allows for the possibility that flight operations that at the present time are not plausible can return in the future. For instance, the network could place special events in the small former airports and are connected to a certain type of productivity—agricultural, micro-productivity or cultural activities—linked to the characteristics of the site for a km0 effect. Another dimension of flight transportation could be utilized, like a network of small-specialized airports, re-activating the aviation system. Finally, in a few relevant cases, a mixture of aviation use and urban functions may coexist. The potentiality of airports on-hold is that they generate the opportunity to activate a new life cycle without a definitive recycle. This condition could also open the possibility of a return of aviation as a future step. Even if the commingling of transport and urban functions is rare, because the strength of one is the weakness of the other, the on-hold state allows a potential combination of functions because it refers to a phase of transition. The result is the activation of a new cycle, not strictly connected to a recycle strategy, which implies a loss of meaning and value after a phase of decommissioning and abandonment: reuse and recycle are alternatives and challenges.

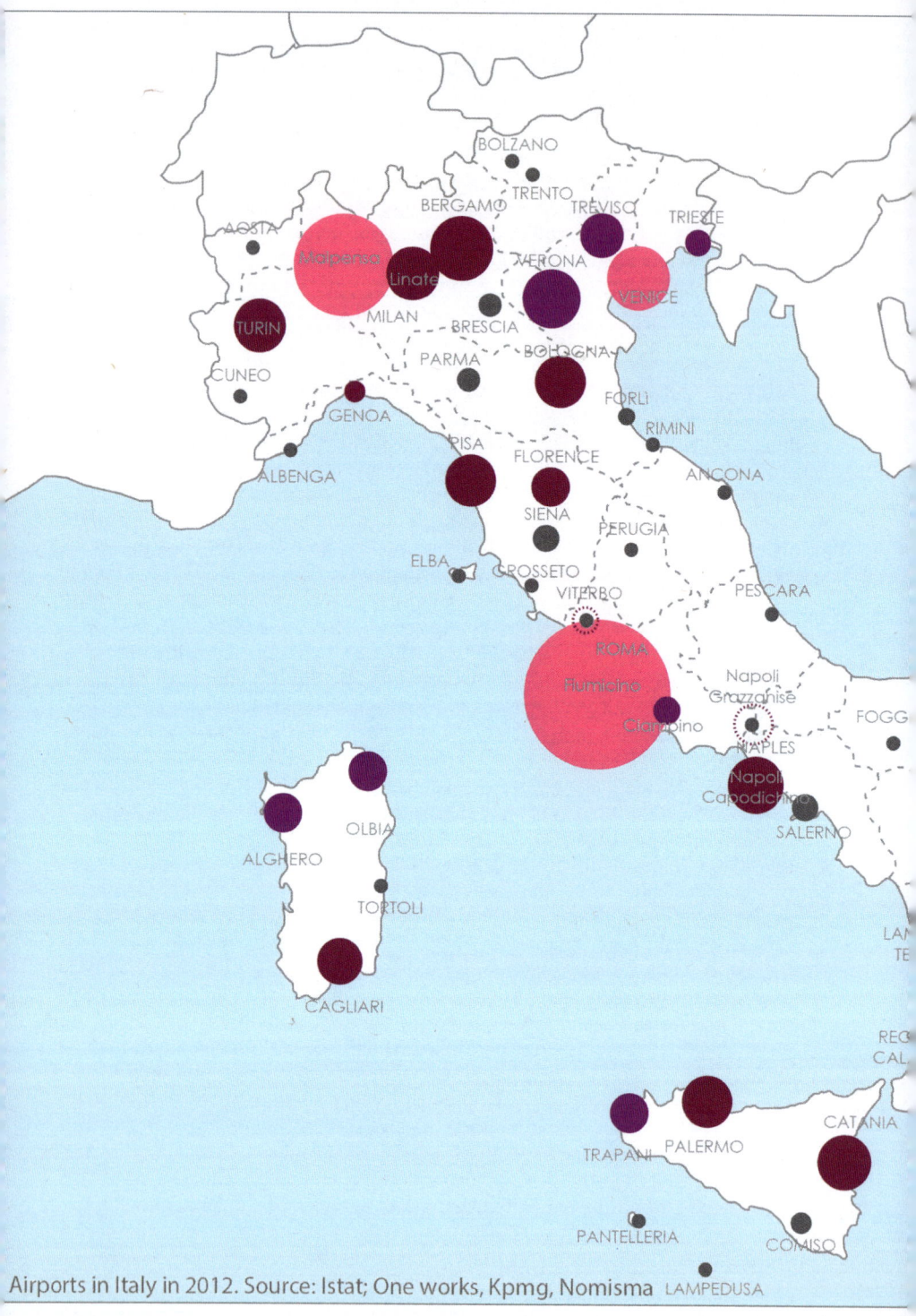

Airports in Italy in 2012. Source: Istat; One works, Kpmg, Nomisma

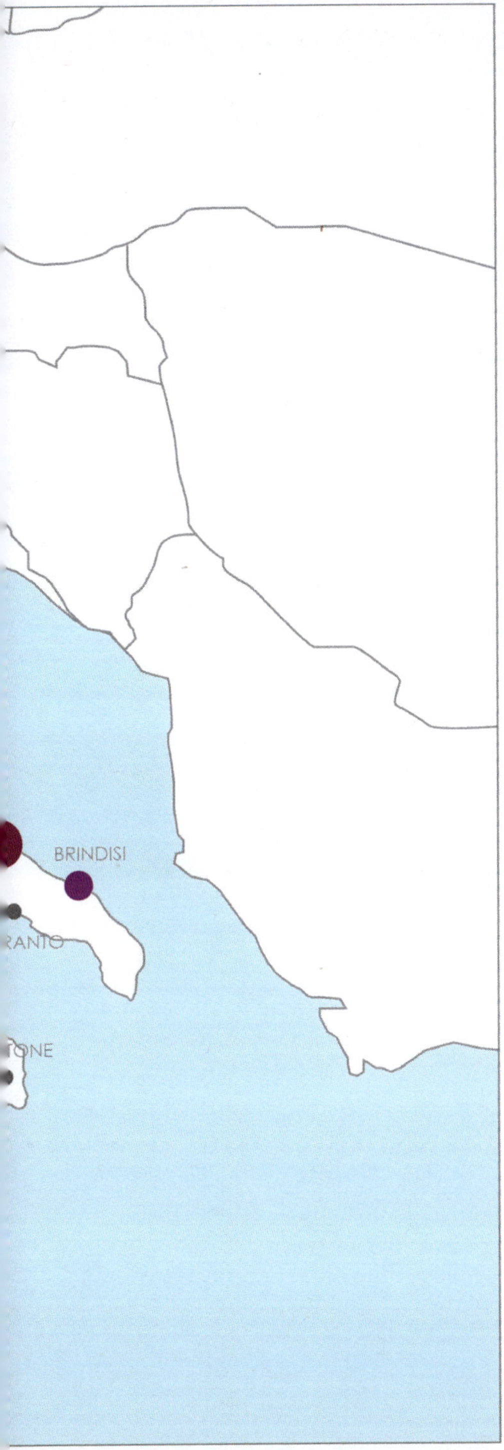

3 International Gates

11 Strategical Airports

8 Primary Airports

26 Uncertain future

BRINDISI

RANTO

ONE

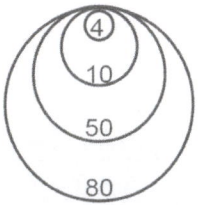

Passengers in millions (2012)

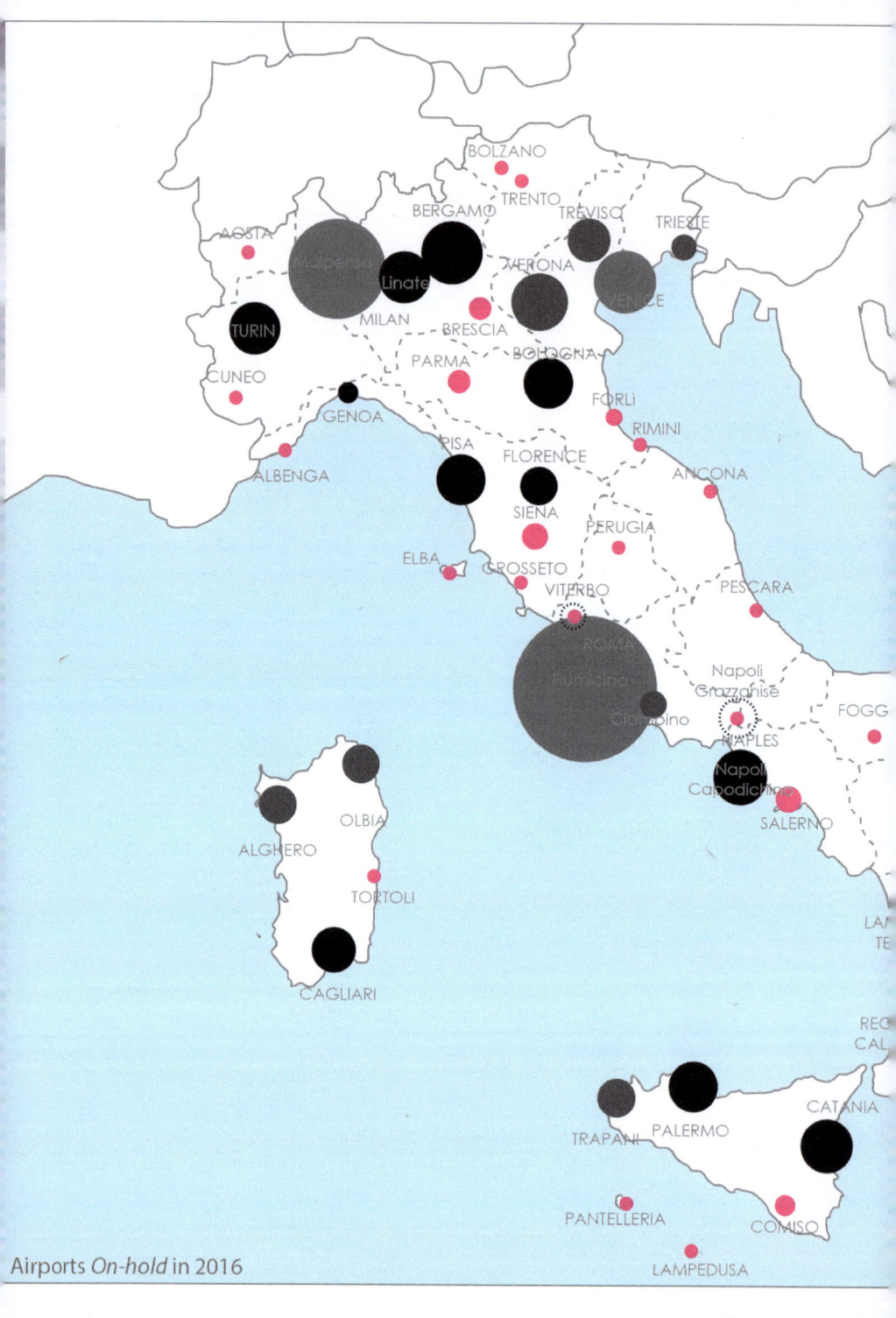

Airports *On-hold* in 2016

3 International Gates

11 Strategical Airports

8 Primary Airports

26 Airports *On-hold*

BRINDISI

RANTO

ONE

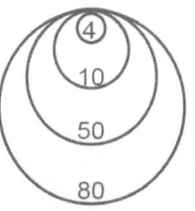

Passengers in millions

2.3 MAPPING AIRPORTS ON-HOLD

We have built runways and control towers in every corner of Italy, often at a distance of a few kilometers from each other. Was it an inordinate anarchy of projects or to answer real local needs? Of the 112 Italian national civil airports only a few of them could manage a positive income and of them just the big hubs. The others are ghost airports with the up-keep costs falling to local authorities. From Bolzano to Foggia there are many cathedrals in the desert: empty waiting rooms, check-in areas with more employees than passengers, firefighters waiting for planes that never arrive. Barman, radar men and border policemen engaged 24 hours a day—very often at the expense of taxpayers—twiddle their thumbs waiting to take care of a sparse 21 passengers per day. "It is a trend that has increased due to the low cost carriers. At the same time, being cathedrals in the desert does not make the small airports attractive for freight traffic."[14] Hundreds of millions of Euros of public money are spent on airports where few pass anymore. Once huge investments for the nation, now large debts for local authorities: this is the sprecopoli of small-Italian airports.[15] The funding to local authorities has substantially decreased and, unless there is the intervention of private capital, many ghost airports soon will become non-existent.

This condition is not exclusively Italian: many other European countries are in the same situation. The role of architecture for large infrastructure is to build the image of urban competitiveness. The effects of these processes on urban and territorial development have been enormous. It has lead to an overestimation and overproduction of airports across the European territory, becoming burdens on the local economy. This has significantly compromised the financial stability of the cities in Europe. During the height of the construction boom, authorities rushed to take advantage of opportunities to plan new airports. Many of the newest regional and secondary airports did not see a single passenger through their terminals. In Europe, this process has significantly affected two specific contexts: Italy and Spain. These Mediterranean countries have strongly believed in the myth of infrastructure as carrier of development. However, even though the contexts are different, the dynamics have been the same: the excessive over-construction has left two countries full of derelict airport infrastructure. "Jungles of waste," "bonsai airports," "cathedrals in the desert," or "ghost airports:" they can be called with many different names but all refer to those structures that have higher maintenance costs than benefits.[16] It is evident that the risk of closure is very high for the majority of these structures. Maybe, in the future, the network will expand again, and those airports will come back to life, or maybe not. The future is not predictable but the reality is demanding attention.

European contexts: Italy and Spain
Nowadays in Italy there are 112 operative airports with only 31 identified as airports of national interest.[17] Of the 112 airports, 90 are civilian airports (43 opened to commercial traffic and 47 with non-scheduled flights); 11 are military airports opened to civil traffic (3 opened to commercial traffic and 8 opened to

civil traffic with non-scheduled flights); 11 are used only for military operations. In addition, there are hundreds of airfields and heliports suitable for landing. Therefore, there are a total of 46 commercial airports: 43 civilians plus 3 military (Grosseto, Pisa and Trapani Birgi).[18] The 31 airports of national interest, are ranked according to their importance and traffic: 10 are included in the Core Network, that are considered to be of strategic importance to the EU as relevant city or primary nodes; 19 are in the Comprehensive Network, including those with traffic in excess of 1 million passengers per year and those with a traffic in excess of 500 thousand passengers per year and with specific territorial characteristics. To this list another two airports must be added because it is forecast that their flows will expand.[19] The distinction between strategic and non-strategic is based on the property. Local authorities own all Italian airports. Therefore, the reorganization of the Italian airport system provides the enhancement of international airports, while minor airports, considered by the Government as non-strategic or "not of national interest", will be entrusted to the management of the Regions.[20] Different scenarios will be possible for these cases: the ability to operate with a regional concession or the addressing of other functions or their closure. Unioncamere has estimated that the reduction in these minor airports could have significant repercussions on businesses and citizens, as well as the territories they served.[21] This picture shows the enormous proliferation of airports and the supply's fragmentation, concerning not just the geographical location of the airports, but also their management.[22] Many of these airports are in crisis.

In the political and economic debate in Italy, airports have often a predominant role. However, only in Northern Italy there is an airport every 50 kilometers: 17 airports are only between Albenga and Trieste, crossing Milan, Venice and Bologna.[23] Between being a lot and being too many, the limit is weak and it depends on their real utility and economic sustainability. On one hand, the entire aviation sector—considering airlines, airports, aviation industry and service providers—contributes 15 billion euros to the national GDP, employs 500 thousand people and handles 149 million passengers.[24] On the other hand, the Italian territory has an extremely high number of airports. After a initial success of the EU Directive "Open Skies", which liberalized the sector, the reform of Title V of the Constitution assigned to the regions the coordination of territorial infrastructures, which was often a failure.[25] Between the 1970s and 1980s there were 41 airports authorized by ENAC, but between the 1990s and 2000—in the highest moment of liberalization—they increased to 49. Almost one airport has been built each year. According to the statistics of Bureau Van Dijk, in the financial statements of 2009-2010, the Italian airports have accumulated a red balance of 3.4 billion euros in total. Municipalities, provinces and regions head 32% of the stake and, consequently, of the debt. Already in 2010 half of the airports had to downsize or even close because they had an insufficient catchment area.[26] Instead, new airports continue to be built: Perugia, Pantelleria, Lampedusa, Comiso[27] are just a few names of the recently constructed airports. In January 2013, the Ministry of Infrastructure and Transport issued an act to address the National Plan for airport development in order to rationalize the Italian airport system.[28]

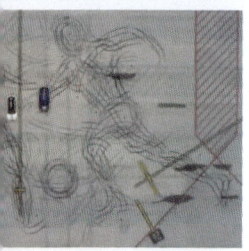

*"Passion leaves its marks"
Spot campaign for Audi,
during the Spanish derby
("El Clásico") Real Madrid-
Barcelona DDB Spain | 2011*

According to the Chamber of Commerce this will be damaging for the territory, arguing that these airports represent an engine in the local economies and a resource for development. Ferruccio Dardanello—President of Unioncamere since 2009—doesn't exclude that a rethinking of the airport system is required. However, he said that the discriminating criteria cannot only be the economic results and the costs per passenger, but other criteria should be identified, taking into account the benefits to surrounding territories. The reorganization of the airport system cannot be done on accounts: the cost-benefit has to be considered and not just the revenue cost, otherwise the challenges the country faces will be lost from the beginning.[29] From the other side, the ex-Minister for Infrastructure and Transport has noted that the National Airport Plan is not intended to close the smaller airports. Ciaccia argues that it is a waste of public resources and the alternative for airports not included in the National Plan is to create a network, joining and becoming economically sustainable. He claimed that nobody does the accounting and the intentions are not to close airports but the government want to verify how they can become an element for development. Localism is a problem and an airport alone does not generate development, but the development is created if the airports work in networks and make critical mass.

Spain seems to be a country with more airports than provinces as AENA manages 48 airports including some that may still be under construction or in planning, and there are 50 provinces.[30] If we include in the count airfields and private aerodromes, the numbers are tripled: in Spain there are about 150 airports and aerodromes, with hundreds of airfields. Thus, there are more airports than provinces. There are obviously very different structures for different uses. Furthermore, there is a very low percentage of positive income airports: in the AENA network, no more than nine airports are deficit free. The most obvious reason is that the infrastructure is not consistent with the actual demand. During the economic and the new-dwellings boom that characterized Spain until 2008, many local authorities have planned to build new airports by taking advantage of benefits induced by low-cost airlines. Actually, many of the newest of these airports have not see a single passenger pass through their terminals. La Seu d'Urgell Airport, Santander Airport, Huesca-Pirineos Airport, Lleida-Alguaire Airport, Ciudad Real Airport, Castellon Airport and Logroño-Agoncillo Airport are just a few of the underused and speculative airports—generally secondary or regional airports—with close to 1 million passengers per year, or even less. In many cases, political motivations and economic interests guided the investment decisions rather than real need. Their construction promised to create a gateway in an undiscovered region, providing jobs for locals struggling in a country with a high unemployment rate, and delivering tourists tempted by cheap deals to some of Spain's most beautiful landscapes. Thus, following the proliferation of routes with low passenger traffic, some of these airports have been called regional or secondary airports. Others prefer to call these infrastructures ghost airports or white elephants. They are all examples of the waste of public money on mega-infrastructure that covers the Spanish landscape.[31] In fact, of the 48 regional commercial airports built in the debt-ridden country in less than 20 years, only 11 make a profit.

According to a recent report of the National Competition Commission *(Comisión Nacional de la Competencia - CNC)*, in the past four years, state governments and several regional and municipal authorities have invested 247.3 million euros in public subsidies to support airlines in launching new routes or in maintaining existing ones, in the hope to promote the activity of many of these airports. However, as noted by some management committees of regional airports, this is not always true univocally: "It is normal for an autonomous region or a municipality to promote the activity of its airports. The presence, or not, of flights is relevant for the growth of tourism or local businesses. However, it does not make sense to maintain unprofitable routes that are only sustained by public money. There are flights that no airline would operate without these funds."[32] Additionally the demand for air travel has decreased during the current economic crisis. Very often the majority of small airports were not necessary at all. For many people it is a frustrating situation but for others it's an indispensable business necessity and, for that reason, eligible for public subsidies. Some experts argue that the economic activity of these airports could regenerate their local environment, allowing for a social function that transcends their negative impact on the income statement of AENA. This could be possible through the expansion of the companies settled in the surrounding areas and with the creation of hundreds of direct and indirect jobs. Furthermore, as described above, future trends show that the concentration of air traffic will grow in those airports connected to worldwide or low-cost companies. Therefore, all those airports that are not able to attract one of the two types of carriers may be the big losers in this traffic concentration.[33] While the amount of State subsidies was increasing, the number of passengers in Spanish airports was falling in recent years. In small regional airports, the most common scene is to see empty halls with few passengers, few airline or airport employees, and the information screens announcing flights scheduled for the next day.

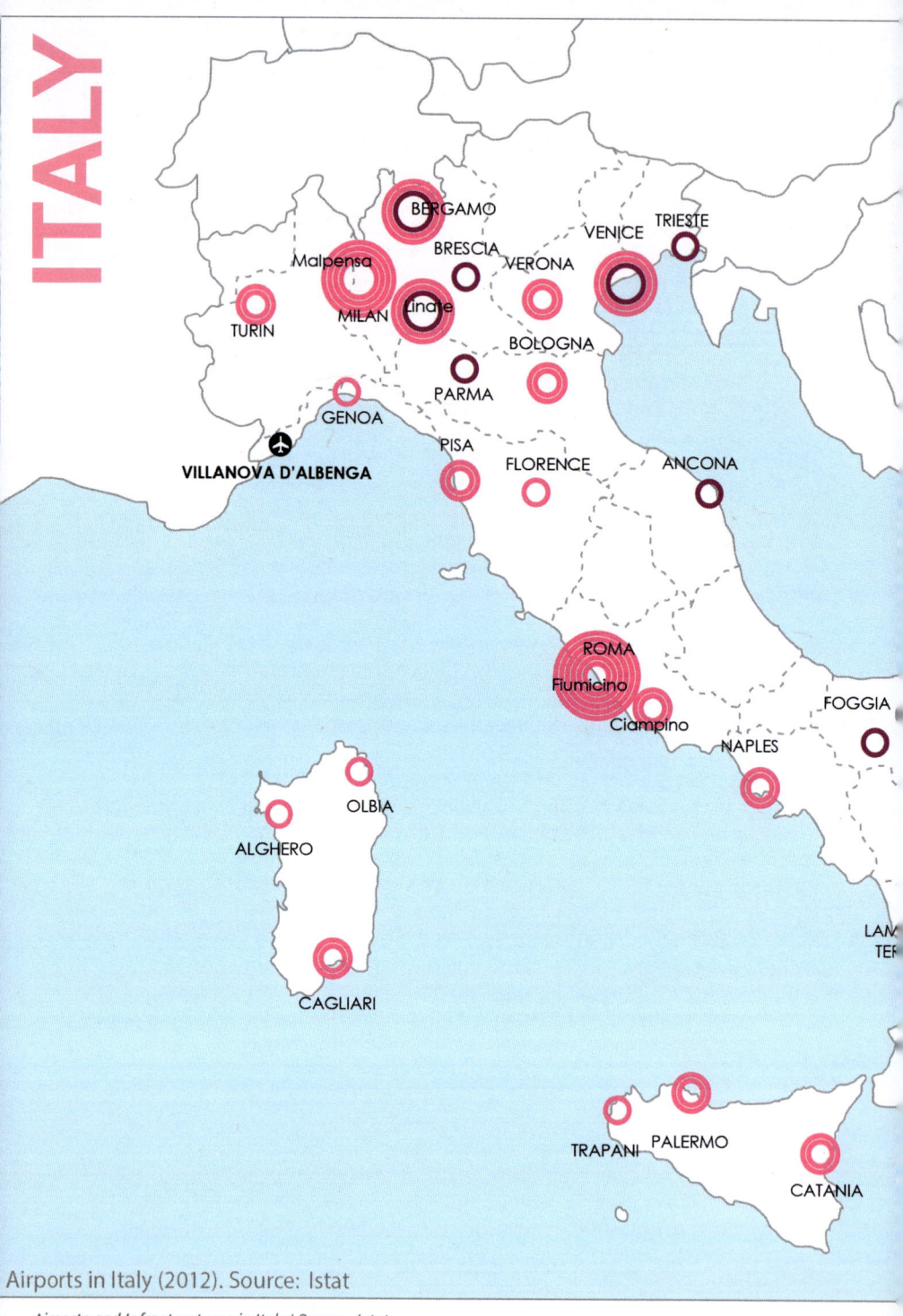

Airports and Infrastructures in Italy | Source: Istat
Drawing by Sara Farvagiotti | 2013

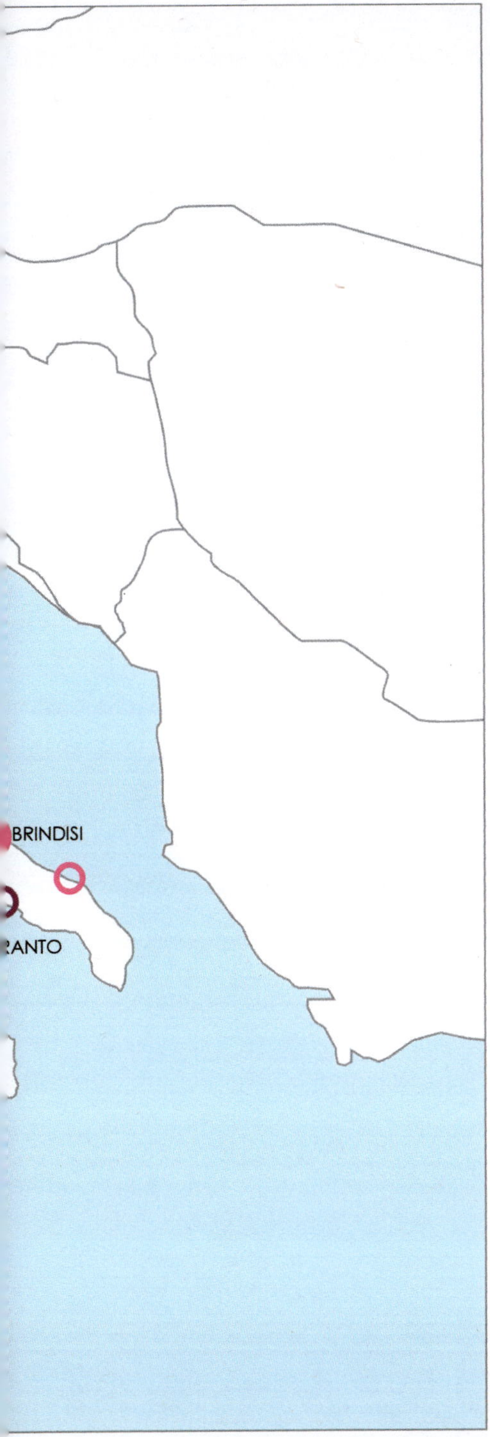

Infrastructures in Italy

MOTORWAY
6.661 km

RAILWAYS NETWORK
24.179 km

MAIN AIRPORTS
31

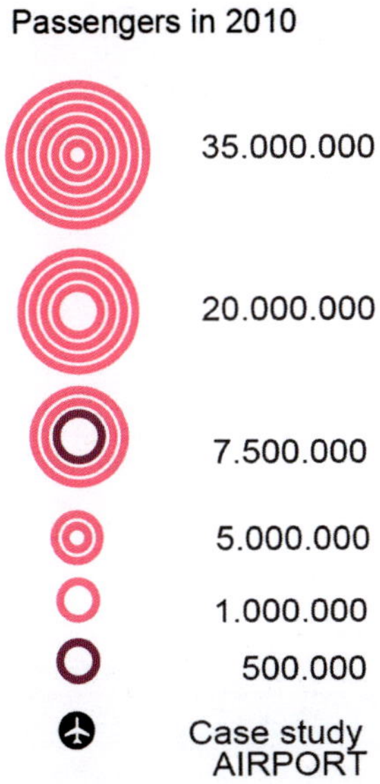

Passengers in 2010

 35.000.000

 20.000.000

 7.500.000

 5.000.000

 1.000.000

 500.000

 Case study AIRPORT

SPAIN

Airports in Spain in 2013. Source: Aena

Airports and Infrastructures in Spain | Source: Aena
Drawing by Sara Farvagiotti | 2013

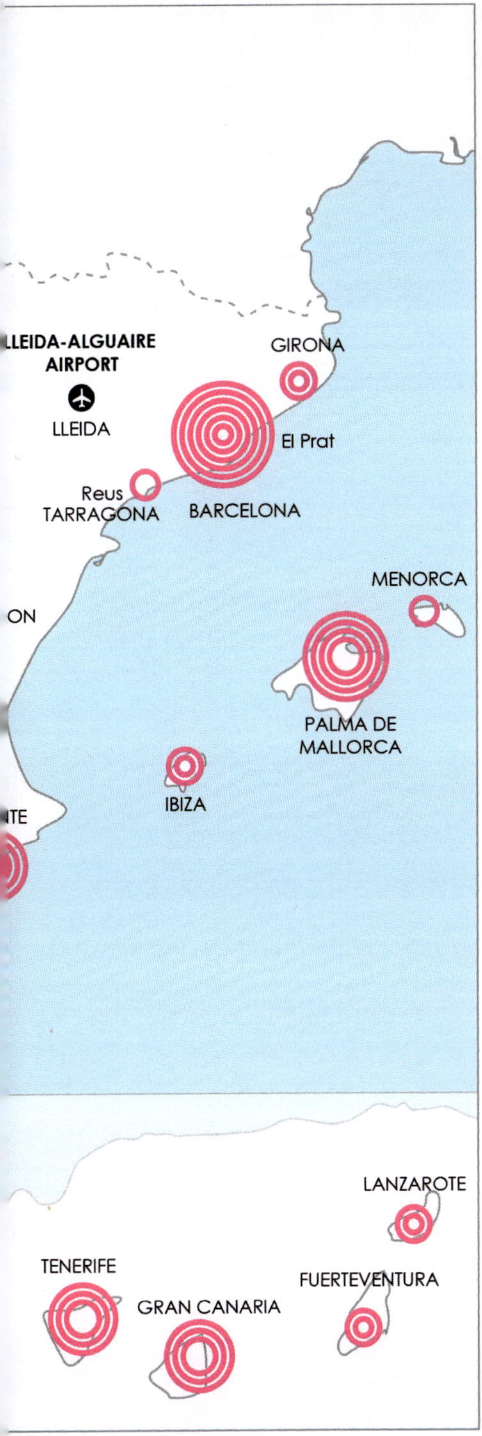

Infrastructures in Spain

MOTORWAY
13.872 km

RAILWAYS NETWORK
15.288 km

MAIN AIRPORTS
28

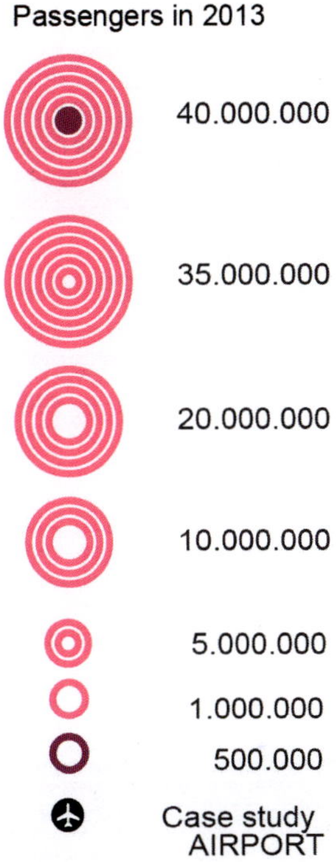

Passengers in 2013

 40.000.000

 35.000.000

 20.000.000

 10.000.000

 5.000.000

 1.000.000

 500.000

 Case study AIRPORT

CHAPTER 2. AIRPORT ON-HOLD

[1] Data obtained by national agencies combined and implemented with Internet researches. North America information gathered from U.S. Department of Transportation, Federal Aviation Administration and Office of Bureau of Transportation Statistics; confirmed by Luis Loarte, FAA Office of Airport Planning & Programming - National Planning and Environmental Division, during a telephone interview on May 5, 2016. Europe information gathered from interpretation of data from EUROCONTROL and national aviation agencies.

2.1 Airport, City and Territory

[2] Hugh Pearman, *Airports: A Century of Architecture*, Laurence King Publishing, 2004, p. 236.
[3] Efrén Mundina, "¿Hay Suficientes Aeropuertos en España?" Available at: www.nosoloaviones.com, March 13, 2012. Source: AENA.
[4] Stefano Paleari, Renato Redondi, "Piccoli aeroporti perché non sono troppi". In: *LaRepubblica.it*, December 6, 2010.
[5] See the essay of Chiara Rizzi, "Time Table. Evoluzione Spazio-temporale del Trasporto Aereo". In: Mosè Ricci, *iSpace*, Meltemi (collana Babele), 2009, pp. 24-25.
[6] See the research of Ramon Tremosa y Balcells, "Importancia de los Aeropuertos Regionales como Complementos de los Grandes Centros Aeroportuarios en el Territorio Arco Latino," supported by Arco Latino with the sponsorship of Lleida Municipality, 2008-2009.
[7] *Ibid.*, p. 37

2.2 Airport Life Cycle

[8] The life cycle model Richard Butler provides is a series of evolutionary stages that connect tourism and territorial transformations. Richard Butler, "The Concept of a Tourist Area Cycle of Evolution: Implications for Management of Resources". In: *Canadian Geographer*, n. 24, 1980. pp. 5-12.
[9] Mohsen Mostafavi, "Why Ecological Urbanisim? Why Now?" Introduction to Ecological Urbanism, p.30. See also Andrea Branzi, "For a Post-Environmentalism", pp. 110-113. In: Mohsen Mostafavi and Gareth Doherty (eds.), *Ecological Urbanism*, Lars Muller Publishers, 2010.
[10] *Ibid.*, p.30.
[11] See "Foreword. An Interview with Charles Waldheim," in this book. Interview conducted at the Graduate School of Design, Harvard University, on November 12, 2013, on the occasion of the conference "Airport Landscape: Urban Ecologies in the Aerial Age" and edited in July 2016.
[12] Adverb, 2. indicating continuation of a movement or action: *she burbled on, he drove on, and so on*. Further forward; in an advanced state: *I'll see you later on, time's getting on*. Adverb, 4. (of an electrical appliance or power supply) functioning: *they always left the lights on*. Source: *Oxford dictionary*.
[13] See the definition of "substitution effect" in Stephen Graham and Simon Marvin, *Telecommunications and the City: Electronic Spaces, Urban Places*, Routledge, 1996, pp. 330-331.

2.3 Mapping Airports On-hold

[14] Antonio Vanuzzo, "L'insostenibile lusso Italiano di un aeroporto ogni 50km". In: *Linkiesta*, January 9, 2013.
[15] The name "ghost airports" referrers to the article of Sandrine Morel, "Aéroports Fantômes," in: *Le Monde*, January 17, 2012.
[16] See Ettore Livini, "Aero Flop Italia. La sprecopoli dei mini aeroporti: 150 Milioni bruciati in tre anni," in: *LaRepubblica.it*, March 1, 2013.
[17] During the XVI Italian Legislature, the evolution of the airport system was at the center of a thorough investigation made by the IX Commission of Transport. On that occasion, there were also changes to the discipline of contracts, between ENAC and

airport management companies, and to airport fees. In January 2013, the government filed the official document *Notice of Address for the definition the National Plan for Airport Development* (*Atto di Indirizzo per la Definizione del Piano Nazionale per lo Sviluppo Aeroportuale*), Rome, January 29, 2013.

[18] Source: Assaeroporti, 2013; ENAC, 2013; and *Airports National Plan* (*Piano Nazionale per gli Aeroporti*), 2015.

[19] The ten big hub are: Bergamo Orio al Serio, Bologna, Genova, Milano Linate, Milano Malpensa, Napoli, Palermo, Roma Fiumicino, Torino, Venezia. Other thirteen airports have with over a million passengers per year are: Alghero, Bari, Brindisi, Cagliari, Catania, Firenze, Lamezia Terme, Olbia, Pisa, Roma Ciampino, Trapani, Treviso, Verona. Six airports have an air traffic over 500 thousand and a main-land connection are: Ancona, Pescara, Reggio Calabria, Trieste. Two more are necessary for a main-land connection: Lampedusa and Pantelleria. The two "salvaged" airports are Rimini and Salerno. They are not part of the European networks, but they are relevant in the Italian context. In fact, the first is an air traffic base near to a million passengers with a growing trend; the second, is designed to relocate the traffic of Naples Airport. See the official document from the Italian Department of Infrastructures, *Airports National Plan* (*Piano Nazionale per gli Aeroporti*), and also the document *Identification of Airports of National interest* (*Individuazione degli aeroporti di interesse Nazionale*), article 698, Government Act n. 173, June 2015

[20] According to the "Transport Statistical Pocketbook" of European Commission of 2011, the majority of Italy's airports are small, that means with a transit between 100 thousand to 5 million passengers a year. For instance, in 2011 the air route Milano Linate-Rome Fiumicino has served 1.5 million people, compared to the train route from Milan Central Station to Roma Termini that has carried 8.3 million people only in the first six months of the year. It is an unfavorable comparison, aggravated by the substantial dependence on the low-cost carriers. Available at: http://ec.europa.eu/transport/facts-fundings/statistics/doc/2011/pocketbook2011.pdf

[21] The risk airports are: Cuneo, Aosta, Brescia, Albenga, Forlì, Parma, Grosseto, Marina di Campo (Elba), Perugia, Foggia, Taranto, Crotone, Comiso and Tortolì, with a traffic of 1.1 million passenger in 2012. According to Unioncamere, if these structures are closed, 500 thousand people would lengthen their journey times to over 60 minutes, with a higher cost, in time spent, to around 52 million euro.

[22] See Laura Cipriani, "The airport landscape of Italy". In: *Ecological Airport Urbanism. Airports and Landscapes in the North East*, published by Università degli Studi di Trento, Trento, 2012, pp. 27-37.

[23] Source: ENAC, 2013. ENAC is the acronyms for *Ente Nazionale Aviazione Civile* that is the controller of Italian ivil aviation.

[24] Source: "Unioncamere: a rischio 15 aeroporti al servizio dei territori," press release by Unioncamere, Rome, April 18, 2013.

[25] "Open Skies" is an international policy concept that calls for the liberalization of the rules and regulations of the international aviation industry—especially commercial aviation—in order to create a free-market environment for the airline industry. Its primary objectives are: to liberalize the rules for international aviation markets and minimize government intervention as it applies to passenger, all-cargo and combination air transportation as well as scheduled and charter services; and to adjust the regime under which military and other state-based flights may be permitted. However, giving the coordination of territorial infrastructures to the regions was mainly a failure because it created paradoxical situations such as the airport of Salerno where 100 million euros was "invested" to fly planes with a load factor that was close to zero.

[26] See the Report titled the *Study on the future development of the national airport network as a strategic component of the organization's infrastructure territory* (*Studio Sullo Sviluppo Futuro della Rete Aeroportuale Nazionale quale Componente Strategica dell'Organizzazione Infrastrutturale del Territorio*) commissioned by ENAC to One Works, Nomisma and KPMG. Source: ENAC, 2010. Document Available at: www.enac.gov.it/repository/ContentManagement/information/N234315289/rapporto2010_web110711.pdf

[27] Comiso Airport was opened on 2007 by Massimo D'Alema. On that occasion he

claimed "[Comiso Airport] is the future flywheel not only for the economy but also for intercultural exchanges with the Arab world." It was an investment of 47 million euro, and still today it does not provide for any flights.

[28] This document does not aim to close the smaller airports. It wants to be rather an act of encouragement and promotion of the territory and it needs to be confronted by the Joint Conference. Because—as claimed the ex-Vice Minister for Infrastructure and Transport by Mario Ciaccia—112 airports in Italy are not economically sustainable. Source: Italian Department of Infrastructure and Transport, Notice of Address for the definition the *National Plan for Airport Development* (*Atto di Indirizzo per la Definizione del Piano Nazionale per lo Sviluppo Aeroportuale*), Rome, January 29, 2013.

[29] Reaction of Ferruccio Dardanello, president of Unioncamere, to the *Notice of Address for the definition the National Plan for Airport Development*, April, 2013.

[30] AENA is the acronyms for *Aeropuertos Españoles y Navegación Aérea*. It is a public entity under the Ministry of Public Works, with legal personality and independent assets of the state. All key aspects of the activity of Spanish airports, like the investments in upgrading or expanding capacity or the negotiations with airlines, are the responsibility of AENA.

[31] See the article of Fiona Govan, "Spain's White Elephants – How Country's Airports Lie Empty," in: *The Telegraph*, October 5, 2011.

[32] David Page, "España llena aeropuertos con dinero público: las aerolíneas reciben 250 millones en ayudas durante la crisis," October 25, 2010.

[33] Referred to the research coordinated by Jordi Martí-Henneberg, Francisco J. Tapiador and Angel Pueyo Campos, "La Eenclosión de los Aeropuertos Regionales Españoles". Documento de Síntesis. University of Lleida and University of Castilla-La Mancha, 2006-2007. Available at: fundacioabertis.org.

CHAPTER 3

Panorama of Flughafen Tempelhof
Berlin | May 2010
Photo by Olaf Hoech @flickr

> The world is full of useless things and forgotten places. We hanker incessantly after new ones, and rarely take note of those that are disappearing. Yet obsolescence, far from being a pejorative term, is the birthmark of every artifact and every building. It simply implies that time passes, things change, and that we seek other ways to engage the manifold realities around us.
>
> Kurt W. Forster, *The light at the end...*, 2010

PLANNING OBSOLESCENCE

3. PLANNING OBSOLESCENCE

Objects may become functionally obsolete when they do not function in the manner that they did when they were created. In Latin, the verb *obsolescĕre* indicates the concept of "wear out "or "fall into disuse". Obsolescence is the state of being that occurs when an object, service or structure is no longer wanted even though it may still be in good working order. Obsolete refers to something that is already disused, discarded or antiquated.[1] This may be due to natural wear or due to some planned break down. Obsolescence occurs frequently because repurchasing has more advantages than the inconvenience related to the replacement of parts; or when the cost of repairs is higher than the cost of buying a new one. In that sense, obsolescence is typically preceded by a gradual decline in popularity. The concept was identified in the 1930s when the entrepreneur Bernard London argued that the only way to revitalize the economy from the economic collapse of 1929 was to stimulate consumption. He proposed to make "planned obsolescence" a compulsory business practice that involved the deliberate reduction of product life to increase consumer consumption. Referring to that practice, in 2011 Cosima Dannoritzer claimed that products are intentionally designed to have a fixed lifetime. In her documentary, she scientifically investigates how producers deliberately reduce the life of a product to increase its consumption, with relevant impacts on the global economy and the environment. In contrast to planned obsolescence, Serge Latouche calls for a change in thinking: a cultural shift in which reuse, recycling and reinvention could bring new uses and second life for many objects.[2]

Similarly, this aging process can happen to airports infrastructures when they become inadequate to still be airports due to physical, technical or environmental conditions. Obsolescence becomes a more complex issue when it refers to infrastructures because it implies a triple aspect: technological, economical and aesthetical obsolescence. In a way, an abandoned airport is another brownfield.[3] In contrast to the general category of brownfield, the airport is typically too large, too peripheral and too contaminated to be redeveloped. They are complex and specific at the same time: they have a wide horizontal space and a singularity to their buildings. What is unique to airports is that most typically they are public, in a way that most brownfields are not. Because airports are mostly public, they can more easily be converted than many brownfields can be.[4] Airports are therefore challenging case studies because they are very difficult to try to put back into the old structure of the city. They have a combination of centrality and connections because they are planned to be very far away but they become the center of the many cities, geographically. They have this horizontality where most of the space is really empty space that's engineered for a margin of error or accident. At the same time, they are among the most economically productive sites in the cities that they served. They are also among the most environmentally problematic. This combination of centrality, emptiness, environmental contamination and economic capability makes a good case for study from a landscape perspective. Landscape architects have reasserted their historical claims to the airports in the last fifteen years. According to Charles Waldheim, describing the airport as a landscape is already an important conceptual break through: just claiming it as a landscape, not just as a simple engineering or architectural project, but within a more coherent framework. According to this new the point of view, it becomes significant to shift the perspective from "a planned obsolescence" to "planning for obsolescence."

Tendencies

The imagery of future cities has frequently inspired all forms of artistic expression like cinema, art, literature, and of course architecture. In those scenarios, infrastructure networks and technological evolution have been given a predominant role. From 1927's Metropolis to 2002's Minority Report, film's futuristic cities—utopias, dystopias, and those somewhere in-between—have asked what our urban future is going to look like. Colossal and vertical cities with glitzy skyscrapers,[5] have high-up freeways linking the buildings, criss-crossing the sky, on which automobiles, trains and monorails casually run. Those cities enjoy the benefits of the digital and technological revolutions, with moving posters, hi-tech places, and emotive artificial intelligence.[6] Wherever people are, they can enter a capsule and easily say "Energy,"[7] becoming dematerialized and re-materialize in a new location. Even many modern architects, of course, have dreamed up visionary plans for city centers. On many occasions, these urban design ideas for the future draw perfectly symmetrical city expressions of egalitarian communities, in which infrastructure networks are centralized, standardized and ordered. The beginning of 1930s is characterized by a concept plan that shows an alternate universe where airports weren't giant fields on the edge of cities. Airports were physical parts of the cities that literally float. On the one hand, runways float on rivers in the middle of cities. On the other hand, airports float above the city on stilts or via a structure like an overhead railroad. These concepts are not as unpractical as they appear, by using short-takeoff, city airports could become flexible and dynamic realities. Others have become a reality with projects such as military aircraft carriers floating on the water.[8] In *Ville Contemporaine* by Le Corbusier the houses are connected by roads which emphasize the use of personal vehicles for transportation. Also, Frank Lloyd Wright had planned, in his *Broadacre City*, multiple cars per family and an airplane in every front yard. In effect, airplanes—the means of transport and symbol of modernity par excellence—have played a predominant role in the collective imagination.

The future is unpredictable and, in a way, it exists as "an act of belief or imagination."[9] This is even more evident when we talk about infrastructure. In the past 200 years, the system has embraced a new means of transport every 50 years or so: barges, trains, autos and airplanes. All of these have significantly influenced territorial transformations and urban developments. Furthermore, airports are specifically manifesting an earlier obsolescence that brings a complexity of problems not solely related to mobility and transport systems. In this context, it is possible to outline some tendencies that have characterized recent decades and may continue in the future. The problematic conditions in which many airports find themselves show the premature state of obsolescence of technology. Airplane technology is quickly becoming outdated but it is not clear which alternative mode of transportation will replace it. Will vertical take-off aircraft, sky cars, teleportation, magnetically levitated systems or maglevs be the future of transportation?[10] Or, will we no longer need to move anymore because drone technology will move things for us? In both cases, what type of structure or urban space will these new vehicles need? How this will affect city transformation? Several contemporary researchers approached these topics, proposing new transport systems and prototypes but even in the most successful cases, these new modes of transport do not seem to be as popular as the previous. The diffusion of vehicles for the masses is still very slow due to economic and safety reasons and restricts them to a limited group of users. There seems to be a gap in the development of replacement technology so the airplane may remain the modern and most popular mode of transport for many decades to come. By contrast, this impasse in technological improvements, has led to a renewed focus on landscape. The melancholy for the natural environment that has been contaminated combined with climate change and a scarcity of renewable resources has brought forward an urban and social approach that seeks to reclaim and compensate what has been destroyed. In the meantime, recycle has become more common as urban and architectonical processes to renew abandoned places looking for new meaning. Recycle, in a way, is the opposite of technology. Behind the good effects of ecological excuses and poetic arguments, the technological resources employed in the reuse and recycling of spaces seem to justify the sins committed in the name of the progress.[11] However, the combination of these approaches allows to give a new interpretation of technology, from the point of view of recycle, like in the technological redesign of the landfill as public park.

3.1 TECHNOLOGY

Train, motor vehicle and plane are the highly successful machines that have significantly improved and accelerated the ways of moving. In contrast, their diffusion has been relatively slow: each has taken from 50 to 100 years to saturate its niche. Each machine carries a progressive evolution of the daily distance travelled that significantly surpasses the 5 km of mobility by foot. Their outcomes are, on one hand, a concrete steady increase in mobility and, on the other hand, the product of a collective futuristic imagery. In the 1960s and 1970s the future was thought about in a much more optimistic way than in the subsequent decades. This period—characterized by a rapid technological changes and an economic boom both in North America and Europe—generated a collective optimism. Even the charm of early space travel led people to strongly believe in technology and scientific progress. The future of humanity was imagined as a technological paradise on Earth and in space.[12] People began to wonder whether applied science would achieve its earlier promise that the life would inevitably improve through technological progress. It was a time in which the belief in progress was able to imagine any type of application or prototype. The basis of this belief was the assurance that inexhaustible resources would support the progress. One of the most fascinating issues was the improvement of infrastructures that were realistic but often imaginary. Airports have often been the focus of numerous representations and futuristic visions. Floating and rooftop airports—like the *New York City's Dream Airport* or *London's Rooftop Circular Airport*—would bring air service right into the heart of cities and eliminate the necessity of travel to and from existing airport locations.[13] At the same time, airplane became the extreme symbol of transport's democratization: it had been imagined as the personal vehicle for the family, in urban or suburban contexts.[14] As Wright claimed, the airplane is the first and fundamental step in human evolution. "The flying machine is yet a more or less extravagant, experimental form, unwieldy in scale, and with its exaggerated wings imitating a bird it is yet a hostage that gives itself to the mercy of the elements. No more than a primitive step in evolution."[15] In the late 1960s, a centralized system of vehicles was imagined, through which passengers would have the opportunity to travel in individual capsules toward select destinations. Ideally, this system would give people almost the same comfort level offered today by private car, but without the need to drive and without traffic. Magnetic levitation trains and prototypes of futuristic cars were abounding during these years. Among others, there were cars with technology derived from aeronautics or the Paul Moller *Flying Car* with vertical take-off.[16] They all seemed to be great revolutionary vehicles, but many of them were soon revealed to be unrealistic.

Several decades later, the technology of flying cars returned to predominance in international debate, influencing urban design research. On the landscape and urban scale, one of the more interesting research was Skycar City coordinated by Winy Maas and Grace La which began as a speculation upon greater questions like urban densification, landscape consumption, land management and fossil fuel depletion.[17] In Skycar City the city structure changes with streets on every level. According to Winy Maas, "in this city, traffic lights are replaced with car's onboard navigational system. Parking problems disappear as cars park directly in the sky, hooked or docked to all types of programmatic elements, in any location."[18] However, the impact of this change does not seem so revolutionary. Except for the physically innovative shapes—cars with wings and more rounded forms—the performances and the needs that of the Skycars City's communities remain the same as nowadays: like parking lots, streets, and mobility services are consequent to the presence of a vehicle.[19] At this point the technology didn't provided a realistic alternative for the future. But what is interesting in the majority of alternative visions for the evolution of transport systems explored above is that they bring in a personalization of the transports. Frequently, the small plane (or similar) is property of an individual, a family or a community of people. This fact expresses the need for a higher comfort level thought a closer proximity to home. Something similar to this is happening in Brazil with helicopters. In the center of Sao Paulo, the helicopters fly very close to roofs. Every day hundreds of people leave home and go to work by helicopter, landing directly on the rooftops of their offices. As for Brazil, these new technologies are limited to an elite minority of users. In fact, the cost of production doesn't yet have a market value for mass distribution, in addition to the safety and regulatory aspects that are not yet resolved. On the other hand, if these issues were settled and this scenario could become a global reality, the problem of obsolete airports would increase exponentially: probably, a high percentage of airports would not have a future, at least in Italy. Airports, even the larger ones, could be quickly abandoned. But this scenario is not predictable yet.

Sky cars were also one of the main issues developed by Small Airports research, focusing more on the effects to the landscape and urban context. In fact, these vehicles could easily become the main operators of small airports, generating a sprawled network system. Indeed, requiring only a small landing strip of ten meters in diameter, the platform for Skycar could easily find a placement in small urban areas: on roofs or on the last level of parking blocks.[20] Although there are already prototypes, tested and implemented, these vehicles still have poor reliability and are high risk, especially in the absence of specific traffic regulations. However, the Small Airports research highlighted a clever point of view for airports. It argues that the structure of small airports could establish a different relationship within their spatial context compared to larger airports. In fact, they are small terminals but equipped with advanced facilities, where hotels, restaurants, conference rooms allow for the airports themselves to become the privileged place for meeting and business exchange. From this point of view it is interesting that the design approach for obsolete airports as urban and territorial facilities has been changed, defining what Stan Allen has defined as a shift "from technologies of production to technologies of reproduction."[21]

Somehow this is what is happening at Liege Airport (Wallonie). Twenty years ago many secondary airport terminals, that today are overcrowded, were abandoned and deserted places. Throughout Europe, the indirect subsidies for low-cost carriers have been crucial to the operational survival of secondary airports. In fact, the boom in low-cost traffic was the result of an attempt to save ghost-airports from failure. Thus, the low-cost companies, attracted by low airport fees and the potential air traffic capacity, have renewed many secondary airports into new efficient operational bases. Ryanair, one of the most popular low-cost carriers, constitutes a paradigmatic case. Ryanair's strategy relies on the European network, consisting of over 150 secondary or regional airports. The majority of these terminals were military airfields with a few civilian airports hosting occasional private flights, relief flights or charter flights to tourist destinations. However, these small and medium-size airports, despite providing specific services, were often in crisis.[22] Similar to the urbanization dynamics that drive the location choice for the construction of a new outlet center, many small airports become knots in a low-cost system inside an attractive system. [23] Several marginal or secondary airports have transformed into low-cost bases, providing a variety of functions and facilities. In fact, by inserting a strong attractor, the airport becomes a geographic and economic centrality.[24] The case of Liege Airport show how the combination of low-cost flight activities can supporting and be supported by the technological investigation. It is a regional airport but also a center of technology and aerospace innovation. The regional network of the Liege Airport, Charleroi Airport and the Euro Space Centre base in Wallonie, demonstrate the implementation of activities related to designing prototypes for the aviation industry. They also show the importance of the impulse for studying the universe for educational purposes, exploring issues related to space research and, finally, the development of cultural, social and business tourism in the area of innovative projects, education and entertainment.

The design for the conversion of airports needs to rely on a sound foundation of infrastructure and operating systems. Existing obsolete airfields have been adapted and implemented by new technologies in order to create unified park systems and to improve alternative energy productions. Several projects strive for on-site generation of renewable energy thought a variety of technologies. This transformation allows to reduce the use of fossil fuels and emissions of greenhouse gases by using the vast area of the site to produce renewable energy. This is the case of Templin (Brandenburg) in which the vast space of an abandoned airfield has been turned into a solar park. It served as a "Sonderlandeplatz," a private special airfield in Brandenburg. From 1955 to 1994 was used by the Soviet Air Force and it was the largest military airfield in the area of DDR. The airfield is closed since March 2012. In September 2011, Siemens, one of Germany's largest electronics companies, began building a test track for alternative power sources for trucks, the Siemens eHighway. Between June and September 2012, a 128MW solar power plant was erected on the main runway. It was connected to the German power grid in April 2013. The airfield has been converted into a Solar Park, which is the outgrowth of Germany's political commitment to sustainable development, with a focus on renewable energy and energy efficiency, and an ultimate goal of diminishing dependence on fossil fuels and nuclear power. The project presents the installation of solar technologies to generate renewable energy on-site, using a variety of technologies such as photovoltaic array, for renewable energy generation.

3.2 LANDSCAPE

Nowadays, the ideological perspective of the design process on the territory tries to maintain good relations with landscape. The trend is moving away from the modern attitude of domination and submission that characterized previous decades towards a mechanism of atonement for the excesses of the past, towards an attitude of understanding and balance with the legacy that has been inherited. People have felt obliged to repair the damage caused by several generations of their forefathers. This moral recovery, beyond that of a simple physical recovery, implies atonement for actions committed, by reinstating existing values in the case of the natural environments or by recovering uses within the urban environments. Furthermore, landscape supplants architecture's historical role as the basic building block of urban design. As Waldheim claims "in a context of decentralization and decreasing density, the 'weighty apparatus' of traditional urban design proves costly, slow and inflexible in relation to the rapidly transforming conditions of contemporary urban culture."[25] Additionally, a landscape is not a pretty image but a living environment governed by cycles (seasons, day and night, tides, climate variations, flora and fauna) forces of growth, fast and slow movement, migration and transhumance. The separation between city-dweller and nature is not only spatial, but also temporal. In contrast with modernist town planning, which reinforced a division between urban rhythms and

Templin Solar Power Plant
Photo source: corriere.it

nature, the remit—through the strong presence of landscape on the sites—is to encourage the introduction of operational processes based on the maintenance or regeneration of their "Ecorhythms."[26] The idea of landscape as a model for contemporary urbanism has also been articulated by the newfound relevance of landscape in describing the temporal mutability and horizontal expansion of the contemporary city, especially in the context of complex natural environments. As Waldheim puts it, "landscape is a medium, it has been recalled by Corner, Allen and others, uniquely capable of responding to temporal change, transformation, adaption, and succession. These qualities recommend landscape as an analog to contemporary processes of urbanization and as a medium uniquely suited to the open-endedness, indeterminacy and change demanded by contemporary urban conditions."[27]

Landscape architects have recently reasserted their historic interest in the airfield as a site of design through a range of practices that most often involve biological and ecological strategies for dealing with the management of the airport. In fact, the economic centrality, environmental impacts and cultural relevance of airports, as well as their abandonment, has provided landscape architecture with new territories and opportunities to be explored. Even if the slow rhythms of the landscape inevitably collide with the incoming mass of passengers, with the restless rhythms of shopping and of low-cost economy, landscape becomes a medium that generates processes of recovery also for airport infrastructures.[28] Specifically, many decommissioned airfields and military air bases have been provided city governments and landscape designers new and, until now, unforeseen opportunities, providing grounds for experimentation with old and new theories of ecological succession and landscape reclamation. [29] The airport is claimed as a site of and for landscape. [30] Airports can have a new meaning, by conceiving airport transformation through Landscape. According to Charles Waldheim, describing an airport as a landscape is already an important conceptual break through: just claiming the airport as an ecological and environmental field to be managed. [31] The conversion of an abandoned airfield is not just a matter of simple engineering or a solely architectural project. Planning, design, development and re-use of airport sites is accomplished by focusing on the relationship between the human and the non-human, as well as on the flows of people, wildlife, machines, energy, water and waste.[32] The aim is to design within a more coherent and interdisciplinary framework. And most often it is a mechanism that also allows one to plan for the ecological function of the site over time. This allows one to think about what is outside the airport and what is on the airport, in relationship to each other. In fact, thinking in a "landscape way" supposes thinking about buildings, land use and ownership. The landscape approach allows one to plan a new airport, thinking about the entire life of the airport, including its decommissioning as one long life cycle. And it is an international process.[33] Many projects show the conversion of abandoned airports for a variety of new uses from public parks to natural reserves, from productive fields to new urban districts.

At Crissy Field (San Francisco) the decommissioned airport provided the opportunities to reclaim, restore and reconstruct large stretches of land as habitat. These projects build on the natural and cultural heritage of the former airfield site to create a legacy. The layers of the site's history are unearthed and used as generators for design and restoration plans. The creation of new habitats for wildlife is paired with the design of environments for recreational and public use. Crissy Field is a park in San Francisco. It was originally an airfield, part of the U.S. Presidio Army base. In 1990 all military operations ceased and the base has been definitely closed. Redesigned by Hargreaves Associates in 1994, Crissy Field transformed itself, from a military airport into a public open space. Today, it is part of the Golden Gate National Recreation Area. A wetland and dune landscape has been restored in the context of cultural landmarks. In fact, Crissy Field is divided into six major natural zones: the rehabilitation of a 1920s grass airfield; a mile-long promenade; wetlands; beach and dunes; a picnic area; and East Beach. This conversion of the Crissy Field Airport into a park revitalized the heart of San Francisco.

As Mozas outlines, "two guises have been applied to architects in recent decades: firstly, that of destroyer of the past and secondly, that of interpreter of history. Now, they are becoming ecologist. Ecological morality recognizes Humanity's sins and proposes redressing them though Re-processes that reintegrate humankind back into the environment. From an environmental perspective it seems that there is no other remedy than to resist the great immorality of the industrial production treadmill and that this resistance may leverage recovery Re-processes which remove the guilt for the damage done."[34] Projects at this scale require an interdisciplinary collaboration across local agencies and professional experts in a convergence of ecology, engineering, social policy, political processes and urban design. This design process is profoundly changing the disciplinary and professional assumptions behind the design of the built environment. This is particularly significant when

Aerial of the Presidio of San Francisco | 2004
Crissy Field, Fort Mason and the Marina
Photo by Wolfgang Schubert @flickr

we have to deal with the transformation of a complex system like an obsolete airfield. Airports have given significant impulse to the landscape urbanism and ecological urbanism design approach. They are not just engineering projects and architectural objects but more complex urban ecologies with significant environmental implications. Operating and abandoned airports comprise complex urban ecologies. Landscape is an opportunity to address airport's critical environmental issues and public health hazards. Landscape systems typically cost less to build and maintain than conventional infrastructure, creating an economic benefit. Therefore, architects and planners have engaged in the design of airports, mitigating and remediating the adverse environmental impacts of aviation. Airport planning, design and development have led to the creation of new landscapes, event programs and synthetic ecologies. We can talk about a Landscape Airchitecture, a design approach established on the specificities of the airfields, in which we can see the fusion of landscape and urban and with the help of the ecological approach in new ways. Among the characteristics of airfields are their large size, openness, and horizontality. The sites have been engineered to reduce biological and hydrological processes. Many designers have therefore interpreted airfields as blank slates for topographic and hydrological invention and intervention. Cut and fill, insertions and landforms have been prominent in the work of many landscape architects on airport sites. These practices are often used in connection with the day-lighting of streams and creeks, the restoration of wildlife habitat and the implementation of extensive water systems that generate new topography.

This is happening at Orange County Great Park (Irvine) where streams and creeks were day-lighted and provided the structure for the park design. Orange County Great Park is the official name of a plan for the public, non-aviation reuse of the decommissioned Marine Corps Air Station El Toro in Irvine, California. It is located in the geographic center of Orange County, in the Southern and Central California Chaparral and Oak Woodlands, an eco-region largely lost to agricultural and urban expansion. The master plan for the Orange County Great Park sets a new standard as a great metropolitan park for the 21st Century. The wise and conservative use of energy, water, and other scarce resources is central to the 1300-acre redesign of the former El Toro Marine Corps Air Station. The Department of the Navy has adopted the park as a model for future military base redevelopment. The plan for Orange County Great Park is an integrated design process. Through an international competition, the Great Park Corporation

Orange County Great Park | 2009
Photo by Be Jonny @flickr

(a non-profit charged with the design, construction and maintenance of the park) selected a design team of experts from diverse fields to form the Great Park Design Studio. The project team and associated consultants include architects, landscape architects, engineers and consultants in a variety of fields, including hydrology, soil science, transportation, environmental design, historic preservation, habitat restoration, energy and urban forestry. The group continually evaluates strategies and design options from their various perspectives. Public participation has been an integral part of designing the masterplan, and in general, continues to shape the park's design and program. Orange County Great Park calls for a wide array of passive and active uses, including miles of walking and biking trails. Most of the park areas is dedicated to open space, education, recreation, exercise and a place to connect with the local natural heritage. A tree-lined terrace and pedestrian plaza link cultural facilities including a library, a museum, cafes and restaurants. The park also hosts Orange County's largest sports park and a botanical garden. Through the park's master plan, the agricultural heritage of Orange County will be preserved and the military history of the former air base will be honored.

3.3 RECYCLE

At the global level, there are many examples of recycled airports. Many abandoned airports have already developed renewal strategies to recover the airport land. Food crises, urban food deserts and public health concerns have led many decommissioned airfields to be considered as sites for urban agriculture. As large open sites, former airfields are also being used to produce renewable energy. As parkland, they can modify and create atmospheres and environments for human experience.[35] The renewal of these infrastructures could activate processes of growth, development of transport and communication networks, and increase the availability of landscape and places in which to live. The conversion of airport infrastructures increases quality and development of the surrounding urban and social condition, transforming abandoned airports into catalysts for urban processes. Therefore, the recycling of airports becomes an operative strategy for other urban transformations. This is a contingent and adaptive strategy. However, recycling airports is not as linear or simple as it might appear. It is a very large and complicated issue because it can propose

Stapleton | 2013
Photo by Michael Ciavatta
ciavattaphoto.com

Landingslaan at Ypenburg | 2013
Photos by Sara Favargiotti

several alternatives. The recycle approach is not limited to proposing the substitution tactic.[36] This common tactic uses the airport landscape to offer new uses and to delete the original one. Stapleton Airfield (Denver) has transformed the site of Denver's old airport into a shiny, new neighborhood with loads of open space and trails.[37] Designed in 1995, the master plan emphasized a pedestrian-oriented design rather than the automobile-oriented design. However, the area is fifteen minutes driving from downtown Denver. In Stapleton new shopping and restaurants are conveniently located so residents don't need to leave the area. The new community is zoned for residential and commercial development, including new lofts, townhouses, single-family houses and mini-mansions in a variety of architectural styles. Even if nearly a third of the airport's site has been redeveloped as public park space, the project reveals itself as a big real estate operation, with the removal of all traces of the former airport. Here the airfield has been considered like any other abandoned place, erasing the physical characteristics of the airport and creating new urban development.

In contrast, recycling takes into account the original characteristics of the airport, highlighting the former airports peculiarities, technical or geographical, and transforming them into a landmark for a new landscape. This process is not exhausted with the total assimilation of the infrastructure into the city. After the transformation and re-activation, the airport leaves physical traces of its memory and of the presence of the previous life or of the former activity. Like in Ypenburg (The Hague) in which the former runway has been converted into an ecological landmark and urban promenade, called Landingslaan. The former runway has been maintained in the original location and the concrete has been turned into a long water channel. Additionally, recycling can also offer different possibilities of action, including the opposite: the enhancement tactic proposes to add new uses to obsolete airports in order to reinforce the aviation activities. [38] As Mostafavi already outlined in 2010—speaking about abandoned industrial cities—this urban recycling "benefits from the unexpected and given context of the site that needs to be remade, a context far from a tabula rasa. [...] The site acts as a mnemonic device for the making of the new. The result is a type of relational approach between the terrain, the built forms and the viewer's participatory experiences."[39] This is particularly evident in the recycling of airfields. It is an experimental idea that stresses the interpretation of recycling as an adaptive practice carried out by specific tactics.

In many cases, these design opportunities seem to show

the airport in terms of archaeology, as a place to be rethought rather than as a place of innovation and progress.[40] This is the case of the transformation of Maurice Rose Airfield (Frankfurt am Main) shows an extraordinary conversion of a field formerly used by the armed forces. The project leaves the signs of airports' activities through the re-elaboration and re-interpretation of the concrete and asphalt into urban parks and ecological environment. After the end of the Second World War, the United States Army opened up an aerodrome, which was provisionally named after General Maurice Rose. Over time, a control tower and several auxiliary buildings were added to the land adjoining the runway and the installation became a major military heliport. In 1994 the United States Army ceased to use the airfield. After closing down, Bonames seemed to remain as a relic of the cold war like a contaminant in the near-natural floodplains of the river Nidda. The buildings were occupied by Werkstatt Frankfurt e.V., an association working to find jobs for the long-term unemployed. The surrounding land was unused and neglected until, slowly and spontaneously, new users from the city discovered that the runway had considerable appeal. In 2003, after acquiring the old aerodrome property, the Frankfurt City Council opted for a subtle intervention. The literal restitution of the old riverside fields seemed, however, to be an anachronistic operation and, paradoxically, one that was not very sustainable. Demolishing and totally dismantling the installations would have meant a costly operation so a less unwieldy project was chosen with the aim of facilitating the transition towards a more natural state while also making the most of popular support and, to some extent, conserving the historical connotations of the place. The four and a half hectares of asphalted surface, set in an ideal environment and, in particular, well away from traffic, offered the perfect setting for bicycle riding, roller skating and skate-boarding. The auxiliary pavilions have also been conserved and they still function as Werkstatt Frankfurt e.V. workshops. A café has been opened in the control tower and from this height it offers good views over the Nidda and surrounding fields. The new park grounds were incorporated into Frankfurt's greenbelt. The design of the airport offers a new approach for creating a public park in which the history of its military use can still be experienced. The concrete and asphalt relics have generated an interesting plant mosaic. [41] In fact, the design's basic idea was to modify the original airfield and its materiality so gently that the military character of the area was able to build a new unity with the surrounding nature. The project is considered an exercise in respect for and enhancement of the past activity of the area: with minimal

Renewed concrete runways at Maurice Rose Airfield | September 2015 | Photos by Sara Favargiotti

Lleida-Alguaire Airport | 2011
Photo by Sara Favargiotti

economic investment, the recycle project has consolidated the natural character of the space. Simultaneously, the former airfield was opened to the public for recreational outdoor uses. The intervention preserved intact one third of the runway, thus keeping one and a half hectares of hard, flat surface that can still be used as a recreation area and skating surface.

The re-significance and renewal of this infrastructure could activate processes of growth, develop transport and communication networks, and increase the availability of landscape and places in which to live. The recycling of airports could also become an operative strategy for other urban transformations. Furthermore, with the dispersion of the contemporary city and the privatization of buildings and activities, open space increasingly gains importance as the place of relationship in the city; pursuing environmental sustainability objectives is a necessity. In that sense, recycled obsolete and underused airports are imagining as latent public spaces, with relational engines and ecological devices. As Muñoz claims, it is more interesting to propose a multi-activity tactic for recycling airports.[42] It is more interesting to think of a more complex treatment recycling, you can get multi-activity and thus a way of recycling is to keep the airport use but add other uses in order to reinforce the original. This is the approach that the Muñoz team followed in the revitalization of Lleida-Alguaire Airport (Catalonia). Recently the airport has a signed agreement with the U.K. in order to reinvigorate tourist use of the airport and their surrounding territories.[43] Making use of resources from the English National Trust.[44] The Muñoz research team proposed, among other initiatives, to include in the airport a bird-watching area and ornithological research center, in order to make the airport itself more attractive. Therefore, it can be possible to gain a reinforcement of airport activities with new tourist use. Going back to the previous topic, the replacement of the airport use is not necessarily the only way to think about airport recycling, it can be achieved by adding new activities that will reinforce the airport use.

The conversion of former airports has provided designers with the opportunity to experiment with new models for urban development and in the public realm, engaging citizens in the shaping of the urban landscape. At Tempelhof Airfield (Berlin) a form of temporary urbanism is being practiced wherein citizens are invited to propose provisional uses for determined plots on the field.[45] The airport has been engulfed by the city and has been naturally transformed into Tempelhofer Park: today it is a new productive field, a contemporary urban square, the greatest open public space

Tempelhofer Park | 2015
Photo by Sara Favargiotti

of the city. Berlin's Tempelhof Airport, often called the City Airport, ceased operations in 2008 during the process of establishing Schönefeld as the sole commercial airport in Berlin. During its post-airport usage it has hosted numerous fairs and events. It's not often that a European metropolis that is hundreds of years old has the opportunity to create a massive new public park directly in its city center. But that is exactly what the German capital of Berlin intended to do with the former Tempelhof airport. In the two years after the runway went silent and the enormous terminal was shuttered, the stream of proposals for transforming the field into a public space illustrated the riches of the city's creative class. Most of the plans that made the final round of the competition utilized the existing layout of the airport: one of the pre-conditions for the landscape designers was that they retain the runways and other historical features, including the terminal. Officially reopened in May 2010 as a city park, today more than 200,000 Berliners have visited the park to enjoy its wide-open spaces for recreation ranging from biking and skating to baseball and kiting. Despite city officials wanting to use about a third of the land for housing because of Berlin's growing population, citizens claimed the former airport as a public space and urban park. On May 25th, 2014 over half of voters backed a referendum to preserve the airport as a leisure space. In this way, Berliners have blocked plans to develop a big part of the former Tempelhof airport.

Urban garden at Tempelhofer Park | 2015 Photo by Sara Favargiotti

The relevance of the recycle process is clear, consolidating its urban action, and it is an increasingly common practice, sometimes utilized as a popular trend, other times for sustainable environmental principles. However, today seems to be more relevant to understand and distinguish what should be recycled and what should not. Already in 1995, Koolhaas—referring to the Generic City—claimed that "the great originality of the Generic City is simply to abandon what doesn't work—what has outlived its use—to break up the blacktop of idealism with the jackhammers of realism and to accept whatever grows in its place."[46] In a way, Re-processes, when applied to remediating the excesses of consumer society, should assume the generic condition of the city as a contemporary quality and learn to abandon whatever has accomplished its mission.

CHAPTER 3. PLANNING OBSOLESCENCE

[1] Fowler HW and Fowler FG (1st ed.), Thompson Delia (ed.). The Concise Oxford Dictionary of Current English, 9th Edition, Clarendon Press, Oxford, 1995.

[2] Referred to the conference of Serge Latouche at Genoa on March 5, 2014, and to the book of the same author, *Usa e getta. Le follie dell'obsolescenza*. Bollati Boringhieri (collana Temi), 2013.

[3] During the past thirty years there has been an economic restructuring of production and society. This creates, among other consequences, many brownfields and former industrial sites. In the North American Urban Planning, a brownfield site (or simply a brownfield) is a land previously used for industrial purposes or some commercial uses. The land may be contaminated by low concentrations of hazardous waste or pollution, and has the potential to be reused once it is cleaned up.

[4] According to Charles Waldheim, converting an abandoned airport is easier because one person or one city owns them. "In our culture, the ownership of the brownfield is very important. Because a private company owns them, they have a very little interest in accepting the liability or the risk for the contamination that's there." See "An Interview with Charles Waldheim," foreword of this book. Interview conducted at Harvard Graduate School of Design on November 12, 2013.

[5] Referred to the following movies: Ridley Scott, *Blade Runner*, 1982; Fritz Lang, *Metropolis*, 1927; and Michael Anderson, *Logan's Run*, 1976.

[6] Referred to the following movies: Steven Spielberg, *Minority Report*, 2002; Katsuhiro Otomo, *Akira*, 1988; and Spike Jonze, *Her*, 2013.

[7] Referred to the teleportation in the American science fiction television series *Star Trek* created by Gene Roddenberry, 1966-1969.

[8] The design of monumental utopian airports started between late 1920s and early 1930s. Designers from North America to Europe proposed astonishingly large runway platforms located in midtown of Manhattan, London, Paris or utopian buildings. Among others, it is referred to the projects of Virgilio Marchi, *Terrazze della Città Superiore*, 1924; Frank R. Paul, Rooftop airport from Amazing Stories, 1928; Norman Bel Geddes, Floating airport off Wall Street; M. Lurcat, Floating airport in middle of Paris, 1932; *Rooftop Circular Airport* from "Illustrated London," 1919; *London Airport over Thames* from "Popular Science Monthly," 1934; and William Zeckendorf, *New York City's Dream Airport*, 1946.

[9] Joseph J. Corn and Brian Horrigan, Yesterday's Tomorrows: Past Visions of the American Future. John Hopkins Press, 1984.

[10] The maglev is a vehicle without a motor—thus, without combustibles aboard—and without wings and wheels, which is suspended magnetically between two guardrails that resemble an open stator of an electric motor. It is propelled by a magnetic field that runs in front and drags it.

[11] See Javier Mozas, "Remediate, Reuse, Recycle. Re-processes as atonement". In: *Reclaim. Remediate, Reuse, Recycle*, a+t architecture publishers, issue 39-40, 2012, p.10.

3.1 Technology

[12] These futuristic visions refer to the Retro-Futurism tendency. Today, this word implies artistic creations in which there is a significant technology component. These works imagine a sort of parallel reality, never realized. The Retro-Futuristic locations are usually placed in utopian society. The Retro-Futurism tendency has as one of its themes a discomfort with the present, providing an ideal alternative. In contrast with dystopian imaginary scenarios, which draw a future plagued by environmental degradation and disasters, the Retro-Futurism suggests a positive idea of scientific-technological progress, drawing a future lived in harmony with technology and with its comfort.

[13] Norman Bel Geddes was probably one of the greatest technological visionaries. He was an industrial designer who lived in the first half of the twentieth century. Among other projects, the greatest work was the construction of the pavilion for the *Futurama Exhibition* (1939).

[14] Le Corbusier designed *Ville Contemporaine* (1922) as an orderly home to three million people where housing, industry and recreation all occupied distinct areas connected

by roads that emphasized the use of personal vehicles for transportation. Frank Lloyd Wright in his *Broadacre City* (1932) puts each homeowner in a self-built single-family home on an entire acre of land brimming with gardens. Complete with multiple cars per family and an airplane in every front yard.

[15] Frank Lloyd Wright, *The Disappearing City*, William Farquhar Payson, New York, 1932, p. 43.

[16] The Firebird designed by General Motors was one of the first cars to have adapted an aircraft turbine as engine. Even the Lincoln Futura, introduced by Ford, provided a system able to plan a route and carry passengers to their destination automatically. In 1933, Richard Buckminster Fuller began the design of the Dymaxion Car, a car equipped with technologies derived from the aerospace.

[17] For more information see "Skycar City" in *Chapter 5. Positions* in this book. According to Grace La "Skycar City research began as a speculation upon the notion of Skycars in relation to the problem of density—a critical response to the ills of inefficient land management, inevitable fossil fuel depletion, and extreme population growth, among others." See: Grace La, "On Boids and Beauty". In: Winy Maas, Grace La (eds.), *Skycar City. A Pre-emptive History*, Actar, p. 232.

[18] Winy Maas, "Skycar City". In: *Ibid.*, p. 22.

[19] See to the essay of Alberto Bertagna, "La Città Sublime. Ovvero, dalla Città Sublimata." In: Pippo Ciorra and Fernanda De Maio (eds.), *Piccoli aeroporti. Infrastruttura, città e paesaggio nel territorio italiano*, Marsilio, 2008, p. 86.

[20] See the essay of Marco D'Annuntiis, "Levitazione. Nuova Frontiera?" In: *Ibid.*, p. 90.

[21] Stan Allen, "Infrastructural Urbanism." In: *Points and Lines: Diagrams and Projects for the City*, New York: Princeton Architectural Press, 1999, p. 49.

[22] Frequently, they have been subsidized by the State to promote regional development in close proximity to some urban centers. The local governments subsidize their landing at specific sites, allocating the marketing expenses. Then, the low-cost companies find attractive conditions to provide flights intended to reverse the fortunes of these airports. It was also the second company to have received more public money for its operations.

[23] Thinking on the Serravalle Scrivia Outlet, it is the center of a "city" of 15 million inhabitants or potential visitors.

[24] According to Laura Cipriani, the radical change, introduced by the new airlines in secondary airports, consist precisely by giving rise to a new low-cost culture corresponding to a consequent urban and social landscape. See: Laura Cipriani, *Airport urbanism. Aeroporti low cost e nuovi paesaggi*, Aracne, 2012, p. 22.

3.2 Landscape

[25] Charles Waldheim, *The Landscape Urbanism Reader*, Princeton Architectural Press, 2006, p. 37.

[26] According to one of the main "Europan 12" topics named *Ecorhythms*, new urban development has to be based on a strong synergy between urban and natural environments in order to break from a principle of opposition that has separated city dwellers from natural environments and gradually undermined those realities. More information available at the official website: www.europan-europe.eu.

[27] Charles Waldheim, *The Landscape Urbanism Reader*, Princeton Architectural Press, 2006, p. 39.

[28] See Laura Cipriani, *Airport urbanism. Aeroporti low cost e nuovi paesaggi*, Aracne, 2012, p. 82

[29] See Sonja Dümpelmann and Charles Waldheim, eds., "Succession," in *Airport Landscape: Urban Ecologies in the Aerial Age*, Harvard Design Studies, Cambridge, MA, 2016, p. 157.

[30] See the research *Airport Landscape: Urban Ecologies in the Aerial Age* directed by Charles Waldheim and Sonja Dümpelmann, Harvard University Graduate School of Design, Cambridge, MA, 2013.

[31] See "An Interview with Charles Waldheim," foreword of this book.

[32] See to the pamphlet for exhibition and conference *Airport Landscape: Urban Ecologies in the Aerial Age*, October 30 - December 19, 2013, Harvard University, Graduate School of Design, Cambridge, MA.

[33] The best case studies are from Germany or Scandinavia. However the operating airports Schipol Airport, Oslo Airport and Munich Airport are good examples. In America there are many examples of decommissioned airports being converted. Furthermore, there are many others interesting international examples such as in Morocco, Island, or Taiwan.
[34] Javier Mozas, "Remediate, Reuse, Recycle. Re-processes as Atonement." In: Reclaim. *Remediate, Reuse, Recycle*, a+t architecture publishers, issue 39-40, 2012, p. 24.

3.3 Recycle

[35] Referred to the pamphlet *Airport Landscape: Urban Ecologies in the Aerial Age*, Harvard University Graduate School of Design, Cambridge, MA, 2013.
[36] According to Graham and Marvin, it is clear that a range of different relationships exist between the physical form of urban places and the development of electronic spaces. They highlighted four key aspects of city-telecommunications relations: physical and development synergies, substitution effects, generation effects and enhancement effects. Precisely, "substitution effect" refers to the relative or absolute substitution of physical flows by electronic flows and physical spaces by virtual electronic spaces. Stephen Graham and Simon Marvin, *Telecommunications and the City: Electronic Spaces, Urban Places*, Routledge, 1996, pp. 330-331.
[37] Stapleton Airfield was opened on October 17th, 1929 as Denver Municipal Airport. Changing the name after a 1944 expansion. By the 1980s, plans were under way to replace Stapleton Airfield with a new airport. In fact, Stapleton Airfield was plagued by a number of problems concerning inadequate physical and technical structures for flights, noise and pollution problems. Meanwhile, the new Denver International Airport (DIA) officially opened in north-eastern Denver. The runways at Stapleton were marked with large yellow "Xs", which indicate it was no longer legal or safe for any aircraft to land there. While Denver International was being constructed, planners began to consider how the Stapleton site could be redeveloped. The former airport site (4,700 acres) has been redeveloped by Forest City Enterprises. Construction began in 2001 of single-family houses, row houses and condominiums. Stapleton Development Plan proposed the transformation of the Denver's old airport into a shiny, new neighborhood with loads of open space and trails. Designed in 1995, the master plan emphasized a pedestrian-oriented design rather than the automobile-oriented design. However, the area is fifteen minutes driving from downtown Denver. In Stapleton new shopping and restaurants are conveniently located so residents don't need to leave the area. The new community is zoned for residential and commercial development, including new lofts, townhouses, single-family houses and mini-mansions in a variety of architectural styles. Even if nearly a third of the airport's site has been redeveloped as public park space, the project reveals itself as a big real estate operation, with the removal of all traces of the former airport.
[38] Referred to the "enhancement effect" which means the use of telematics to increase attractiveness, efficiency and capacity of physical networks (road, rail, water, and energy). In: Stephen Graham and Simon Marvin, *Telecommunications and the City: Electronic Spaces, Urban Places*, Routledge, 1996, pp. 332-333.
[39] Mohsen Mostafavi, "Why Ecological Urbanism? Why Now?". In: Mohsen Mostafavi and Gareth Doherty (eds.), *Ecological Urbanism*, Lars Muller Publishers, 2010, p. 28.
[40] Referred to the essay of Sara Marini, "Spazi del volo e territori. Risonanze europee." In: Pippo Ciorra and Fernanda De Maio (eds.), *Piccoli aeroporti. Infrastruttura, città e paesaggio nel territorio italiano*, Marsilio, Venezia, 2008, p. 145.
[41] GTL Gnüchtel Triebswetter Landschaftsarchitekten, "Old Airfield. Frankfurt am Main - Bonames, Germany." In: *Paisea. Revista de Paisajismo/Landscape Architecture Magazine*, Cicatrices/Scars, issue 016, March 2011, p. 31.
[42] See "Conversation with Francesc Muñoz" in this book. The conversation has been carried out at the Universidad Autonoma de Barcelona, Barcelona, on August 23, 2013.
[43] In the hope to improve the Lleida-Alguaire Airport's activities, recently a commitment was signed for five years between the U.K. and Lleida-Alguaire Airport. The U.K. has agreed to perform flights to the airport over the next five winter seasons. This agreement gives a boost to the Lleida-Alguaire Airport and it will improve the use of the skiing area by British tourists.

[44] The National Trust for Places of Historic Interest or Natural Beauty, usually known as the National Trust, is a conservation organization in England, Wales and Northern Ireland. The trust owns many heritage properties, including historic houses and gardens, industrial monuments and social history sites. It is one of the largest landowners in the United Kingdom, owning many beauty spots, most of which are open to the public free of charge. It is the largest membership organization in the United Kingdom, and one of the largest UK charities by both income and assets.

[45] Referred to the presentation of Eelco Hooftman "Tempelhofer Freiheit. A Prairie for the Contemporary Urban Cowboy" at the conference *Airport Landscape: Urban Ecologies in the Aerial Age*, November 15, 2013, Harvard University Graduate School of Design, Cambridge MA.

[46] Rem Koolhaas, "The Generic City." In: OMA, Koolhaan R., Mau B., *S,M,L,XL*, Monacelli Press, New York, 1995, p. 1252.

Airports Reference Cases

[1] Crissy Field | US-CA. [2] Orange County Park | US-CA. [3] Stapleton | US-CO. [4] Quito | EC. [5] Downsview Park | CA. [6] Floyd Bennett Field | US-NY. [7] Hispaniola Airport | DOM. [8] Caracas Airbase | YV. [9] Anfa Airport | MA. [10] Girona Airport | SP. [11] Charleroi Airport | BE. [12] Liege Airport | BE. [13] Schipol Airport | NL. [14] Ypenburg | NL. [15] Weeze Airport | DE. [16] Templin | DE. [17] Oslo Airport | NO. [18] Kraufbeuren | DE. [19] Fliegerhorst Oldenburg | DE. [20] Bonames | DE. [21] Dübendorf Military Airport | CH. [22] Skavsta Airport | SV. [23] Munich Reim | DE. [24] Gatow | DE. [25] Tempelhof | DE. [26] Vicenza Airpark | IT. [27] Hellenicon Airbase | GRE. [28] Kai Tak Airport | CN. [29] Taichung Gateway | TW. [30] Auckland International Airport | NZ.

CHAPTER 4

Lleida-Alguaire Airport
Catalonia | Spain
Photo by Enric Seres

"

The world is full of useless things and forgotten places. We hanker incessantly after new ones, and rarely take note of those that are disappearing. Yet obsolescence, far from being a pejorative term, is the birthmark of every artifact and every building. It simply implies that time passes, things change, and that we seek other ways to engage the manifold realities around us.

Kurt W. Forster, *The light at the end...*, 2010

"

RESILIENT LANDSCAPE RESERVE

4. RESILIENT LANDSCAPE RESERVES

Since the earliest research on airports there have been no great leaps forward in the modes of transport. But it is not possible to exclude forecasts in which technology could create sudden changes. Infrastructure innovation is changeable and there seems to be a technological "gap" despite on-going studies. The issues are still open to discussion. Many airport facilities will become obsolete, many will serve other functions and many will begin new life cycles generating new trade within the cities, landscapes and territories they serve. It seems that the destiny for many airports will be adaptation as points of territorial aggregation with multiple functions: environmental, touristic, and leisure. The reconversion of airports into parks or land for city expansion seems to be a contemporary trend. The projects described in *Chapter 3* show the reconversion of the existing airfield into an urban park: a re-naturalized park providing new economic and social activities—like re-naturalization, park facilities and temporary installations. These re-interpretations of the airport landscape allow us to understand the crucial step that many small and medium airports are currently facing: they conceive the airport not only as transport infrastructure but also as a key element for the development of territories. On-hold infrastructures may become the new backbone of the city, improving the quality of urban life and becoming a place to live instead of a place to leave. But, when neither the landscape nor the city has the chance to expand towards the airport, how can the relationship between the cities and the airport be changed? Among all the possibilities and trends, the option of destroying the infrastructure does not seem to be the most convenient. Rather, relying on its physical existence creates more interesting results to understand the value of its resilience.

In 1999, Stan Allen claims "rethinking infrastructure is only one aspect of a larger move away from the representational model, one of the many implications of architecture understood as a 'material practice.' [...] They do not work primarily with images or meaning, or even with objects, but with performance: energy inputs and outputs, the calibration of force and resistance. They are less concerned with what things look like and more concerned with what they can do."[1] According to this, the temporary condition of the on-hold airport allows the possibility to transform the undetermined and suspended perspective of the on-hold state into an opportunity to start a second life for the existing airport infrastructure, maximizing its potential through different re-development strategies that work with specific performances. This approach is focused on re-thinking not only the abandoned and unused infrastructures in search of new identities, but also on all those infrastructures that are already in use but poorly operating and unproductive.

Airport infrastructures are a combination of opposite characteristics: they are "islands" but connected to the cities, they are large but constrained and they combine mobility functions with urban services. They are complex systems used in a specialized way. Airports offer a large amount of available space that could become an agricultural field, a park, a productive landscape or new urban district.

Additionally, on-hold airports, thought temporarily unused, can still be returned to usefulness. Due to these physical and territorial characteristics, airports are resilient landscape reserves able to be adapted to accommodate or either anticipate the future and adapt to its unpredictable environmental, cultural, social and economic changes. The concept of resilience—towards the landscape— offers the change to recreate a place that lives with the density of its history, the romantic side of abandonment and the adaptability to other kinds of experiences. Therefore it becomes an interesting challenge to use this approach for airport infrastructures. Normally infrastructures of mobility are considered as the driving force of development. They are fixed and unique. Starting from the edges and re-interpreting the airports, could give provide alternatives for achieving a creative resilience, in other words, adapting to a changing environment. Resilient and ecological airport infrastructures could generate a reserve for cities in which the function of aviation could remain active as possibility, overlapping with other ecological and urban systems. In the competition project for Taichung Gateway Park, Stoss' project shows how an airfield can be transformed into a productive landscape by considering the airport as a potential site for recalibrating larger ecological urban systems, especially in terms of water management or energy production. As previously mentioned, the concept of ecological resilience comes from the indeterminate nature of the future, the structural weaknesses of the human ecosystems and the poor adaptability to ecological stresses. Resilient airports have therefore the ability to regain value as infrastructure with renewed and combined functions, such as leisure, cultural and productive activities.

4.1 AIRPORTS' SECOND LIFE

Many abandoned airports have already become part of by the urban fabric: they have been engulfed by the growth of the city. Others airports are insulated from the city. Others on-hold airports are more marginal in the urban context. These categories of centrality are referred to as a system of flows and land use, rather than to a physical and geographical proximity to the city. Airports can be engulfed, insulated or marginal according to a system of centrality, flows and attractors that determine the territorial value. Until the end of the 1900s cities had grown steadily. In the first decade of 2000, with the environmental and economic crisis, cities tended to grow much more slowly, especially in the countries of Western Europe. So, the aforementioned categories that once rapidly changed with an isolated airport becoming engulfed into the fabric of urban sprawl; or a marginal airport could be easily accessed by the city expansion. Today, these categories tend to be more stable. Furthermore, the European condition with its overestimated production of airports, each one larger than the next, collides with an uneconomic condition. Then the on-hold state becomes even more a condition of stability and urgency. These categories are crucial to activation of their second life. Some airports are insulated, even though the city has expanded, and they are not at the center of a transformation process. So, they need an "injection" of central functions. Others are marginal but they can quickly be reached from the city.

Their re-activation is easily facilitated and they need less central functions. For instance, an insulated airport like Lleida-Alguaire Airport finds its second life from a strong economic expediency with the tourism system of Andorra. Differently, Templehof Airport has been engulfed by the city of Berlin and it was naturally transformed into park, a new public space, because the city is now surrounding it.

Worldwide case studies and research experiments show different ways to activate airports' second life, starting the process that Sonja Dümpelmann has defined as *Airport Afterlives*.[2] After decommissioning, many former military airports were not re-used and they have remained in an abandoned state for years. But due to growing populations and the high demand for new housing, many of these airports have been re-developed as a new part of the city. Starting with the transformation of the air connection infrastructure—runway or technical street— into roads and streets and continuing this new urban development with houses, public services, commercial and business areas. The addition of public urban parks will add value to the gradual renovation of existing structures and the new urban development area. This development is extremely well connected to the nearby cities, but the memory of the airport is almost completely removed. This is the case of Stapleton City in Colorado or München Riem in Germany. In other cases, many problematic airports no longer present themselves in the potential range for urban expansion. These airports, which were once peripheral, have now been engulfed in the urban context, becoming physically central in the city. This simplifies their re-conversation into urban park space. These cases can make the transformation into public urban parks as clearly shown by Tempelhofer Park in Berlin or Downsview Park in Canada.

The proliferation of low-cost companies started to promote the revitalization of secondary airports. After the post war decommission of many small and medium airports they remained unused for years until local municipalities focused their attention on these airfields to find alternative use solutions. The fundamental role of these airports as strategic hubs in the new low-cost air model and their moderate but well connected dimensions make them crucial airport infrastructures on the local and European scale. They generate a rapid transformation of land use and of the infrastructure network relating to land transportation. Stockholm-Skavsta Airport in Sweden and Liege Airport in Belgium clearly show how the integration of new economic, cultural and leisure activities at these airports contributed to a dynamic renewal of the surrounding territories and improved local businesses. In this way, the secondary low-cost airports became landmarks in the territory and important elements for the local economies. In all these projects, airports have been able to be readapted and activated a new productive and operative phase in their life cycle. Similar to cities, resilience should be the ability of an infrastructure exposed to hazards to resist, absorb, accommodate and recover promptly the efficiency from the effects of the hazard. In this scenario, the hazard exists as temporal event or premature obsolesces. Airport's resilience value consists of two factors: the large amount of available space that could become an agricultural field, a park, a public space or a square and in being an infrastructure that is limited and used in a specialized way. Additionally, on-hold airports, thought temporarily unused, can still be returned to usefulness. In the end, airport resilience is the capability of structures to regain value. It may come back in value as infrastructure or as open space, or as a combination of both.

Additionally, the environmentally sensitive approach has its origins in the ecology and environmental engineering disciplines, but nowadays, is strictly integrated in architecture, landscape and urban design. Designers consider the city and its metabolism through "behavior models" as patterns for an activation of new life cycles. In fact, to view the city as something that can be recycled means to consider its rhythms, its life cycles and its metamorphoses. The conversion of airport infrastructure, in fact, increases quality and development of the surrounding urban and social condition, transforming airports on-hold into catalytic processes. These new infrastructures generate trade with landscapes but also allow us to see new landscapes. Therefore, the airport infrastructure can be considered as a place of permanence and not just a transition, as a biological material originating from the surrounding area and as an integral part of the new housing situation.[3] The airport becomes a place to live in, not just a doorway to another destination. From airports to arrive in and to fly "beyond" to a far away destination, to airports in which to go and stay in, as attractors of flows related to activities associated with the local area and the structure of the airport. In this sense, the airport infrastructure becomes a place to live instead of a place to leave. It is organized to satisfy not only one specific sector (flight operation) but it adapts itself and its efficiency in relation to the surrounding context, it can exchange flows (physical and immaterial) with the surrounding territory and accommodate multiple functions. Valuing and anticipating the correct strategy of re-cycling for airports is an increasingly urgent necessity, in order to anticipate the inevitable decline of these structures and to activate recovery processes in synergy with the different urban realities. According to this idea, the airport becomes a place to live instead of a place to leave. It establishes a stronger relationship between the infrastructure and the surrounding territories. At the same time, economic improvements and new uses for the airports are gained, allowing the economic growth of the territory without the construction of new infrastructure. In that sense, the regenerated airport is organized to satisfy not only one specific sector (flight operation) but adapts itself and its efficiency in relation to the surrounding context and business, it exchanges fluxes (physical and immaterial) with the surrounding territory and accommodates multiple functions. Therefore, airports are resilient landscape reserves due to their capability to return into the landscape either to generate a new productive landscape.

4.2 DEVICES FOR AIRPORTS ON-HOLD: 4 TOOLS

Airports are architectural and landscape structures with an urban function: in most cases they lack a physical and spatial integration with their landscape and urban contexts. This is more evident in those unused, obsolete and on-hold airports. The reconnection to their surrounding landscapes either the creation of new landscapes can be gained by working on the in-transition phase, transformed from a problem into a potentiality. Valuing the specific strategy for airports on-hold can anticipate the premature decline of these structures and to activate recovery processes in synergy with the different urban and territorial realities. So, the indeterminate condition of these airports could be transformed into an opportunity. The application of specific tools—after discussions and meetings with a trans-disciplinary team of experts and local authorities—has been applied to specific stakeholder airports, allowing different operative renewal strategies and future development scenarios. The state of transition of on-hold airports also allows for considering the airport as an app-lication. By proposing specific tools for obsolete airport development it is possible to react to the potentials of the airport system before it enters its deep decline slope. These could be the operative strategies for airports to recalibrate their fundamental function within their physical contexts: the integration of air traffic transportation facilities with activities that regenerate their life and their surroundings. These processes are driven by different devices that offer a series of possible alternative scenarios. The experimentation on specific case studies—described in the following paragraph— has elaborated and applied four tools: airport as environmental sensor, airport as services center for local activities, airport as hub for local transportation and airport as network. They are architectural devices and their application, individual or integrated, of these devices, guides the re-conversion process of on-hold airports.

Tool1: Airport as environmental sensor

The first tool deals with the environmental and landscape implications of airports, such as mitigation of impacts and risks. An airport is an environment detractor. Its impacts are produced by the ground structures—land use, light pollution, interference with wildlife and vegetation—and by the aviation activity of the airport - pollution emissions and interference with bird migrations. This tool defines an environmental code in order in order to compensate and mitigate the impacts that an airport has on ecosystem. It invests in policies of environmental protection. In this sense, the project becomes a landscape project, where noise barriers, new green areas and permeable soils (for instance runways in grass) are no longer considered mere technical devices, but an integrated piece of a new landscape. This allows for the reduction in consumption of resources and the protection of biodiversity, especially through the preservation and integration of green corridors. The buffer zone is a barrier but it is also a place, a filter to reconnect parts of the territory through environmental linear infrastructure (ecological corridors) as well as heterogeneous and punctual elements (stepping stones). According to this device, the airport hosts the technologies for the production of renewable energy like wind, solar, biomass and photovoltaic plants.

Tool2: Airport as services centre for local activities

This tool stresses the integration of the airport in the territory by including services connected with local production. In this sense, improving the airport as a logistic hub is a priority. In fact, the development of economies, businesses and settlements enhances the attractiveness of local contexts. Regional offices of corporations and institutions, centers for conferences and business meetings, technology and communication industries, and high-tech research centers could be settled in the airport propriety, by taking advantage from the capillarity of the flight connections offered. At the same time, the airport becomes more valuable in the market and adds to the resources and specificity of the region. This tool defines an integrated process to share functions and opportunities between airports and cities. This refers not only to flight operations (for example storage of planes, production of planes, business aviation or schools of aviation), but also includes productive functions at the airport that allow it to become a new territorial center of local production. This will expand the opportunities and benefits to the airport even when it is not used for flight operations.

Tool3: Airport as hub for local transportation

Around airports and along the infrastructure accessibility systems, there is a growing concentration of activity that creates new forms of urban settlement. The airport and the immediate area around them are themselves trading centers and transport modes that induce new territorial dynamics and influence new landscapes. The guidelines of the European Infrastructure Development Plan for 2014-2020 calls for an increase in airport connections within the smaller networks of the surrounding territory in order to bring the airports into better condition and to improve the organization of those networks. This device proposes the integration with local transport systems such as railways and local bus lines. This creates integration with the planning of local infrastructure systems. Better train links to the nearest main cities will increase the attractiveness and the accessibility of the airport and, indeed, of the entire region.

Tool4: Airport network

A territorial synergy (networking) between nearby airports drives cooperation among airports. It will increase complementarities and, at the same time, specialization of each airport. In that case, the airport network strengthens and creates growth opportunities from a European perspective. A governance system will drive this cooperation. Representatives of each airport will be involved in the management of the other nearby airports. All representatives of these airports will approve a shared management policy: a specialization of airports to avoid competition among them. The possibility of developing cooperation agreements with other neighboring airports is seen as a window of opportunity, especially in terms of commercial activities and market segmentation. This is something that many European secondary airports could consider and adopt as strategic and programmatic plan.

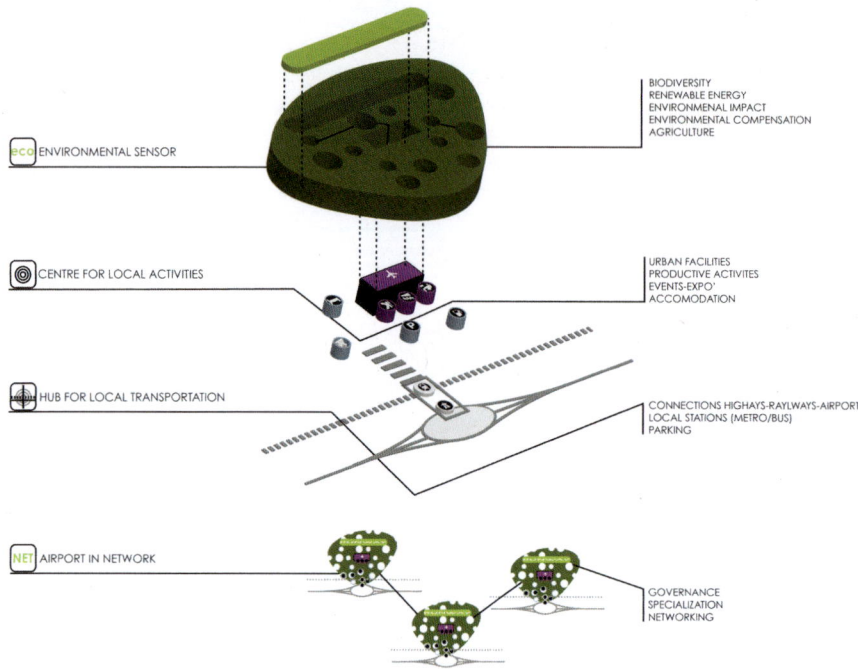

Tools

4.3 EXPERIMENTATIONS: 3 CASES[4]

Many European peripheral regions encounter difficulties in keeping up or developing their competitiveness. In this era of declining resources and generally poor economic development due to slow urban growth, making airports' central in the urban development plan is very challenging. In many cases, policy makers don't see a real convenience in strengthening scheduled flights or improving the technical and physical characteristics of these infrastructures. When it does happen, airports dramatically burden the regional economy. This is what happens in Jyväskylä Airport (Central Finland); Araxos Airport, Aktion Airport, Andravida Airport (Region of Western Greece); and Villanova d'Albenga Airport (Italy). These airports show different examples of the widespread phenomenon of underused airports stuck in a pre-decline phase. They are all airports on-hold. It is even more urgent to think about their future in order to transform these airport infrastructures into urban re-activators, before the airport is definitely abandoned. For all these airports, the development into a big hub for travel is not realistic. This is because the catchment area is modest and the physical dimensions of the airport cannot allow for a huge traffic of passengers. Furthermore, transport service is a consequence of the creation of a request for those services. In the future it is possible that more tourists will arrive with new flights carriers. However, tourists do not come simply by the creation of new flights. The creation of a touristic offer, the offer of hospitality and the promotion in Europe in the world will attract tourists. The goal is to have those airports fill that role in the territory. In this way, the research stresses the idea of the airport as resource. The airport is considered not only for its functional role but also for its image in the territory, whose development has to be taken in account during regional planning. According to this idea, the research analyses different renewal strategies for reactivation of these obsolete airports. Their conversion could increase the quality and development of the surrounding urban area and improve social conditions: from airports on-hold to airports as catalysts for regional improvement.

The re-significance of these infrastructures can activate processes of growth and mobility to develop transport and communication networks, but also processes answering to the need for landscape and places in which to live in. This can be the operative strategy for these airports to recalibrate their fundamental function in their physical contexts: the integration of air traffic transportation facilities with activities that regenerate their life and the surrounding context. From this perspective, the main research objectives aim to highlight that the improvement of accessibility can improve the economic situation of a region. However, each region must carry out a thorough analysis to decide the most efficient way to improve accessibility. In some cases (like in a remote area in Finland) this might be the strengthening of an airport (expansion of the physical structures and creation a better flight schedule). In other cases (like in the Greek regions), it might be the subsidy of scheduled flights to the next large hub. In a few cases, it is recommended to completely abandon airport activities in order to transform it into an urban facility that will have stronger positive effects on the economic performance of the region. In still other cases (like in the Italian regions) it may be best to integrate urban functions in the airport areas and the temporary interruption of flying activity, waiting for a possible future return of them.

Recommendations for airports on-hold

Due to the heterogeneity of the case studies, it isn't possible to draw one general model to adopt in all stakeholder regions. The research proposes three design strategies for renewal of these on-hold infrastructures. The logic for intervention in various areas is obviously different, depending on the contextual analysis conducted and results obtained. The combination of four tools described above drives the realization of each strategy: airport as environmental sensor, airport as services center for local activities, airport as hub for local transportation and airport as network. They allow for establishing stronger relationships between the infrastructure and their surrounding territories. At the same time, they gain

economic improvements and new uses for the airports. In that sense, the renewed airport is organized to satisfy not only one specific sector (flight operations) but it also adapts itself and its efficiency in relation to the surrounding context and business, it can exchange fluxes (physical and immaterial) with the surrounding territory and it can accommodate multiple functions. In that way, three different design strategies (Reload, Reuse, Recycle) have been identified to guide the airport renewal process:
- Reload. Expansion of the existing airport: increasing the number of flights, adding new functions to neighboring industrial and commercial areas
- Reuse. Maintenance of airport operation (even if temporarily suspended): improving by the hybridization with other activities related to the local context and with the integration of urban functions
- Recycle. Abandonment of airport function in favor of a comprehensive recycling action: reclaiming land from the old infrastructure, creation of a park and public facilities for the city.

The Reload design strategy provides for the maintenance of existing airport facilities and strengthening it with new facilities and equipment. In particular, it proposes the development of the potentials found in the analysis in an attempt to enlarge the airport and ensure economic growth in the local context. This design strategy is the approach used in the cases of Jyväskylä and Aktion airports. In Central Finland, the military aviation is located in the Jyväskylä Airport and the military traffic still has a strong role. It will also secure good conditions for commercial air traffic in the future. Moreover, the development of Jyväskylä air traffic—today, not so negative—will concentrate on international connections that will improve transfer passengers functions. At the same time, rail transportation will be developed, even for domestic travel). Jyväskylä Airport aims to become an important junction for Central Finland. Aktion Airport, in contrast, points to a strengthening of the existing airport facilities and increasing the number of flights only during the summer to support tourist traffic. This airport could become a strategic hub with regard to the tourist sector. Tourism, even when not taken into account in the algorithmic formulas, can have a fundamental role in the development of the Greek region, especially with the connections to the port of Lefkada, among others, that bring people to the Mediterranean islands. According to this idea, Aktion could become a seasonal airport with the activity of low-cost carriers. In that sense, it is realistic to think of enhancing the attractiveness of the airport hub (terminal and surrounding territory).

The Reuse design strategy provides for the maintenance of airport operation improved by the insertion and hybridization of other activities related to the local context and with the integration of urban functions, in an attempt to find alternatives to the use of flight activity not entirely necessary in these structures. This design strategy is approached to the cases of Araxos and Villanova d'Albenga airports. Araxos Airport (next to Patras) is a typical airport that can work when and if it is required. It would be a better solution to integrate with the city of Patras through the de-localization of activities from the city (for instance the University and research institutes) to the airport. Even more so today, with the good connection between Athens and Patras, it seems irrelevant to transform Araxos airport into a big airport hub. In this way, it provides an activity structure that lasts year round and provides the local context with new areas of economic growth and productive equipment. The air traffic, in this case, will be concentrated during the summer and connected to tourism in the region. Villanova d'Albenga Airport is "an essential piece to strengthen the infrastructure system in the Province of Savona."[5] The concept of airport's resilience has been stresses by proposing a hybrid infrastructure through the transformation of the on-hold airport into a light mobility system integrated to the existing urban mobility infrastructure as well as the city center. According to this, the reconversion of airport infrastructure could become an operative strategy for other landscape preservation and urban transformations. Their re-significance could increase quality and development of the surrounding urban and social conditions. The urban design approach aims to rethink on-hold airports, imagining them as latent public spaces, in synergy with engines of change and ecological devices. Additioanlly, Villanova d'Albenga airport was therefore represented in the local and provincial framework in order to make realistic developments in infrastructure and technological innovation, integrated with the landscape: the small airport becomes an integrated structure within the urban fabric, open to the community because it is equipped with urban facilities.[6] Therefore the development strategies of Villanova d'Albenga airport stress two directions. On one side, the possible further development of the airport is only in business aviation, or executive jet, because of the impossibility of accepting all typologies of airplanes. On the other side, it's possible to imagine that the land is used to cultivate flowers and agricultural products, in a further vision in which there is synergy between agricultural and touristic sectors (for instance open air exhibition in the countryside or a contemporary art events). Another interesting vision could be to work with the industrial sector that could find its localization in the flat land of Albenga. In this way, the growth of the airport could generate new possibilities to know the surrounding territories and enrich the poor local context. And finally, the relationship with Nice and Cannes airport is crucial because it is a cross-border network and it will create a relationship that strengthens and generates growth for a European region.

The Recycle design strategy provides for leaving the airport function in favor of a comprehensive recycling, by reclaiming land from the old infrastructure, and through new landscapes with the creation of parks and public facilities. Specifically, the development of the potentials found in the analysis is proposed, in an attempt to recycle the airport and give it back to the city. The primary aspect related to the recycle of small airports is the re-interpretation and requalification of the original systems and services with new meanings. The signs of the past, the memory traces of the activities ended, remain visible elements of the airport second life. To evaluate and anticipate the correct strategy of airport recycling is an increasingly urgent requirement to anticipate the inevitable decline of these structures and to activate recovery processes in synergy with the different urban realities. This design strategy could be the approach used in the case of Andravida Airport for a long-term future vision. Andravida Airport is an airport exclusively used for military purpose. Located a few kilometers from the airport of Aktion (30km), it is in a strategic position in the region of Western Greece. This area is ranked among the privileged areas of Greece in terms of existing natural, cultural and tourism advantages. In particular, it has the advantage of countless natural and cultural attractions: the inland and the mountainous areas, the purity of the sea, the rich and rare ecosystems, the monasteries, the modern sports facilities, the convention centers and the growing and modernized tourist facilities. These all comprise the variety of comparative advantages. The growth potential of both the agricultural and tourism industries is high if the airport's development is combined with local development projects. Such projects could be hotels and thematic tourist attractions, and combined transport services and usage of modern cultivating methods for agriculture. Moreover, the strategic position of the region can foster both a collaboration with local agricultural producers and the touristic activity. Furthermore, two airports already support the region of Western Greece. It doesn't really need a new airport for transport operations. With the possibility that the military may abandon Andravida airport, a more realistic and desirable vision for the future of this airport is the complete recycling of it. Andravida airport could be in a privileged position if transformed into a new natural attraction and urban facility. Aviation must be abandoned in favor of a transformation of the land into an urban park, with the localization of recreation facilities, in order to improve the value of the surrounding territory.

Lastly, two are the general recommendations. The first, according to the guidelines of the European infrastructure development plan for 2014-2020, is to increase as much as possible, the airport connections with smaller networks in the surrounding territory, in order to guarantee a more coherent organization of flows and connected networks, with less consumption of landscapes. The second, specific for local stakeholders, is to increase the diversification of activities in the airport. This refers not only to flight operations—such as production of planes, business aviation or aviation school—but it includes productive, social and cultural activities. All of these allow the airport to be used as a new landscape for local production over the lifetime. The new airport landscape offers a wide range of opportunities even when the airport is not in use for flight operations to be adapted as new centralities in their territorial and economic systems.

CHAPTER 4. RESILIENT LANDSCAPE RESERVES
[1] Stan Allen, "Infrastructural Urbanism." In: *Points and Lines: Diagrams and Projects for the City*, Princeton Architectural Press, New York, 1999, p.52

4.1 Airports' Second Life
[2] "Airport Landscape: Urban Ecologies in the Aerial Age" Exhibition, curated by Charles Waldheim and Sonja Dümpelmann, assembles canonical cases, projects and practices, as well as specific species and selected sites in support of this claim. The exhibition was organized within two broad thematic categories: Operations and Afterlives. Cases included in "Airport Operations" embody the status and role of landscape as a medium of design for operating airports. Those featured in "Airport Afterlives" describe the status and role of landscape as a medium of design for envisioning the future of abandoned airports. *Airport Landscape: Urban Ecologies in the Aerial Age Exhibition*, October 30 - December 19, 2013, Harvard University, Graduate School of Design, Cambridge, MA.
[3] The infrastructure is considered as a place of permanence and not just a transition, a biological material originating from the surrounding area and an integral part of the new housing situation. This is the definition of *osmotic infrastructure:* an infrastructure in osmosis with the surrounding area. These new infrastructures generate trade with landscapes but also allows us to see new landscapes. See Mosè Ricci, *New Paradigms*, LISt Lab, Barcellona/Trento, 2012.

4.3 Experimentation: 3 Cases
[4] These experimentations on real case studies and recommendations on airports on-hold have been developed throughout the ESPON-ADES research project. ADES is the acronyms for *Airports as Drivers of Economic Success in Peripheral Regions*. It was a Targeted Analysis founded by the European Community and involved in ESPON 2013 Programme. This international research was the good environment to investigate and experiment the role of regional airports in economic development in European peripheral regions, proposing alternative strategies to improve small regional airports. In particular, the project was targeted to the situation and needs of three stakeholder regions: Province of Savona (Italy), Regions of Western Greece (Greece) and the City of Jyväskylä (Finland).
ESPON-ADES Research Credits and Participants. Local Stakeholders: Province of Savona, Italy (Lead Stakeholder); Region of Western Greece, Greece; and City of Jyvaskyla, Finland. Lead Partner: Department of Sciences for Architecture – University of Genoa, Italy. Project Partners: BAK Basel Economics AG, Switzerland; Knowledge and Innovation Intermediaries Consulting LTD, Greece; Jyväskylä University School of Business and Economics, Finland. Research Team: Prof. Arch. Mosè Ricci, Arch. Sara Favargiotti, Dr. Arch, Federica Alcozer, Arch. Beatrice Moretti, Arch. Romina Ghezzi (DSA, Genoa); Prof. Dr. Urs Müller, Christoph Strueby, Larissa Müller (BAK Basel Economics, AG, Switzerland); Yiannis Geragotellis, Dr. Konstantinos Fouskas, Charis Loupassi (Knowledge and Innovation Intermediaries Consulting Ltd KiNNO, Greece); Prof. Hannu Tervo, Dr. Kirsi Mukkala, Kari Itkonen, Pekka Pyyny (Jyväskylä University School of Business and Economics, Finland). Project Expert at the ESPON Coordination Unit: Nuno MADEIRA.
[5] Luciano Pasquale (Unioncamere) during the press conference *The Revitalization of the Villanova d'Albenga Airport* (*Rilancio dell'Aeroporto di Villanova d'Albenga*) at the Airport of Villanova d'Albenga, October 10, 2013.
[6] See the essay of Marialessandra Signorastri, "L'aeroporto di Alberga nel quadro delle scelte strategiche per l'albenganese". In: Mosè Ricci, *iSpace,* Meltemi (collana Babele), 2009, p. 113.

Comparison of surface, population and density of Stakeholder Regions

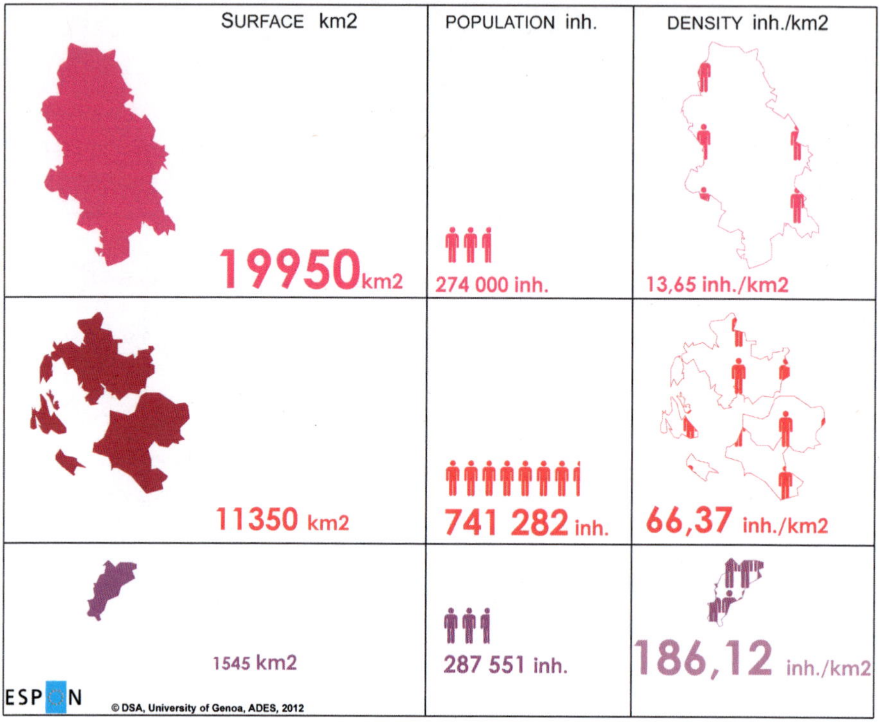

	SURFACE km2	POPULATION inh.	DENSITY inh./km2
	19950 km2	274 000 inh.	13,65 inh./km2
	11350 km2	741 282 inh.	66,37 inh./km2
	1545 km2	287 551 inh.	186,12 inh./km2

© DSA, University of Genoa, ADES, 2012

Legend
- Central Finland
- Western Greece
- Province of Savona

ID_Jyväskylä Airport

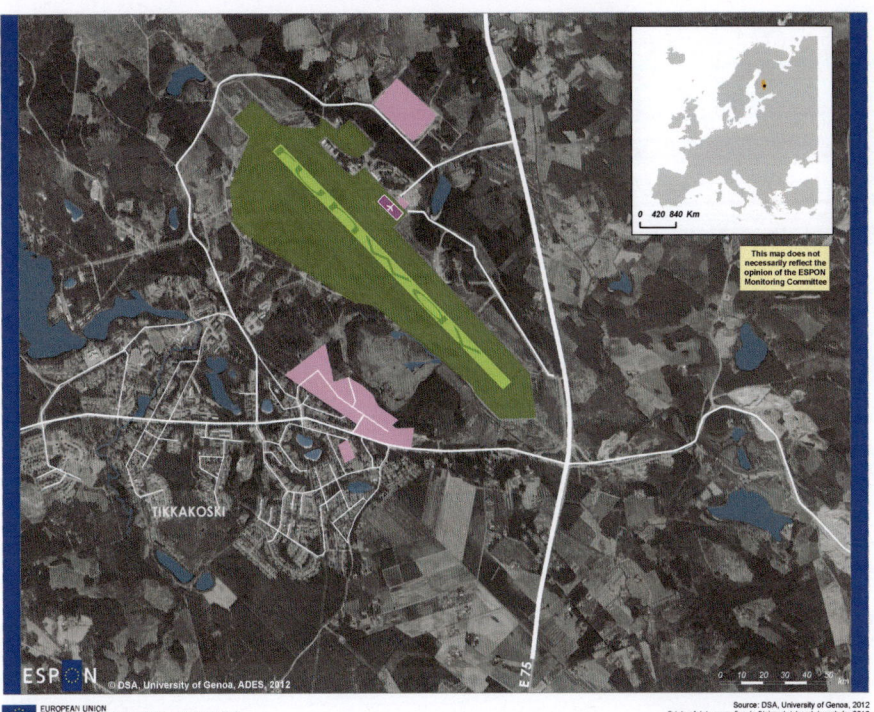

Legend
- Airport terminal
- Runway
- Buffer zone

JYVÄSKYLÄ AIRPORT JYV
62° 23' 58" N   25° 40' 42" E

- ELEVATION (SLM) **140M**
- RUNWAY LENGHT **2601M**
- SURFACE **ASPHALT**
- TYPOLOGY **CIVIL AND MILITARY**

- LANDINGS **14812 (in 2010)**
- PASSENGERS **88608 (in 2010)**

- FACILITIES RESTAURANTS, BARS, SHOPS, POST OFFICE, TELECOMUNICATION SERVICES, FIRST AID, FIRE SERVICES, PHARMACY, LEFT-LUGGAGE, CHILD FACILITIES, VIP LOUNGE, DISABLE FACILITIES, PARKING, TRAVEL AGENCY, CAR RENTAL, POLICE STATION, INFORMATION SERVICES, AIRLINE OFFICES, CONFERENCE ROOMS, MANAGEMENT SERVICES,
- CONNECTIONS JYVÄSKYLÄ

ID_Villanova d'Albenga Airport

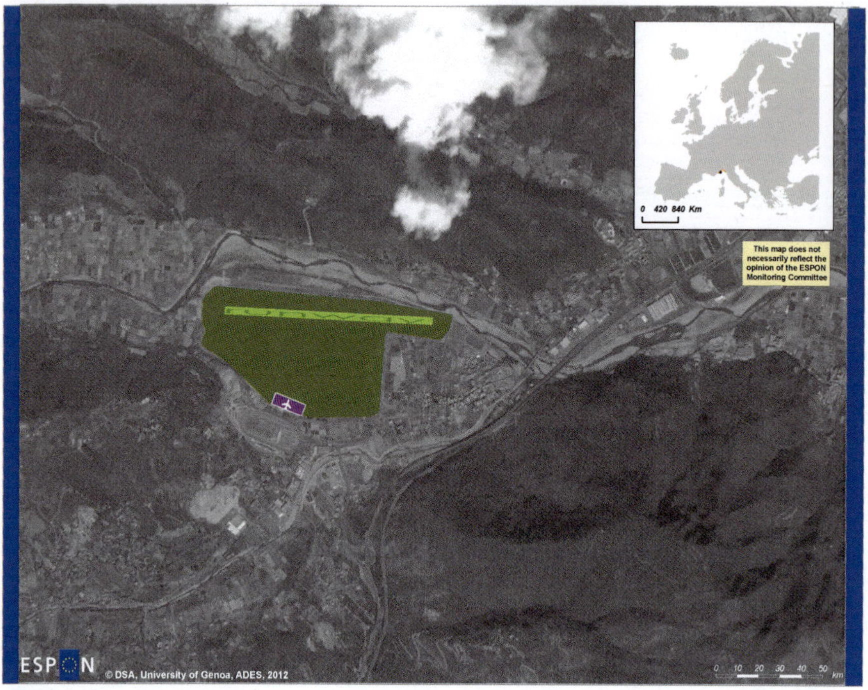

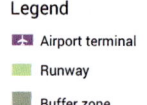

Legend
- Airport terminal
- Runway
- Buffer zone

VILLANOVA AIRPORT VLA
44° 02' 45" N   08° 07' 45" E

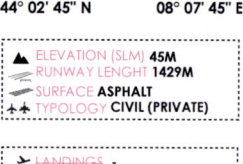

ELEVATION (SLM) **45M**
RUNWAY LENGHT **1429M**
SURFACE **ASPHALT**
TYPOLOGY **CIVIL (PRIVATE)**

LANDINGS -
PASSENGERS -

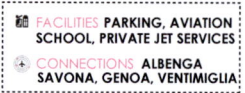

FACILITIES **PARKING, AVIATION SCHOOL, PRIVATE JET SERVICES**
CONNECTIONS **ALBENGA SAVONA, GENOA, VENTIMIGLIA**

ID_Aktion Airport

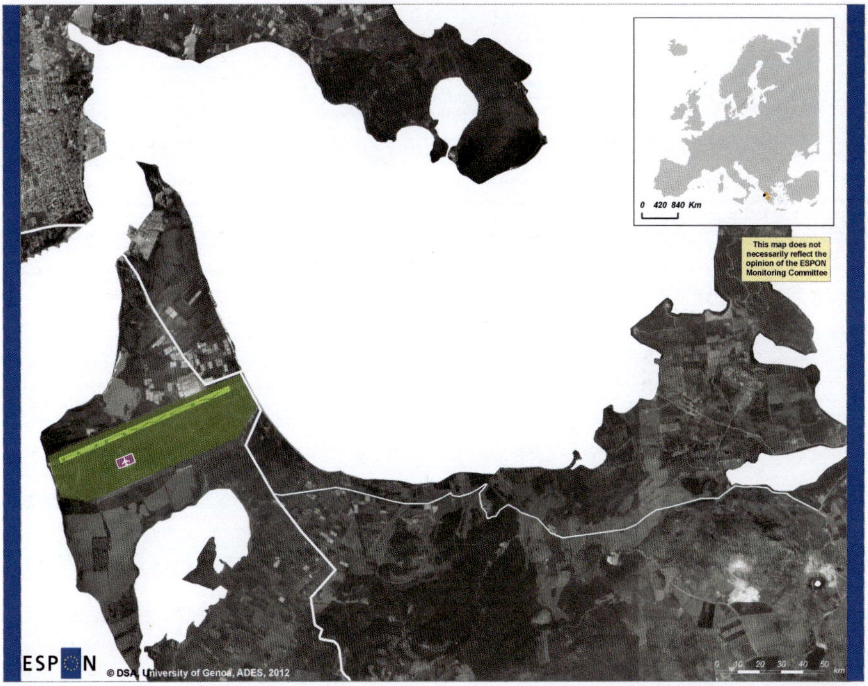

EUROPEAN UNION
Part-financed by the European Regional Development Fund
INVESTING IN YOUR FUTURE

Regional level: NUTS 3
Source: DSA, Universiy of Genoa, 2012
Origin of data: www.hcaa-eleng.gr/preveza.htm, 2012
© EuroGeographics Association for administrative boundaries

Legend

- Airport terminal
- Runway
- Buffer zone

AKTION AIRPORT **PVK**

38° 55' 32'' N **20° 45' 55'' E**

ELEVATION (SLM) **3M**
RUNWAY LENGHT **2871M**
SURFACE **ASPHALT**
TYPOLOGY **CIVIL AND MILITARY**

~~LANDINGS~~
PASSENGERS **292394 (in 2010)**

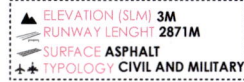

FACILITIES **RESTAURANTS, BARS, SHOPS, BANKS, POST OFFICE, TELECOMUNICATION SERVICES, FIRST AID, FIRE SERVICES, PHARMACY, LEFT-LUGGAGE, CHILD FACILITIES, VIP LOUNGE, DISABLE FACILITIES, PARKING, METEOROLOGICAL CENTER, TRAVEL AGENCY, CAR RENTAL, POLICE STATION, INFORMATION SERVICES, AIRLINE OFFICES, MANAGEMENT SERVICES**
CONNECTIONS **PREVEZA**

ID_Araxos Airport

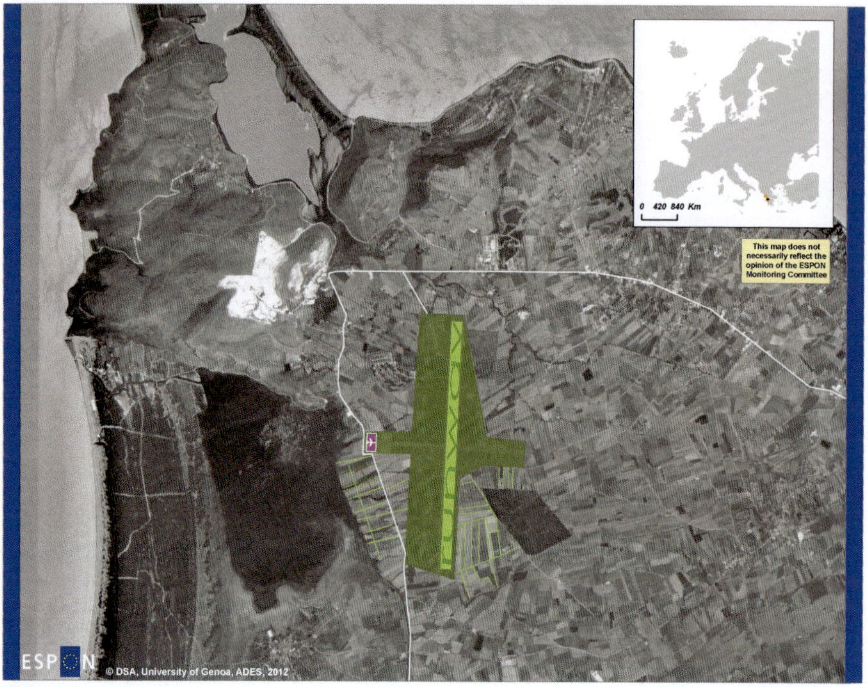

EUROPEAN UNION
Part-financed by the European Regional Development Fund
INVESTING IN YOUR FUTURE

Source: DSA, Universiy of Genoa, 2012
Origin of data: www.araxos-airport.com, 2012
© EuroGeographics Association for administrative boundaries

Legend

- Airport terminal
- Runway
- Buffer zone

ARAXOS AIRPORT **GPA**
38° 9' 4" N **21° 25' 32" E**

ELEVATION (SLM) **14M**
RUNWAY LENGHT **3352M**
SURFACE **MACADAM**
TYPOLOGY **CIVIL AND MILITARY**

~~LANDINGS~~
PASSENGERS **292394 (in 2010)**

FACILITIES **RESTAURANTS, BARS, SHOPS, LEFT-LUGGAGE, PARKING, TRAVEL AGENCY, CAR RENTAL, POLICE STATION, INFORMATION SERVICES, AIRLINE OFFICES, MANAGEMENT SERVICES**

CONNECTIONS **PATRAS**

ID_Andravida Airport

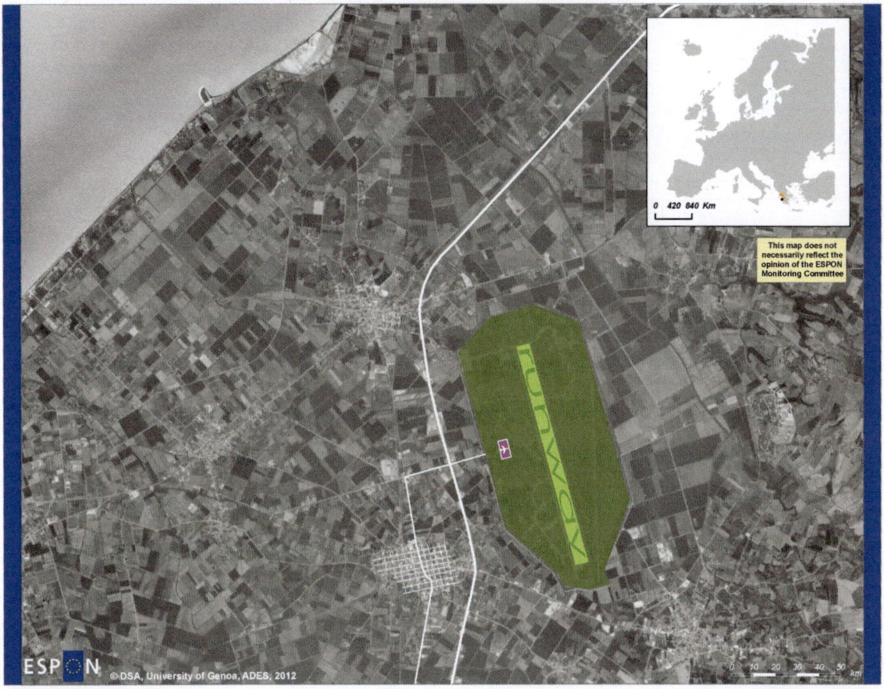

Legend
- Airport terminal
- Runway
- Buffer zone

ANDRAVIDA AIRPORT PYR
37° 41' 0" N 21° 28' 0" E

ELEVATION (SLM) **17M**
RUNWAY LENGHT **3139M**
SURFACE **ASPHALT**
TYPOLOGY **MILITARY**

LANDINGS -
PASSENGERS -

FACILITIES **MILITAR FACILITIES, PRIVATE JET SERVICES, PARKING**
CONNECTIONS **IONION SEA PATRAS**

REload strategy in Jyväskylä Airport: Military Park Airport

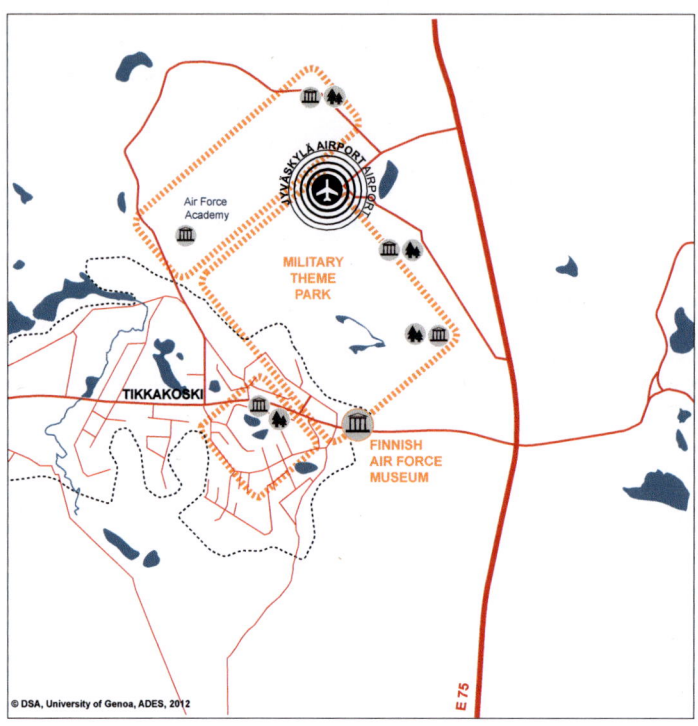

Legend

- ✈ Airport
- ⊪⊪⊪ Military Theme Park
- 🏛ﾠMuseum and Cultural facilities
- 🌲 Park and Green

- 🟩 ENVIRONMENTAL SENSOR
- ⚫ CENTRE FOR LOCAL ACTIVITIES
- HUB FOR LOCAL TRANSPORTATION
- AIRPORT NETWORK

REload strategy in Jyväskylä Airport: Industrial Airport

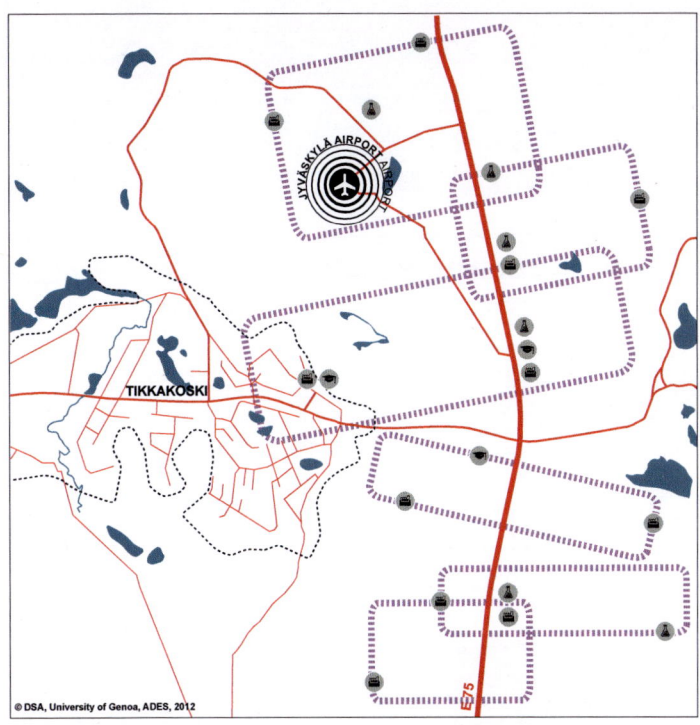

Legend
- Airport
- Industrial Platform
- Industries
- Research Institutes
- Universities
- ENVIRONMENTAL SENSOR
- CENTRE FOR LOCAL ACTIVITIES
- HUB FOR LOCAL TRANSPORTATION
- AIRPORT NETWORK

Airport Network Strategy in Jyväskylä Airport

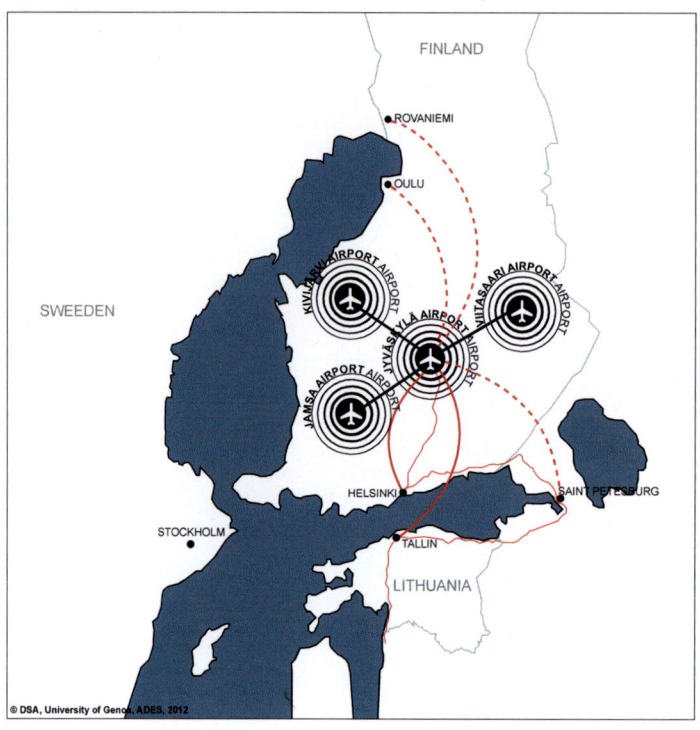

Legend

⊕ Airport
— Existent Flight connection
···· Proposed Flight connection
 Flows of passengers

ENVIRONMENTAL SENSOR

CENTRE FOR LOCAL ACTIVITIES

HUB FOR LOCAL TRANSPORTATION

NET AIRPORT NETWORK

Airport Network Strategy in Villanova d'Albenga Airport

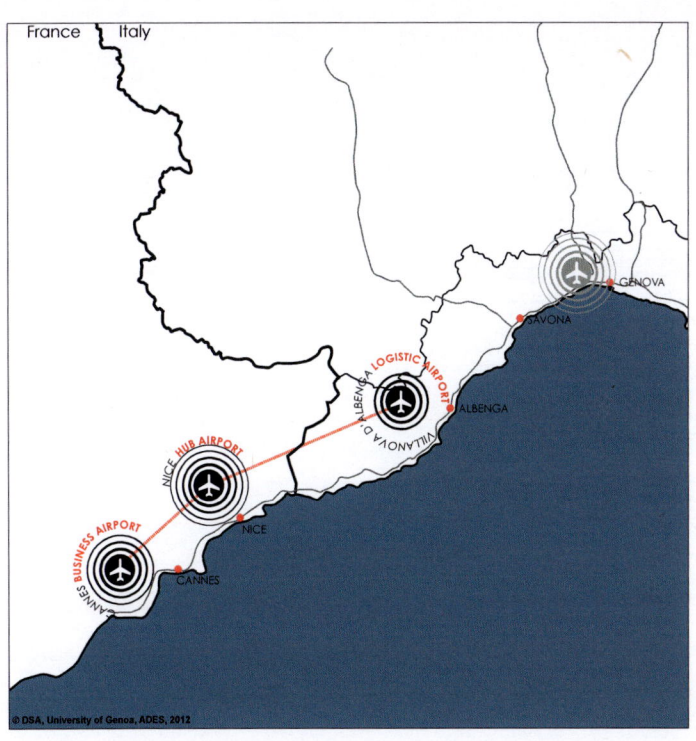

Legend

- ✈ Airport
- — Connection
-  Flows of passengers

- ENVIRONMENTAL SENSOR
- CENTRE FOR LOCAL ACTIVITIES
- HUB FOR LOCAL TRANSPORTATION
- AIRPORT NETWORK

REuse strategy in Villanova d'Albenga Airport:
ECO-Agriport

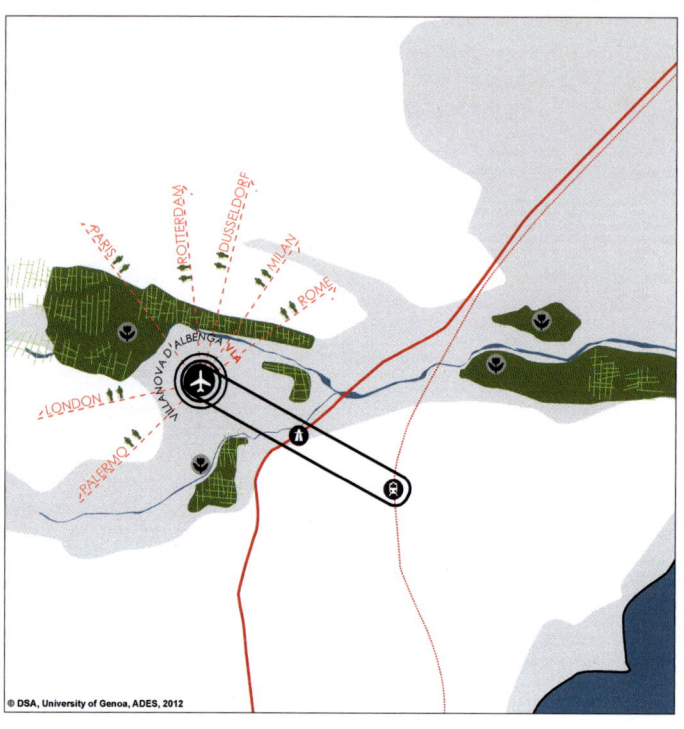

© DSA, University of Genoa, ADES, 2012

Legend
- ✈ Airport
- ✈ 🚗 🚆 Connection highway- railway- airport
- Agriculture
- Fruits
- Flowers
- ♦city New destinations

- ENVIRONMENTAL SENSOR
- CENTRE FOR LOCAL ACTIVITIES
- HUB FOR LOCAL TRANSPORTATION
- AIRPORT NETWORK

REuse strategy in Villanova d'Albenga Airport: Industrial Airport

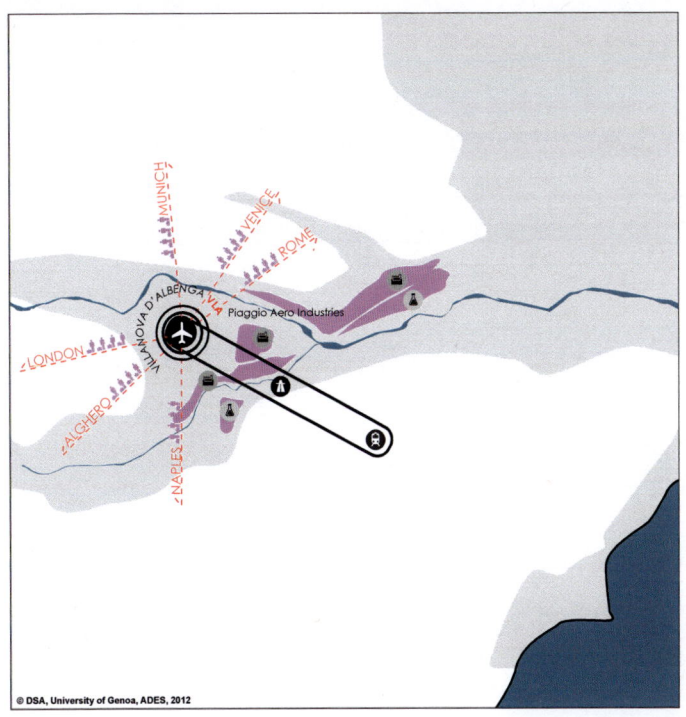

© DSA, University of Genoa, ADES, 2012

Legend

- ✈ Airport
- ✈ 🏠 🚂 Connection highway- railway- airport
- 🏭 Industries
- 🏛 Research Institutions
- city New destinations

- ENVIRONMENTAL SENSOR
- CENTRE FOR LOCAL ACTIVITIES
- HUB FOR LOCAL TRANSPORTATION
- AIRPORT NETWORK

REload strategy in Aktion Airport: Touristic Airport

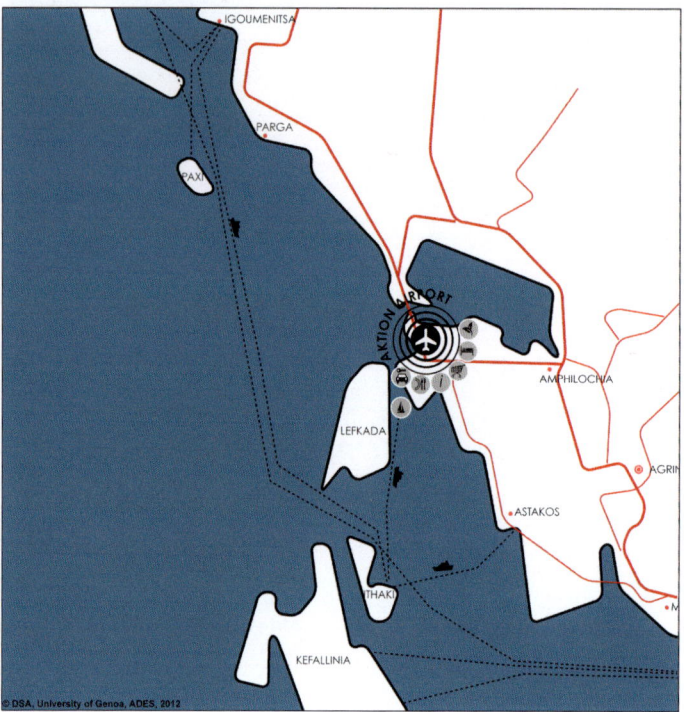

Legend
- Airport
- Harbour
- Car rental
- Restaurants-Bars
- Information
- Shops
- Accomodation
- Renewable energy

- ENVIRONMENTAL SENSOR
- CENTRE FOR LOCAL ACTIVITIES
- HUB FOR LOCAL TRANSPORTATION
- AIRPORT NETWORK

REuse strategy in Araxos Airport: Platform Airport

Legend
- Airport
- Industries
- Research Institutions
- Univerties
- Industrial Platform
- ENVIRONMENTAL SENSOR
- CENTRE FOR LOCAL ACTIVITIES
- HUB FOR LOCAL TRANSPORTATION
- AIRPORT NETWORK

REcycle strategy in Andravida Airport: *ECO-Airpark*

Legend
- Airpark
- Parks network
- Cultural heritage
- Blue flag

- ENVIRONMENTAL SENSOR
- CENTRE FOR LOCAL ACTIVITIES
- HUB FOR LOCAL TRANSPORTATION
- AIRPORT NETWORK

Jyväskylä Airport Masterplan: *Platform Airport*

Legend

Platform Airport
Industrial Platform
Agriculture
Bike Path
Cultural heritage
Research Institutes
Universities
Cultural heritage Path
Infrastructures
Green Corridors

Villanova d'Albenga Airport Masterplan: *Logistic Airport*

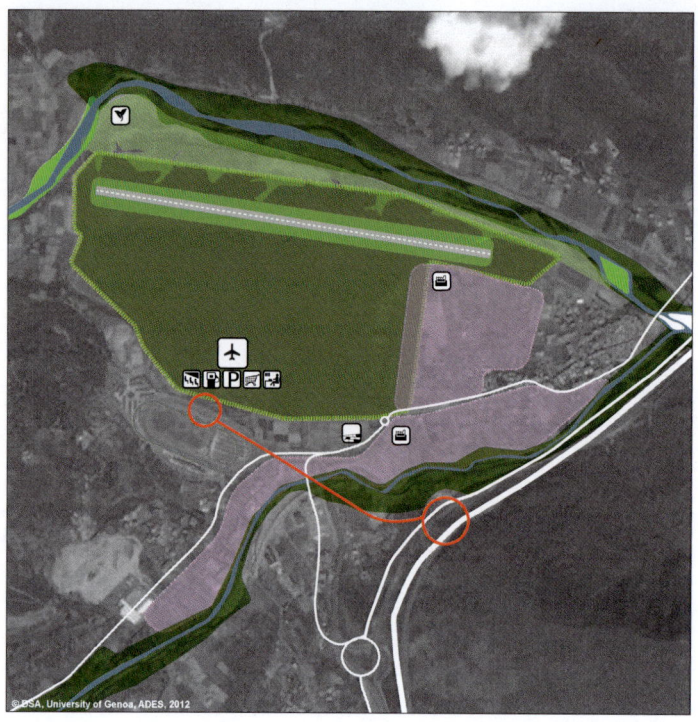

Legend

 Logistic Airport

  Industrial Platform

  Agriculture

  Renewable energy

  Urban facilities

  Connection highway- railway- airport

  Green corridors

  Buffer zone

Aktion Airport Masterplan: *Touristic Airport*

Legend

- ✈ Touristic Airport
- ⚛ Renewable energy
- ⓘ Information
- 🛍 Shops
- 🛏 Accomodation
- 🚗 Car rental
- 🍽 Restaurants-Bars
- ⚓ Harbour
- — Commercial axis
- ⋯ Maritime routes
- ▒ Buffer zone-Green corridors

Araxos Airport Masterplan: *Platform Airport*

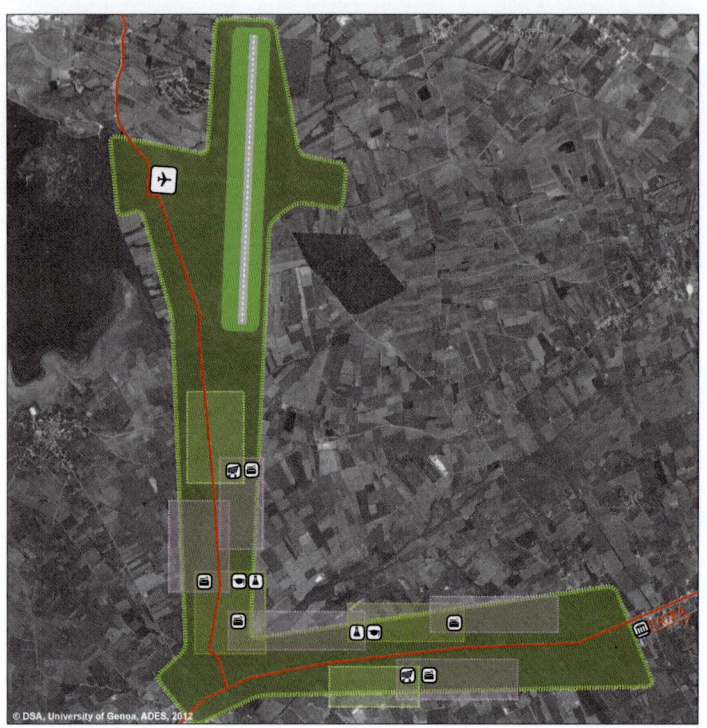

Legend

Platform Airport

Research Platform

Commercial Platform

Industrial Platform

Cultural heritage

Buffer zone

Andravida Airport Masterplan: *EcoAirpark*

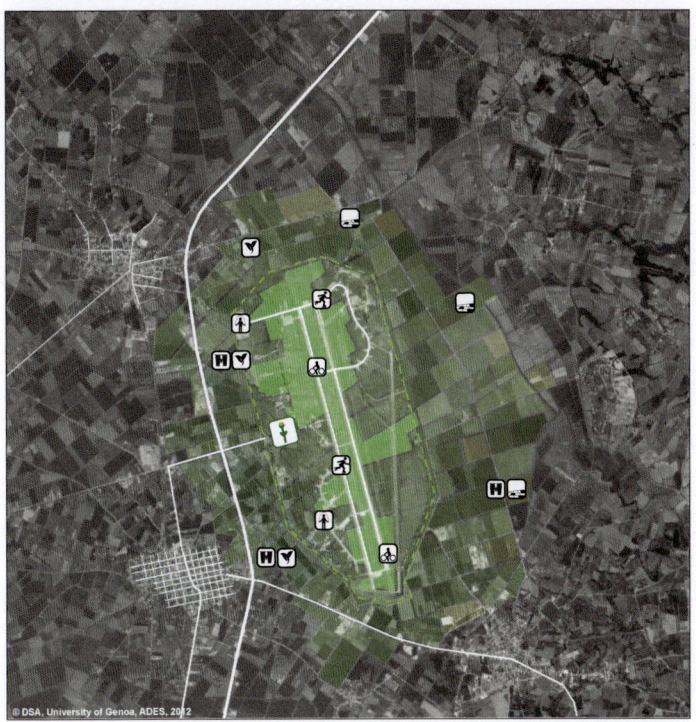

Legend

- EcoAirpark
- Renewable energy
- Agriculture
- Environmental monitoring
- Fitness trail
- Bike path
- Roller-skating rink

POSITIONS

Public viewing area at London (Heathrow) Airport
London | 1955
Photo by John Carter @flickr

> **Describing an airport as a landscape is already an important conceptual break through. Just claiming it as a landscape gives us a kind of coherence, and a way of approaching it that if you simply did engineering or if you simple did architecture, it would lack.**
>
> Charles Waldheim, *Airport Landscape Conference*, 2013

CONVERSATIONS

Research Platforms

Airports International Research

The goals of the European Union are taken into consideration during this research in terms of mobility, territorial cohesion and environmental sustainability, and focusing in particular on the role of accessibility. In fact, the EU 2020 priorities include among others "Inclusive growth - fostering a high employment economy delivering economic, social and territorial cohesion." In line with the priorities of the Territorial Agenda 2020, the aim is to promote polycentric and balanced territorial development and to improve territorial connectivity for individuals and enterprises. In that sense, the contents of the "Fifth Report of Social, Economic and Territorial Cohesion" give important references.[1] The Fifth Report precisely states that regional competitiveness and development prospects are affected by infrastructure endowments, such as transport or telecommunication networks. This document is relevant to reflect the issues of accessibility, infrastructure (in particular air travel), transport systems and regional development. As indicated by many studies, the provision of public infrastructure has a large, positive effect on productivity and growth. Physical infrastructure can adversely affect the environment, especially heavy and long-lasting infrastructure such as roads, motorways, railway lines and modifications to watercourses. In such cases, the trade-off between economic and environmental costs and benefits needs to be explicitly and properly taken into account. The report assumes that a good transport system is important for regional economic development. It reduces journey times and, accordingly, production costs, thereby increasing competitiveness. It improves access to markets for consumers, workers and businesses and is an important aspect of the attractiveness of a region for investors. However, a good transport system in itself is not sufficient to ensure regional development. The effects of investment in transport and other infrastructure on economic performance also depends on the region's capacity to use it efficiently, as well as on investment in other factors important for development, such as in human capital and innovation. This partly explains why the return on investment in infrastructure can vary significantly between regions. Furthermore, air travel has continued to grow over the past few years up until the onset of the crisis in 2008. The highest growth in traffic has been in secondary airports, which are mostly used by low-cost airlines as well as in the airports in the capital cities in the EU-12. This proliferation of low-cost companies started to promote the revitalization of secondary airports. They generated a rapid transformation of land use and of the infrastructure network relative to land transportation. The integration of new economic, cultural and leisure activities at these airports, allowed the surrounding territories to become more dynamic and improve local businesses. In that sense the secondary low-cost airports became a landmark in the territory and an important element for the local economy.

Significance in the European Framework

The EU cohesion goals call particularly for an improvement of the framework conditions of peripheral regions. Better accessibility is one of the means to move towards this goal. And regional airports are an option for improving accessibility. However, building new infrastructure, in this moment of crisis, does not reveal itself as the most sustainable strategy, considering sustainability as an aim in relation to social and territorial changes. Already in 2001, the European Commission's White Paper indicated that it was an absolutely necessary strategy to interrupt the connection between increased mobility and economic growth.[2] Nowadays, the European Union expects air traffic to double over the next fifteen years, as has happened in the last fifteen.[3] However, their prospective reports on airports reflect a significant concern: air traffic can be duplicated in Europe but there are only a few major European airports that can grow physically. Barcelona, for example, can build new runways and terminals over the sea. Many European airports, however, are surrounded by cities, highways, railroads, and industrial sites making the possibility of physical expansion extremely difficult. Another example is in the United Kingdom. In 2008 the Mayor of London proposed to study the possibility of constructing a new airport on the Thames River delta, due to the increasing overburdening of Heathrow Airport. Meanwhile, the European funding plan for the period 2014-2020 is geared towards the development of the corridors with local networks and to the creation of new slight hubs. Furthermore, many local populations will no longer accept the environmental damage to the landscape caused by heavy construction in their territories. The increasing social conflicts regarding the construction of high-speed train lines are grave in peripheral contexts: even this indicates the need to change the paradigms.

The ESPON-ADES Target Analysis contributed significantly to the European debate on transport policy regarding airport renewal in particular.[4] The research project has been developed under the ESPON 2013 Programme, which stands for European Observation Network for Territorial Development and Cohesion. This Programme highlights, among other things, the relations with the regional development policies, placing them in a framework of transnational cooperation involving the 28+4 EU countries. Addressing aspects of European territorial policy, ranging from innovation to knowledge accessibility, the research highlights the position of regions in relation to the objectives set by Europe 2020. In fact, the project gives a comprehensive and detailed view of the problems that European peripheral regions are faced with when trying to keep up or develop their competitiveness in the era of declining resources and generally poor economic development. The research stresses the idea of the airport as a resource and investigates the role of regional airports in regional economic development in European peripheral regions. ADES research findings support an innovative point of view: the construction of a new infrastructure is not always efficient per se and should be supported by innovative actions outlined by the Renewal Strategies. These strategies outline different scenarios, with three basic alternatives to enhance airport development and the local communities' vitality. ESPON-ADES findings and results constituted a source of inspiration to other local and regional authorities in charge of planning, managing and/ or monitoring plans and strategies that acknowledge the positive effects of renewed transport infrastructures in revitalizing local economies.[5] Although the role of accessibility to economic development often results important, it can't guarantee economic development by itself: the modern idea that infrastructure produces economic development in peripheral areas and the belief that there is no economic development without new infrastructure are no longer univocally valid, as explain above. Alternative scenarios for underused airports have been over-appreciated by Stakeholders but also by the European Community during the ESPON Seminar in Paphos, Cyprus.[6]

International Research Platforms

In 1970, the Boeing 747 soon became the fetish of a whole generation of students and teachers. The front elevation of an airplane was the logo of the Bartlett Summer School: the airplane, in fact, was what made it possible.[7] Even before, in 1935, Le Corbusier said that the airplane "is the symbol of the new age. [...] The airplane, in the sky, carries our hearts above mediocre things. The airplane has given us the bird's eye view. When the eye sees clearly, the mind makes a clear decision."[8] These statements reveal how airports have affected the modern imagination and the relation between city, landscape and infrastructure. Even today, the relations between city and airport or the evolutions of aviation are topics that have been investigated by international research platforms. The connection with other research platforms or researchers who study airports in recent years has been a relevant moment for sharing cultural experiences and points of view. Travelling from Europe to the United States, I have met and interviewed the most relevant academics whose work is focused on airports: from the relation between airports and cities, to the investigation of airports afterlife, and into the future with experimental forms of aviation. The following paragraph provides an overview on the state of the art and the specific research points of view. The integral interviews are proposed in the following paragraphs.

Skycar City | UWM + MVRDV | 2006

From the 2006 Marcus Prize Studio at the University of Wisconsin-Milwaukee (UWM), Winy Maas of MVDRV and Grace La (who was faculty of member in the School of Architecture and Urban Planning at UMW) presented the work of twelve students who explored the relationship between infrastructure, architecture and urban form. The research began as a speculation upon greater problems like urban densification, landscape consumption, land management and fossil fuel depletion. This highly investigative studio pushed the physical and conceptual limits of given definitions of city, circulation and program. Tested in two scenarios (one real in Tianjin, China and the other purely hypothetical), the studio severed vehicular traffic flow from its traditional two-dimensional plane and then forecast the potentials of a new, hyper-volumetric city where given urban activity inflate to fully occupy all three-dimensions. Populated by 5 million inhabitants and rising 800 meters high, this new **Skycar City** is buzzing with the flow of goods and people, as they navigate the airways in several models of newly designed air-born vehicles.

Small Airports | IUAV + UNICAM + UNIGE + UNIUD | 2006>2008

This national research, coordinated by Alberto Ferlenga, aimed to investigate architectural and urban implications of a new generation of airports, updated to the newest technologies and to the demands of the The national research Small Airports (Piccoli Aeroporti) was coordinated by Alberto Ferlenga and involved several Italian universities: University IUAV of Venice, University of Camerino, University of Genoa, and University of Udine. The research aimed to investigate architectural and urban implications of a new generation of airports, updated to the newest technologies and to the demands of the new **Very Light Jet (VLA)**. More specifically, the work focused on two main topics: the first highlighted the transformations generated by the new small infrastructure in the urban landscape, especially at the regional scale; the second analyzed the physical changes caused by the technological innovations at the architectural scale of the airport and its services. The research highlighted three main issues: the definition of an airport-model based on the demands of the new transportation system Very Light Jet; the analysis and the evaluation of the localization effects that these infrastructures established at the regional level; and finally, the urban and territorial changes caused by an integrated network of **small airports and local development**. The research findings have been supported by a large number of case studies across Italy, such as Marche, Abruzzo, Lazio, Liguria, Veneto and Friuli Venezia-Giulia. For all of them, the research has proposed specific scenarios for their physical transformation inspired by technological innovation.

Airports ADES - ESPON | DSA + BAKBasel + KiNNO + JSBE | 2012>2013

The ESPON project **Airports as Drivers of Economic Success in Peripheral Regions (ADES)** was developed by the Department of Sciences for Architecture DSA, University of Genoa, Italy (Lead partner); BAK Basel Economics AG, Switzerland; KiNNO Consulting LTD, Greece; and Jyväskylä University School of Business and Economics, Finland. ADES Target Analysis gave an improvement in the European debate on transport policy in particular for airport renewal. Under the coordination of Mosè Ricci, the research stressed the idea of the airport as a resource and it investigated the role of regional airports in regional economic development in European peripheral regions. The research analyzed and proposed alternative strategies to improve infrastructures and services in small regional airports. The project was specifically targeted to the situation and needs of three stakeholder regions: Province of Savona (Italy), Region of Western Greece (Greece) and the City of Jyväskylä (Finland). The target analysis aimed to propose alternatives to the excessive construction of new infrastructure: explore the leverage effect of existing infrastructures in boosting local economies. ADES research findings support an innovative point of view: the construction of a new infrastructure is not always efficient per se and should be supported by innovative actions outlined by the **Renewal Strategies**. These strategies outline different scenarios, with three basic alternatives to enhance airport development and the local communities' vitality. These findings and results constituted a source of inspiration to other local and regional authorities in charge of planning, managing and/or monitoring plans and strategies that acknowledge the positive effects of renewed transport infrastructures in revitalizing landscapes, cities, and communities.

Airport Urbanism | IUAV-POLIMI-UNITN | 2004>2014

Over the years, Laura Cipriani, has specialized in the relationship between infrastructure and landscape, with particular attention to airports. Starting with case studies, the research analyses landscape changes in the areas immediately around secondary airports, as well as infrastructural network developments on a larger scale. Investigating the infrastructural landscape shaped by this network of secondary airports does not only mean studying the new typology of **low-cost airports**, but also, and above all, to examine the physical impact of mass air transportation on the European territory. Industrial districts, new tourist developments, and newly built infrastructures are only some of the physical consequences of this new network expansion where airports are the privileged entry points to the spread of urbanization within Europe and beyond European borders. Airport infrastructure acts as a catalyst of urban evolution/devolution not only for the regions immediately involved in the transformation process, but also for the spread of urban models beyond national boundaries, giving birth to a real airport urbanism that echoes in profound landscape and environmental transformations.

Emerging Infrastructural Landscapes | UAB | 2007>2014

Emerging Infrastructural Landscapes is a research project managed by the Master in Intervenció i Gestió del Paisatge, Department of Geography - Universitat Autònoma de Barcelona - under the coordination of Francesc Muñoz. In particular, the research platform deals with airport infrastructures and the environmental management of the landscape. The research aims to develop intervention plans and landscape management to highlight the relationship between the new airport and the surrounding landscape, in accordance with the various future scenarios. The starting point in this research is the consideration of infrastructures not as isolated from the territory, but rather as elements defined in the environment and landscape of the metropolis today. Since 2011 the research platform is supporting the *Generalitat* of Catalonia to develop future scenarios for the underused Lleida-Alguaire airport. One of the main aims of the research is to consider the airport infrastructure as an element for the territorial development, in close connection and relation with the environment and landscape.

Airport and the City | ETH | 2008>2014

Airports and Cities is a research platform based at ETH in Zurich, chaired by Prof. Kees Christiaanse together with Christian Salewski and Benedikt Boucsein. The research investigates the relationship between airports and their urban regions. Searching for a deeper understanding of their reciprocity, the aim is to find better and more sustainable airport and urban development strategies. Airports and Cities is based on specific case studies, such as Zurich Airport region, Munich Airport region, Singapore Airport region, the Pearl River airport system, and Amsterdam Airport region. Airport and Cities' main themes are: urbanization effects of hub airports; development of airport design and planning; best practices of enhanced reciprocity of airports and cities; conceptual models for airports and cities. From 2012 the research team has been involved in the research **Better Airport Regions: Models and Development Pathways for Sustainable Urban Transformation**. The aim of the project is to research sustainable transformation pathways for Amsterdam Airport Region, while Zurich airport region will serve as the main reference case.

Airport Landscape | GSD | 2013>2016

Airport Landscape is a research project based at the Harvard Graduate School of Design. Airports have never been more central to the life of cities, yet they have remained relatively peripheral in design discourse. Designers in recent decades have reaffirmed their historic assertions about the **airfield as a site of design through a range of practices**. Airport Landscape assembles these practices through case study projects for the ecological enhancement of operating airports and the conversion of abandoned airports. The School recently published the definitive volume on the subject, *Airport Landscape: Urban Ecologies in the Aerial Age* (2016). The publication was co-edited by the Office for Urbanization's founding director Prof. Charles Waldheim in collaboration with Sonja Dümpelmann. The book gathers work from the eponymous exhibition that was held at the Harvard Graduate School of Design, presenting the airport as a site of and for landscape. More recently, the Office for Urbanization is editing a companion volume as a field guide to the transformation of abandoned, decommissioned, and deactivated airports.[9] The Airfield Manual is an Harvard GSD Airport Landscape initiative and it documents case study strategies and best practices for the conversion of decommissioned airports for a variety of new uses from public parks to ecological corridors, from energy farms to new urban districts.

This section reports the conversations carried out between 2013 and 2015 with academic and practitioners involved on landscape and urban infrastructures in a broad sense. The conversations focus on the past or on-going projects of each platforms that deal with landscape, infrastructures and urban transformations to clarify their specific re-interpretation of landscape in the contemporary age. Lastly, they contribute to highlight the network of research platforms involved in the topic of airport landscape across different scales and fields of interest.

*Airport Landscape Exhibition
Graduate School of Design,
Harvard University
Photo by Sara Favargiotti |
November 2013*

CONVERSATION WITH
ALBERTO FERLENGA

Dean and Full Professor in Architecture and Urban Design of the University IUAV of Venice. Among other researches, in 2006-2007 he was national coordinator of the PRIN project Small Airports (Piccoli Aeoporti). The research results are published in the book "Piccoli Aeroporti. Infrastruttura, città e paesaggio nel territorio italiano." In 2012, he was curator of the exhibition "L'architettura del Mondo. Infrastrutture, Mobilità, Nuovi Paesaggi" at the Triennale in Milan. The conversation has been carried at the University IUAV of Venice on January 25, 2014.

SF | What sparked your interest in the study of airports and which paradigms are investigated in the Small Airports research?

AF | The origin is pretty casual. After the Villard Seminar, which dealt for the first time with the airports topic, we decided to analyse the issue in depth and to propose the topic for Research of National Interest, PRIN 2006-2007. The emergence of the theme in terms of quantity was extremely surprising. The high number of these areas in Italy was compelling enough to make our nation a borderline case. In other countries, with different territorial characteristics, the problem was less evident. It is a very important issue. We tried to bring together two, apparently opposite issues: the territorial identity and mobility. The first deals with the idea of conservatism, and the second, focused on aviation, was one of the emblems of modernity. The aim was to understand if these two ideas could be brought together and if, by doing so, we could possibly work to address the fragmentation of both. This required that we dealt with the issue of a multiplicity of identity: an airport—apparently a univocal theme—could have many identities and many declinations when placed in a very uneven territory like the Italian one. Although an infrastructure always requires the same technical structure— such as track length or terminal dimensions—when it is situated in an uneven territory, the landscape affected each case, transforming into unique places. In that sense, the research has dealt with the specificity of the airports in a territory.

After analysing and mapping the problems within a selection of specific case studies, the second part of the research outlined several scenarios for us to explore what happened at the edges of airports, those areas that faced surrounding territories, cities and landscapes. It was a para-projectual issue, trying to define how the edges or the fences of small airports could become a place of permeability in relation to the characteristics of each surrounding context. In that sense, the research proposed osmotic tools to define the edge of an airport as a place of connection between the airport and the city. For example, through other functions or facilities we put in relation the airport with the local productive area - such as the health clinics or the production of flowers. In that way, the airport has been declined in different ways. We reflected on the fragmentation, the osmosis and the hybridization with other urban facilities. And perhaps this seems one of the least plausible operations today.

SF | During the analysis and design of scenarios for your case studies, how did you arrange the relationships with local or national authorities, private investors or companies?

AF | We had very few contacts but this was due to bad management on our side. In some cases, these relationships were created. In other cases, the research was developed together with local authorities from the beginning, such as Ascoli, Genoa and Venice. This helped us to focus the general topic of the project but for them it was very difficult to make forecasts. The development (or not) of a small airport is related to economic and political decisions that definitely are not manageable at that scale. Thus, local managers had hopes, in some cases project ideas, but these were almost always not feasible. And, in fact, these ideas were almost never carried out. For the majority of the airports that we studied, today they are in exactly the same condition as when we left. There has been no progress. Even with the difficulties in generalizing on this issue, we weren't able to activate a discussion on this topic, except for an exhibition in Venice and several publications. But some in cases, explored and connected the national research with European research.

SF | In what sense has the relationship between landscape, city and infrastructure changed?

AF | In the case where a city becomes huge, quantities become huge. Despite modern cultural beliefs, these dynamics and quantities are not controllable through urban planning. The possibility of movement coincides with people's way of life in the contemporary world. And this is what allows them to build more and more infrastructure. The infrastructure dimension, both linear and network, is the only thing that somehow can compete with the expansion of the city. A contemporary change in paradigm is to apply several additional functions to those structures that have always been connected only to technical aspects. If infrastructure is designed with certain paradigms, it can address in a positive way many urban and social issues. For instance, the public space is no longer identifiable just with squares or plazas. It can be defined through a design of certain infrastructures, considering them as a public space. In fact, infrastructures are the places in which people crowd more.

This is one of the main topics addressed in the Triennale Exhibition.[10] In this case, we looked around the world searching for all forms of mixed function. There are cases in which two different functions work together in the same place, such as the metro station that incorporates a museum. In others cases the union of different functions creates a different relationship with the urban contemporary transformation. For example, the wide phenomena of urban transformation in the informal city—like *favelas*, slums, *barrios informales*—see the infrastructure as the unique chance to improve or empower. In these areas, the most interesting projects have built new infrastructure, like funiculars, and often they provide higher value than just the structure itself: at the cable car station we can find a health centre, like in Bogotá, or a library, like in Medellín. Thus, the exhibition considered the most specific actors of our time, in which it is easier to identify the contemporaneity and modernity, as opportunities not only to make things work but also to improve the spaces. This is not an obvious concept. Consider shopping malls, they work well but they do not improve the quality of the place in terms of functionality and aesthetic.

Going back to airports, the issue to understand is if, and how, acting on them it is possible to improve a territory. In recent years, Architecture is more concerned about the localization of enclosed objects. Thus, during the exhibition, we reflected more about relationships and networks: all types of infrastructure represent a contemporary system of relationships. Airports, as well as railway stations, harbours and highways, exist through their networks. Rarely does it have a value in itself, as an object. An added value to an infrastructure can multiply its intrinsic value.

were necessary to quantify the problems at the national level. The exhibition was the way to see the wider implications of these problems and to expand the investigation to what is happening worldwide. Looking back at the airports research, I would pay more attention to regulatory, economic and industrial aspects related to the use of airports than what we had considered. Another thing that I would definitely be interested in exploring more fully is the idea of possible networks between all the small airports. The risk is that considering the airport individually, brings a unique value: as comparing network system at all. That is the relation between the airport and the city, especially when the city has to deal with abandoned airports. The opportunity to consider airports in the network is an interesting topic: what's the achievable network? What is complementary or can be replaced in the network of abandoned airports? The complexity of the issue makes it interesting.

SF | Going back to the research for Small Airports in recent years these issues have returned to the forefront but with new paradigms and modalities. How would you address these research issues today?

AF | The research on airports and the previous work on the A4 highway and the Triennale exhibition are inherently connected. The first two topics

CONVERSATION WITH
LAURA CIPRIANI

Laura Cipriani, Marie Curie researcher at Trento University and adjunct professor in Landscape Urbanism at Venice University IUAV and the Politecnico di Milano, works in urban and landscape research and design. Over the years, she has specialised in the relationship between infrastructure and landscape, with a constant commitment to research and university teaching. "Ecological Airport Urbanism" (University of Trento, 2012) and "Airport Urbanism" (Aracne, 2012) are her latest publications focusing on the relationship between airports and cities. The conversation has been carried on skype on July 18, 2014.

SF | What sparked your interest in the study of airports and which paradigms are investigated in your research for *Low-Cost Airports*?

LC | I started to investigate low-cost airports in 2004. At that time, my interest was to observe the changes in the European landscape that were happening due to the advent of low-cost airports. So, the research started from the need to understand if there would be some changes in the territory or not. At the time when I started to work on this issue, I realized that there were neither studies nor previous work. It was an urgent issue but also a pioneering topic. In a sense, doing research on a topic that had never been studied before always stimulated me. Later, this interest gradually became something else. As the study progressed, I realized that there were many interesting sub-themes. Inside the "airport machine" I identified other topics to be investigated.

One of the most recent results of this research process are the books *Ecological Airport Urbanism* and *Rethinking Treviso Airport Urbanism*. These works came from three issue. At first, I questioned if it was possible to speak about an airport from an ecological urbanism point of view. Usually infrastructure, in particular airports, are always something pollutant. So I wanted to figure out if and how to combine these ecological aspects within airport infrastructures. The second objective concerned the methodology. I tried to figure out how to work on a regional and local level on specific cases like the Italian north-east. The aim was to find a new way of working that could become an explanatory case within the "large airport world." A third reason was that the majority of European airports have problems regarding their territorial development. In fact, they are often in or close to the cities they serve or near highly weak environmental systems. These conditions are all characteristics of the north-eastern Italian area.

SF | In what sense has the relationship between city and infrastructure changed?

LC | As regards low-cost airports, the work analysed the transformation of the territory on a local scale (Points), on a large scale (Lines) and the network of this change (Network). That's why the work was divided into three parts: points, lines and network. On one hand, I approached Airports as points— at the local scale—to figure out what transformation was induced by low-cost airports in the surrounding landscape. The second part of the research concerns the transformation of the city and the territory identified by the connection between two points that are the lines. This happened by a series of transmigrations of urban patterns from one point in the European territory. The third part of the work tried to see this transformation on a much larger scale, on a European scale. In this part I analysed the airport networks to understand how they were engines of change on the European scale.

SF | America landscape architects define airports "as landscape with a complex ecology". What is your opinion about this?

LC | The airport is a landscape. It is an infrastructured landscape, in which there are many very interesting ecological aspects. Those ecological aspects affect the technical impacts like noise or air pollution (as predominant problems). In reality there is a whole series of other complex ecologies connected to the ecological aspects such as the water system or the green system. At the same time, the airport is defined in its interior as a particular landscape, and that is the "point." This landscape is given by the functions that occur at airports through the flows of people and things. Then, in that case, the airport defines a new landscape that grows out of its urban fabric and its limits.

SF | During the analysis and design of scenarios for your case studies, how did you arrange for contacts with the local and national authorities, private investors or companies?

LC | In the first work on low-cost airports, I always contacted authorities, at both the national and local levels, and through case studies and connections with the European insitutions and the Ministry of Infrastructure and Transport in Italy. [11] This helped me to understand the different positions and points of view in regard to air transport. This was at first a theoretical work and so there was some criticism and a number of issues that needed consideration regarding this landscape in transformation. In the last works—*Ecological Airport Urbanism* and *Rethinking Treviso Airport Urbanism*—I wanted to move from theory into practice, due to the urgent need to find a method that would include local and national governments in order to transform the landscape. The idea was not only to study the airport landscape but also to be the actor in this transformation.

Therefore, the first phase of the work was focused on **Venice Airport** following a request from the consulting sector of Urbanism and Landscape for the Veneto region. From this position I searched for a precise methodology. The problems in that case were that the conflicts between different stakeholders (local communities and airports) were so harsh that it was not possible to apply the method studied until the design stage. This work was then given to the region of Veneto.

The second step, however, was actually to do something where there was a tool of "informed participation". I was interested not in participation of local communities who decide in their own way but a participation through to the design and planning stages. Then in the work for **Treviso Airport**[12] we involved not only the airport authorities but also local populations and experts in the ecosystem of the landscape along the river Sile—the river around Treviso Airport. Together we tried to find a meeting point through the project. I was interested that all the actors involved, could participate in the design choices, so that they were part of the transformation. That was the idea, that everyone would share the project. And it partially worked.

Both the local population and project committees and administrations at various levels were able to create the project together. The idea was just to provide an "open project," which then had to be necessarily implemented by a precise political choice. In fact, research suggests a number of solutions and alternative scenarios but it is necessary to exert a serious political willpower to find a convergence for these ideas.

SF | You have been studying airports since 2004: what processes did you defined for the airport re-activation?

LC | One of the objectives of the *Ecological Airport Urbanism* research, supported by the Marie Curie program, was to define a method. Therefore, in the first part named "research by design" I outlined research through the project. The second part defines the *tools*: a set of tools that change over time. Some tools work for the short term, some for the medium term and others for the long term. The idea of time is one of the key variables. From the premises of the first two parts, the third part of the research involves the construction of a "design by research" that is a project through the research. This has provided for the production of a series of scenarios for the short and long term. Those scenarios for the short term must be concerted; those for the long term are extreme visions of what may happen, therefore they do not require public consultation. In particular, in the case of Treviso, the basic idea is to test this methodology and to activate this process through the project.

SF | According to your research experience, which future tendencies most commonly characterized airport development?

LC | Currently I believe we are in the phase of "inertia" and selection of low-cost airports in Europe. It was one of the three scenarios in the first book, that is, the birth of an optimized configuration. We are in an era of economic stagnation, partial reduction of low-cost air traffic and a partial saturation of the market. So what is happening is the selection of some low-cost airports that will continue in the long term. Other airports, which were basically promoted by regional, provincial and municipal institutions, will atrophy and no longer be used.

I recently started work on "Lost Airports" referring to airports that are untraceable. For any typology of infrastructure, there will always be a life cycle that ends and is followed by another cycle that can be unexpected. But the specificity of an airport is, by definition, very different because it is a point and not a line. It means that the airport never separates two territories but is part of the territory. Some of these airports are recycled, while others are lost and are gradually included in the urban fabric or the landscape, whatever their transformation is. It is very interesting how the transformation of these places generated totally unexpected phenomena that were not always predictable. And the transformations caused by unpredictable processes, from a certain point of view, assume a more interesting value for the landscape as they open up unexpected possibilities.

Francesc Muñoz is a geographer and professor at the Universidad Autónoma de Barcelona (UAB). He has specialized in urban planning and design of regional strategies. He has participated as an expert at the Council of Europe concerning these issues and he has been Invited Professor in foreign universities in France, Italy, Slovenia, Portugal and the United Kingdom. He has published several books on the transformation of urban and metropolitan landscapes, among others "urBANALización: Paisajes Comunes, Lugares Globales" (Gustavo Gili, Barcelona, 2008). He currently heads the Observatorio de la Urbanización and Master's program Intervención y Gestión del Paisaje of the Universidad Autónoma de Barcelona. The conversation has been carried at the Observatorio de la Urbanización, Barcelona, on August 22, 2013.

SF | Goals and issues of the *Emerging Infrastructure Landscape* research: which paradigms are imaged by research the regeneration of airports?

FM | There are three key issues to understanding the dynamics of contemporary contexts. The first issue is the **territory**. From the beginning of the 1980s, with consequences until the present time, there have been several territorial changes. With these transformations, the significance of airports has changed. The second issue is infrastructure, particularly **airport infrastructure**. This concerns the new values relating to mobility at the different urban, metropolitan, regional and global scales. The third issue is the **landscape**. The modern approach to conceptually understand the landscapes from binomials - like internal/external, city/country, artificial/natural - have lost meaning. Our position is to view regional airports that are closer to natural contexts, as elements of hybridization, rather than as a dialog between artifice and nature or between urban element (machine) and the field. We consider airports as a common interface, as an eco-infrastructure that provides a view of the "frontier" of urbanization. These are the major themes that overlap in the Master research approach and that brought us to organize our first workshop with the motif of *Low-Cost Landscape*—which was also the first title of the project. The aim of the first workshop - that was in Girona, while the seconded was in Alghero - was to investigate the relation between low-cost airport and landscape: having a low-cost airport does not necessarily mean you have a low-cost landscape. The low-cost infrastructure can be the effect of a high-quality landscape in a broad sense—economical, social, landscape and urban high quality. In the third workshop in Llerida—and in the following workshop at La Seu d'Urgell Airprot and in Odena Airport both in Catalunya —we focused on the emerging airports. We realized that our research interest was not only related to low-cost geography, but the new role of infrastructures in the territories. So, we have changed the name of the workshop to *Emerging Infrastructural Landscapes* to reflect our interests.

SF | In what sense is the relationship between city and infrastructure changed?

FM | In the last decades, we have simplified through words like "country," "periphery," "suburbs" or *"Catalunya interior"* (in Catalunya) those territories that had traditionally been left marginalized by the urbanization. These concepts didn't represent territories but rather they gave them a "label" to define, through opposition, what was not at the center. Since the 80s this process has changed: urban sprawl, population diffusion, the dispersion of urban centralities and the explosion of new urban physical formulas (like edge-cities or hub-cities) have significantly affected the territorial identity. Places previously without any urban content until that moment, suddenly achieved an urban value. Airports became triggers for this process especially for regional airports. In fact, due to the logic of the low-cost economy, they are farther from the city. The low-cost geography, driven by carriers like Rayanair and Easyjet, has increased the value of infrastructure centrality"in physically urban peripheries. Therefore, the airport became an urban growth machine: the airport is not only an infrastructure for flying but - with the advent of low-cost carriers - it is also a generator for rising land prices, the increase of connections to highways and the emergence of *sub-rurban* landscape.[13]

Contemporary territories are fragmented with many infrastructures. Particularly ,high speed railways, harbors, and airports are among the factors that have generated this condition. Infrastructures are no longer something auxiliary in the urban environment. Infrastructures were elements in the service of mobility. This mobility was something residual that served to link local density. Today, this is no longer the case. Mobility is the main parameter to understanding the functioning of cities, even more important than density. Density depends on mobility. In fact, mobility can increase or decrease the density in certain times. In that sense, the temporary use of the territory gives much more importance to mobility. Therefore, territories that serve mobility—such as infrastructures— are much more important and nodal.

Another clever element is landscape, as I have said previously. The definition of landscape as nature and the simplification that the urban is not landscape cannot stand anymore. **We are facing a hybridization process of the urban infrastructural landscape within the agricultural and natural landscapes**. This is an opportunity to conceptually represent the landscape of the 21st Century that no longer works through the opposition of landscape/nature and artificial/natural. We have to think starting from keys of hybridization. The territories where this hybridization between urban and non-urban, rural and urban, mobility and nature are more evident are the surroundings of low-cost airports. Those are landscapes with values that need to be managed, rather to be preserved.

SF | During the analysis and design of scenarios for your case studies, how did you arrange the relationships with local or national authorities, private investors or companies?

FM | We proposed ourselves to administrators as a creative and active think-tank. We didn't support them only through design visions, but by proposing urban plans for the realization of the projects together with advice from public administrations. We proposed an integrated and multidisciplinary approach to the low-cost geography issue by obtaining concrete results and by applying those research findings and workshop results. For instance, The **Lleida-Alguaire Airport** has built a warehouse for aircraft, which was one of the workshop proposals. We hope that this can allow for a continued collaboration.

We have been called the "saviors of airports." I like to think in this sense due to the singular work we do as multidisciplinary consultants.

SF | What is your opinion regarding airport recycling as process to create new landscapes?

FM | If the main conviction of the 20th century was to expand the city and generate urban density, **the main leitmotiv of the urbanism of the 21st century is recycle.** We are in a time of cultural change in society. Similarly for intensity and effects, was the change that occurred in the Modern Age with industrialization. We are going through a culture change that began in the 70s with the conservative *contro-culture* and the advent of the "heritage" concept. Today, we are in a time in which the cooperative phenomenon paradoxically reminds us in some aspects of the utopias of the 19th Century.[14] This has nothing to do directly with architecture and urban planning, but it is part of society. On the other hand, there has been such a rapid change in territories and technologies that many artifacts have lost their original functions. Recycling has to do with the change of use and the finding of new functions for elements. This is what happened with telephone booths—iconic elements of the urban imagery of the 20th Century. This is also happening to airports.

However, the recycling of materials or simple elements—for instance a table or a telephone booth—is very linear. Instead, the recycling of infrastructures gives the opportunity to think according to a *multi-layered* approach. The recycling is not change from one use to another: recycle means to combine several layers of information and uses together in order to generate added value. The recycling of the territory refers to the capacity to generate new synergies. Then, the three issues explored above, characterize airports as a place that allows for unexpected uses. In fact, airports have mobility of people, they have a central role in specific territories, and because they are hybrids, they are attractive landscapes. We are not interested in the reusing, but we are interested in heritage because it is a key element in this new recycle strategy of functions and uses. **Heritage is an element that enriches the experience.**

Culturally we are a generation of curious explorers, *voyageurs*, that needs new experiences. As tourists, we have fewer possibilities to find something new: everything is explored, exploited and seen. Apparently, exotic and distant places are less surprising to us for two main reasons: it is very easy to go there and there are too many people. The dissatisfaction produced is so strong that it generates a need to live new experiences. In this sense, territories that through recycling are able to maintain and project heritage in order to generate new experiences—even related to original functions—will be very attractive to global users.

CONVERSATION WITH
CHRISTIAN SALEWSKI

Christian Salewski is Senior Assistant and Lecturer for Urban Design at ETH Zurich. He is lead for the research platform "Airports and Cities." The aim of the project focuses on developing a deeper understanding of the reciprocity of airport and city development as a point of departure for research and teaching activities on the contemporary city. In all related activities, the airport is used as a vantage point that provides the globality and scale required for understanding cities today. The conversation has been carried at Utrecht on July 10, 2014, on the occasion of the AESOP 2014 congress "From control to co-evolution."

SF | Why are you interested in studying airports? Which paradigms are envisaged by *Airport and City* platform?

CS | It started, basically, when a confluence of observations and situations emerged. Prof. Kees Christiaanse became supervisor of Urban-Design Planning for Amsterdam Schipol Airport. I was working together with Mark Michaeli who was Senior Assistant and Lecturer at the chair and was involved in the *Zwischenstadt* Research, which is about the agglomeration, urbanization of the spaces between cities and peri-urban spaces. It always starts with cases: it stated with Amsterdam and Zurich. And Maurits Schaafsma.[15] had always been invited as guest speaker at our chair, right from the start when Christiaanse became professor in Zurich. And so he always told the story of the "airport city" and "airport corridor," as lecturer and we were very familiar with that. But then if you look out your window in Zurich, and see where the airport is located, it is just in the next valley, outside the border of the city of Zurich but within the urbanized territory of the larger Zurich area and it is more or less built-in at one side. And there was a lot of debate at that time[16] about the emergence of what they call the *Glattalstadt*[17] whereby the valley became a part of the city. Formerly, it'd been smaller villages then smaller towns and actually already functioning as a functional unit for a long time. And the airport was completely missing in this debate.

We were interested in all these approaches, like looking at how to plan an airport in this area, how spatial production leads to the spatial conditions, and how this very important player is not perceived or not put into the discourse at all. And we then very quickly discovered that **we were not really interested in airports: we were interested in the city because the airport gives a very good framework to understand contemporary urbanization**. In fact, it forces the observer to combine scales from the global to the local: there is no other way to understand an airport. Secondly, it allows looking at the city on the scale of the functional city-region because it is how the airport works. Finally, it means incorporating crosscutting themes from technology, planning systems and governance also including human fields like sociology and psychology. So, it is a very interesting perspective from which to study city-regions, even internationally. We said at the beginning that we were interested in large hub-airports, close to city centres, because this leads to case studies of Amsterdam and Schipol Airport. And then we thought that this is basically what we were interested in, where they are so close that you can really observe the interaction at a very good level. After a bit of preparation, we started to contact the airport in Zurich and had very close contact with the Masterplanner. We had contact with local community planners, to the local authorities including mayors. We started right away to build research contacts, to invite everybody doing anything on airports. So we worked right from the beginning to have a big network of people to discuss these things. Right from the start we knew that we were not interested in promoting airports or promoting anti-noise fraction: we wanted to do it as researchers from a neutral position, we wanted to describe what happens and how it happens. And that is also the only reason why all the airports until now were very open to cooperate with us because there was no conflict or a possible conflict or competition between us.

SF | What have you learned from the case studies that you analysed?

CS | What we discovered first is that it is very difficult to make any statement that holds generally for airports and cities because there is a specificity to each situation. So I more and more think that **it is impossible to have a general airport and city model.** Maybe there is one, but I am not sure. What I am very sure about it is the "airport-city" or "aerotropolis" models are not valid to understand it. They are idealized versions that have airport-city as a political or business tool, which sparks a lot of imagination. "Aerotropolis" is based on fundamental research that shows 20% productivity increases in city-regions with large airports in comparison to city-regions without large airports. That is a valid research result. But then it draws very simplified causal relationships as to why it is like that, which are not empirically proven. I had a debate with John Kasarda about that once.

[18] Basically what he does, he just applies the very old Burgess model to get a very old industrial-ecology model that just puts the airport in the centre.[19] And it is highly dubious that it describes anything real. And even he says himself that it doesn't exist, it is just a model to say how it could function, but then he is promoting it as if you can build it. Some people actually do. The "airport city" is a concept that emerged specifically to describe developments at Amsterdam Schiphol. We found out that it is not easily transferable to any other airport. So our hope was to give a better description of how it inter-relates, to make better planning for more sustainable integration. That already implies a hypothesis which is the hypothesis that arenas of planning for airports and arenas of planning for the urban environment are not the same ones: different decision makers, different legislation, different economic reasoning are required. We think that if the development and planning is more integrated it could benefit both the airport and the city region. And that is why we set up this major project, which is called "Better Airport Regions," where we address our hypotheses. And what we learned is we can basically only talk very well about the few cases we have studied in-depth. Once people get into depth, it becomes interesting. There are now few cases.[20] Even with the same cases, you can have different results. In fact, the airport is part of the city which means there is a system boundary that you can draw very easily, depends on what you focuses, or what you want to look at. That's about where we are

at the moment. I think there should be more cases coming up at some point.

SF | How could be described the relationship airport-city?

CS | In the publication by Alain Thierstien called *Airport, Cities and Regions* we tried for the first time to summarize our findings for the three cases. We said we don't have a new model yet, but we have at least some observations, which might be valid for a lot of cases. These are approaches about how to study airports and cities. In that sense, we have defined the effect categories, which are: territorial effects, aviation effects, flows effects, allocation effects and urbanization effects. So we try to make categories of what are the spatial reciprocities just to make it more of a base for future research. The territorial effects are referring to airfields that are large and change urban and spatial development around airports. Aviation effects mainly concern emissions and security restrictions that affect large parts of the airport area. The flows effects—which are less discussed in that article and are part of the "Better Airport Regions" project— are related to how to close the cycles and make them more sustainable. Allocation effects are usually overstated by proponents of airport development but difficult to localize. Urbanization effects are there but are very difficult to quantify and localize at all. These categories are a methodological framework that allows for a more clear and comprehensive approach to the spatial reciprocity of airports and cities, and avoids confusingly mixing up things and scales and issues because the one is talking about economic effects, the other about spatial effects, others about noise and another on governance.

SF | You have been studying airports since 2008: what future tendencies could you imagine in airport development?

CS | Karl Valentin, a German comedian from the 1920s, said that predictions are difficult, especially if they concern the future. The future is something we don't know and nobody does. So it is all speculations, which we still can do. But there is no certainty about that. But then all forecasts are always wrong in the long term because the mobility development is extremely changeable. There is a lot of talk about reducing mobility, of reducing the need for mobility for people - that's a classic topic in urban planning of mixing functions to reduce mobility. And the more I think about it, the more I believe it completely misses the point. I don't think that people have to be mobile; I think that people want to be mobile. If you look at traffic behaviour more than half of the traffic, 60% is not necessary traffic. It is leisure time traffic. I think people like to move around and they will use any means that they have. Depending on the means: it's more kilometres, and more carbon or less. But I think the idea of confining people to local environments, I think is completely an illusion. And it would be a very horrific view of the future. It's back to the very tightly, sometimes violently, controlled village structure that has a direct power relation from top to bottom to keep everybody there. **Mobility also means a lot of choice and freedom, in a way.**

That said globally there is no economic crisis. There is economic crisis in certain places and in other places there isn't. In Italy there might be an economic crisis at the moment, in the Netherlands as well. In Switzerland there is the highest growth rate in a long time, at the moment. So it is spiky, it is not uniform. And then you look globally; we never had such a growth globally, ever, because if you see all the Asian middle-class emerging, not only in China but also in Indonesia, Malaysia, the Philippines, and so forth, there is a huge growth of wealth. At least from the past, we know that growing wealth leads to growing mobility. If you frame it that people have to be mobile, if there in a more labour divided economic system, than you can find the discourse and you have to reduce it. But maybe, and this is just an hypothesis, because this is a lot of speculation now—that's not my field—but if you would frame it as people having the possibility to be mobile, and the first thing most people do once they have a house, is they buy a car. It is globally like that. It doesn't matter where you are. Even in India where you can't even drive cause there are no good roads. There seems to be an urge to be mobile.

For now, there is no other system imaginable for intercontinental travel and no other system imaginable for large continental distances. Talk about oil based fuels, if the world is lucky enough to make a transition from oil, the last things that will run on oil are airplanes because it is the only technology that cannot be replaced easily. So, in a sort of hierarchy of replacement of energy resources, airplanes are the last ones to be replaced because is so difficult to get a fuel that works at 80 degrees plus and down to 50 degrees minus, which are technical reasons. So in that sense, I don't see peak oil as a real threat to aviation, or a reason why aviation should stop. I think generally the increase of the cost of energy is of course influencing mobility because it's all dependant on costs. I'm not saying that it's good. I'm not saying that mobility is good. And if I say growth it's not a total growth because of course we are completely destroying our planet at the same time. If you really calculate, we're doing negative growth already: we are just destroying what we live on. I'm not judging that. I think, of course, an immoral behaviour for society as a whole but that's emergent behaviour also for every individual and a lot of things are illogical. And I think mobility will always be a part of it because we are roaming species. And that is part of my speculation.

SF | Have you ever been interested in small or secondary airports?

CS | Airports are like the big, smelly, noisy guy in the class: he has to find his place as well! In Europe, as Kees Christiaanse always says, it is very unlikely that any new major airport will be built at all, for political reasons, because nobody allows a new airport to emerge. Most airports are locked in their position, which means that they are in urbanized regions. And that is just a fact in Europe. Globally the situation looks very different, of course. But then we have different modes or different stages of development, different conditions, of course. If you look at how many airports have been built at that moment globally, it is a staggering number: in China alone, hundreds of major airports have been built. And for the small airports, Europe is full of derelict "wishful thinking" places which were doomed from the start because it's one thing to build such a thing, and another thing for it to make sense and be run and operated and accepted. There is a lot of wishful thinking about making an airport because it is the plan for the big city and it's getting the big money. And in the end it turns out, it is just wasted money and resources. And I think that is where *Airport and City* research can really contribute to say, "it is not that easy."

SF | According to your experience, what are the more desirable destinies for obsolete airports?

CS | An airport is not the best leisure park you can think of. It is only the second best choice: if you have an airport, then maybe use some of the area as we proposed with the "noise landscape" in Amsterdam. And I think osmosis is definitely the wrong word for an airport because there is such a strict filter around it for security reasons, that it's always an enclave with very controlled ins and outs. There is no real diffusion possible in that sense. And for the time being and probably for a long while because of the economies of scale, which is a very important principle of productivity, airports are not economically valid at all. I think there is no single airport globally that makes a profit on aviation. So what about the very small ones? They will never make a profit, probably, because operations costs are much too high when looking at security standards, technological standards and maintenance standards. We have many small airfields in Europe. Probably, you need to keep them as a reserve, if at some point you have different aviation systems and you need them. There are also a lot of military airfields, we should not forget about those. In Switzerland there are officially one hundred airports, if you count all military and small airfields, including some of the glaciers which can be used for landing and starting these small military aircrafts. But as a commercially viable thing, I think it is usually communities just keeping up the appearances: wasting a lot of money and keeping up an airport that doesn't make sense at that spot. So, I think the best business model for small airports will be to shut down.

With regard to reuse or recycle, it is something that we can debate because it is very hard to imagine any new location being opened as an airport. And we see, for example, in Switzerland that we are running out of large spaces for urban development in more or less accessible locations. So an airfield is a very large space and maybe it is really interesting to keep it as a reserve for uses that we don't know yet. Maybe there will be an aviation use of a different kind in the future, which I can't predict now. But, who knows, maybe there is a form of energy production that we can't even think about now that will emerge in a few decades and which needs large spaces. So, if it is in an area with, for example, a lot of urbanization pressure and demand for urban development, maybe you can reuse it. But if it is not, maybe even exactly there—one could argue about that—maybe one option would be not to reuse or recycle them but keep them. And the question is: what do you do in the waiting time?

CONVERSATION WITH
SONJA DÜMPELMANN

Sonja Dümpelmann is Associate Professor of Landscape Architecture at the Harvard Graduate School of Design (GSD) where she teaches history and theory courses. Dümpelmann's research and writing focuses on nineteenth and twentieth century landscape history and contemporary landscape architecture in the Western World, with a particular focus on the urban environment in Germany, Italy and the United States. Her work explores the transatlantic transfer of ideas, the role of politics, technology and science, and the work of women in the field. Her latest book "Flights of Imagination: Powered Aviation and the Art and Science of Landscape Design and Planning" has been published in 2014 by the University of Virginia Press. The book focuses on the relationship between airports and landscape, with particular interest for "Airports Afterlives." The conversation has been carried at the Graduate School of Design, Harvard University, on November 13, 2013, on the occasion of the conference "Airport Landscape: Urban Ecologies in the Aerial Age."

SF | Why are you interested in studying *Airport Landscape*?

SD | In the past, I worked a lot on urban parks and I realized that there is a particular history in the United States that links landscape architecture and airports to the theme of aerial view. First, I was curious to investigate how the view from above had influenced designers during the twentieth century. But soon I discovered that in the 1920s, some landscape architects had begun to deal with the airport because it was really similar to the treatment of a park. In fact, both were vast lands that could not stay in the middle of the city. Then, flipping through old newspapers of landscape architecture, I found articles written in the 1930s by landscape architects who spoke about the airport. And so this made me considerably curious. **These landscape architects began to question about what to do with this vast airport land, ones that were no longer used.** Already at the time, they suggested that obsolete airports could become parks. So, my interest was in airports, precisely Airports Afterlives from a landscaped point of view. In fact, in the past, many designers had read the airport as landscape: studying the airport infrastructure, and its connections with the city, it also means to deal with the history of landscape architecture. And finally I'm also interested in studying airports because I like to fly!

SF | The exhibition[21] shows different case studies: studies for the design of operating airports and the design of parks on former airports and airfields. How did you select these cases?

SD | The aim was not to make a catalogue with all types of airports conversions but was, rather, driven by the ideas and projects of designers who have been confronted with airports. In fact, many of the projects presented are competition projects. In addition, there is a predominant focus on landscape architecture. **The exhibition shows how landscape architects have discovered, especially in recent years, the airport as a designable land.** Therefore it is a show very much tied to landscape architecture, in urban and suburban contexts. In this way, the exhibition aims to also be a vehicle for students so that they can see how contemporary landscape architects are designing landscapes in non-traditional places. Some projects maybe are not so well represented because there are materials that came from the 1990s, when many offices still drew by hand. So it was very difficult for offices to search for materials. But the message of the show has not changed. It was very interesting to see how many of these offices had done several projects with an attention to the present and the future, but little regard for the past, not bothering to store the material.

SF | In what way is an airport a complex ecology?

SD | In particular, two projects

have been quite important in the change of paradigms of landscape design in the American context. In the late 1990s the *Downsview Park* competition in Toronto was a point of reference for American landscape architects. Following the indications given by the competition brief, many proposed projects acted with the idea of the uncertainty of an ecological open system. Many competition proposals, including the winning project, were based on theories related to the science of ecology. These theories, born in the 1960s, took time to arrive and inspire the landscape field. Downsview Park competition launched the blend of ecology as a tool to draw the landscape.

Another significant project in the United States was *Crissy Field* project by Hargreaves Associates. Crissy Field in San Francisco, at the Golden Gate Bridge, is one of the first projects of restoration of a landscape. For the first time, the designers tried to recreate an ecosystem that existed before the construction of the military base. In addition, Crissy Field is directly inspired by the old airfield: the park is a large surface of grass shaped by the dunes, inspired by those the designers found in old maps. Hargreaves was influenced by the work of Robert Smithson. [22] Smithson, in turn, was inspired by the view from above. Thus, he created many works that play with the shaping of the land and with the figures seen from above. So, from my point of view, there is also a refined but interesting connection between Smithson, aviation and the view from above that landscape architects have resumed.

SF | What are the specifics of airport's renewals? From your experience, what differentiates airfields' recycling from that of other obsolete infrastructures—such as railway, roads or industrial areas?

SD | In industrial areas, in most cases, the soil is polluted and usually it requires a reclamation. However, in many airports this does not happen. For example, *Temphelof Airfield* was opened to people without remediation, despite the presence of contaminated soil. In fact, it has been verified that the soil is not a danger to people because it does not affect the air. However, there are problems that remain open and are not resolved. So I think that pollution is a very problematic issue that concerns the airport. The location of airports is usually a bit different from other types of infrastructure. The airport is characterized by a wide area that is very different from linear infrastructure, such as the tracks of the trains. Furthermore, the approach to airport recycle depends on the typology of the airport: if it is close to or far from the city, if it is a military or civilian base. The contexts are always different and lead significant transformations in airports. Even the localization of airports is usually different from other types of infrastructure. In general—although it is difficult to speak in general—abandoned airports are located near residential areas. Then, their situation changes from the beginning because it is easier if the city is interested to transform them into a new park or to expand into a new neighbourhood. But, of course, the physical characteristics of the land and the structures are different. Airports usually have a certain size while the industrial zones have dimensions that depend on the usage. In addition, the industrial areas have many buildings along the industrial site, while at the airport buildings are concentrated in one part of the area. However, on second thought, although the industrial zones have been built rather peripheral, it is partly a similar matter. Very often, we treat these areas in the same way because the sites are very similar.

CHAPTER 5. POSITIONS

[1] The "Fifth Report of Social, Economic and Territorial Cohesion" presents a range of options for future cohesion policy, all fitting into the Europe 2020 strategy. November 10, 2010.
[2] The European Commission's White Paper in 2001 indicates that it is absolutely necessary to interrupt the connection between increased mobility and economic growth. White Paper: "European transport policy for 2010: Time to Decide", COM (2001) 370. Reviewed in 2006 by the Council Commission Communication and the European Parliament.
[3] See teh research by Ramon Tremosa y Balcells, "Importancia de los Aeropuertos Regionales como Complementos de los Grandes Centros Aeroportuarios en el Territorio Arco Latino" supported by Arco Latino with the sponsorship of Lleida Municipality, 2008-2009, p.35.
[4] The ESPON project "Airports as Drivers of Economic Success in Peripheral Regions" (ADES). The research team have involved the Department of Sciences for Architecture – University of Genoa - Italy (Lead partner), BAK Basel Economics AG - Switzerland, KiNNO Consulting LTD – Greece, and Jyväskylä University School of Business and Economics – Finland. The project specifically targeted the situation and needs of three stakeholder regions: Province of Savona – Italy, Region of Western Greece – Greece and the City of Jyväskylä – Finland.
[5] In relation to the national, regional and local authorities the results of ADES research can provide valuable information. ADES results have mainly been used as background material in regional plans and documents. The research findings have already been very useful in each stakeholder region in discussions with the transport ministry of these regions. ADES research has also drawn attention to possible problems encountered when looking at the future of the air traffic. The research has also influenced the representatives of regional authorities by raising awareness of problems encountered in regional airports with low or moderate levels of both passenger and freight traffic. For instance, in Central Finland, the main results have been cited in the document of the growth agreement between the city of Jyväskylä and the Ministry of Employment and the Economy, and they have also been utilized in Jyväskylä's application to a Finnish development program "Innovative Cities" (INKA).
[6] Referred to the ESPON Seminar in Paphos, Cyprus, on December 5-6, 2012.
[7] "The first 'Summer Sessions' took place at the Bartlett School of Architecture in London. This summer school program brought together architects and students from '24 countries.' The faculty included such figures as Arata Isozaki, Hans Hollein, Nikolaas Habraken, Adolfo Natalini, Yona Friedman, Charles Jencks, Juan Pablo Bonta, Stanislaus von Moos, Peter Cook, Andrea Branzi, Germano Celant, Cedric Price, Gordon Pask, James Stirling, and Reyner Banham, among others." Beatriz Colomina, "Towards a Posthuman Architect." In: *Design of the In/Human International Symposium*, Akademie Schloss Solitude, November 19-21, 2009, p. 8.
[8] Le Corbusier, *Aircraft*, 1935. Reprint Universe Books, New York, 1988.
[9] The *Airfield Manual* is an on-going project started in January 2016 during the author term as visiting research scholar at the GSD's Office for Urbanization. Charles Waldheim and Sara Favargiotti, *Airfield Manual: A Field Guide to the Transformation of Abandoned Airports* (Cambridge: Harvard Graduate School of Design, manuscript 2016, anticipated 2017).

Conversations
[10] In 2012, Alberto Ferlenga was curator of the exhibition *L'architettura del Mondo. Infrastruttura, Mobilità, Nuovi Paesaggi* at the Triennale in Milan. The exhibitions featured, road, railway and airport projects that contribute to the shape of the world and allows it to function. Milan, October 9, 2012 - February 10, 2013.
[11] Giuseppe Rizzo is member of the General Direction for Energy and Transport of the European Commission and he was also one of the tutors of Laura Cirpiani's doctoral thesis entitled *Airport Urbanism. Aeroporti low-cost e nuovi paesaggi*.
[12] Cipriani additionally claims that "the case of Treviso was chosen primarily because I wanted to study the Italian north-east as a methodological case. Secondly, because it

is one of the eight cases of airports in the Italian north-east to be close to waterways or weak environmental systems. In fact, this context is close to a resurgent river, the longest in Europe, that means that is a very vulnerable area. So the work dealt with the conflict between the air transport function and the local environmental needs - like preserving the environmental quality of these SCI (Site of Community Interest) or ZTS (Special Protection Area) areas. The choice, therefore, has not been determined by the low-cost airport but by the environmental characteristics of the area."

[13] Concepts from *suburbia* plus the French concept *rur*. Referred to the book of Francesc Muñoz, *Urbanalización. Paisaje Comunes, Lugares Globales*, Editorial Gustavo Gill, Barcelona, 2008.

[14] New phenomena, like co-working, co-housing, community buying and the interchange of goods between people, are some of the social interactions that permeating contemporary society.

[15] Maurits Schaafsma is head of Urban Planning at Schiphol group. He is an urban planner specialized in airports. His topic is the airport as a "city" and the interaction between airport and metropolitan region.

[16] The research started in 2008. From 2012 to 2014 they have been involved in the *Better Airport Regions* Research.

[17] The *Glatt-Thal-Stadt*, shortened to *Glattalstadt*, is an economic metropolis: a second parallel city.

[18] John D. Kasarda is an American academic focused on global management strategy, aviation and economic development. He is considered the leading developer of th concept defining the roles of aviation and airports in shaping 21st century business location, urban competitiveness, and economic growth. Following this concept, Kasarda works with regions and countries worldwide to leverage airports and their surrounding areas for economic growth.

[19] In 1925, Burgess presented a descriptive urban land use model, which divided cities in a set of concentric circles expanding from the downtown to the suburbs. This representation was built from Burgess' observations of a number of American cities, notably Chicago, for which he provided empirical evidence. The model assumes a relationship between the socio-economic status (mainly income) of households and the distance from the Central Business District (CBD). The farther one goes from the CBD, the better the quality of housing, but the longer the commuting time. Thus, accessing better housing is done at the expense of longer commuting times (and costs).

[20] Johanna Schlaack is studying the Berlin-Brandenburg Airport; Eirini Kasioumi is analysing Paris-Charles de Gaulle Airport; Michel van Wijk is studying Nagoya Airport and Amsterdam Schiphol Airport. Even if Amsterdam Schiphol Airport is a bit to over-studied, it differs on the way it's approached. For example Bart de Jong is doing illustration for governance approach; Michel van Vijk has an institutional approach, which is already different. Alain Thierstein and Andreas Schmit are doing comparative studies about Munich, Frankfurt, Copenhagen and Dusseldorf airports. Finally, Laura Cipriani is working with Treviso airport.

[21] Referred to the Exhibition *Airport Landscape: Urban Ecologies in the Aerial Age* curated by Charles Waldheim and Sonja Dümpelmann at Harvard Graduate School of Design, Cambridge, MA, October 30 - December 19, 2013.

[22] Robert Smithson was an American artist and he was one of the founders of the art form known as earthworks or land art. Smithson's earthworks defined an entirely original notion of landscape. Dissatisfied with the *status quo*, Smithson did not limit himself to any one form or style of art. He moved beyond modernism's hermetic tendencies by abandoning formalism, rules and traditional art materials. Smithson's oeuvre, as an artist and writer, defied convention and produced works that could not be easily categorized. He utilized non-traditional art materials such as language, mirrors, maps, dump trucks, abandoned quarries, hotels, contractors, and earth to produce his radical sculptures, photographs, films, and earthworks. Smithson is most well-known for his provocative earthwork *Spiral Jetty* made in 1970, located in Great Salt Lake, Utah.

Airport is landscape with a complex ecology.
Charles Waldheim

Airport Infrastructure: from flows to events.
Antione Picon

Operative or abandoned airports: we should go back to the spirit of the context.
Christophe Girot

Airport landscape is an experience of temporality.
Mohsen Mostafavi

Airport is an open system: it allows to redefine the ecology.
Pierre Belanger

We are now in the third life of Schipol Airport project.
Adriaan Geuze

Besides creating places or non-places, Airport Landscape also creates spaces.
Sonja Dümpelmann

*Airport Landscape Conference
Graduate School of Design,
Harvard University
Photo by Sara Favargiotti
November 2013*

AFTERWORD

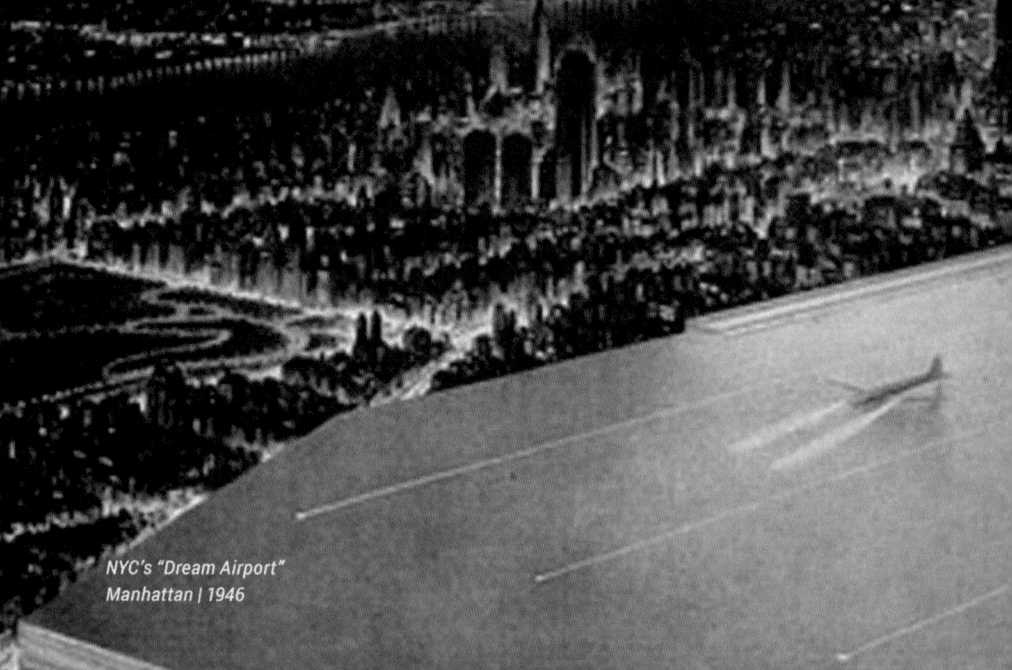

NYC's "Dream Airport"
Manhattan | 1946

"

I'm interested in the coexistence of modernity and endlessly improvised, spontaneous conditions that don't consume much energy or material. For me, a hybrid condition is the condition of the day.

Rem Koolhaas, *Advancement Versus Apocalypse*, 2003

"

AFTERWORD
AN INTERVIEW WITH MOSÈ RICCI

Mosè Ricci—Emeritus of Italian Republic for Art and Culture since 2003—is an Italian architect and urbanist. His research examines the relations between landscape, contemporary urbanism and architecture and concerns ecological performing projects, recycle, resilience, sensitive landscapes design and ecological urbanis. He is Full Professor of Landscape Architecture at the University of Trento.
In 1996-1997 he was Fulbright Recipient and Visiting Scholar at GSD, Harvard University, USA, (1996-97) Visiting Professor of Sustainable Urbanism at Universidad Moderna de Lisboa (2006-2007), at Technische Universitat of Munich (2008-2009) and of Advanced Urbanism at IAAC, Barcelona, Spain (2015).
He is author of several books, such as: New Paradigms (List, 2012), UniverCity (List 2010), iSpace (Meltemi, 2008), RISCHIOPAESAGGIO (Meltemi, 2003). His projects with RICCISPAINI architectural firm have got several prizes in international competitions and have been exhibited in the Biennale of Venice in 1996 and in 2012. His Ghella Offices Building in Rome won the European Solar Prize in 2015.
The interview has been carried at the University of Genoa, on September 4, 2014, and it has been edited in July 2016.

The simultaneous action of three key factors—the economic crisis, the environment and the revolution for sharing information technologies—is so deeply changing our lifestyles and the way we imagine and we want solid shapes in our future. Our design knowledge suddenly appears to be inadequate both to interpret current inhabiting spaces situation or as a device capable of generating new environmental, social, economic qualities and new beauty. Nothing surprising. In the history of architecture and cities the huge technological changes have always produced major transformations in living modes and shapes and consequently in the modes and forms of urban architectural and landscape projects. One of the main theoretical paradigm of modernity was the best possible spatial synthesis between form and function. Today we have the opposite problem to give sense, narrative and uses—even temporary—to places that have already a given form. And turn them into attractive and environmentally efficient living spaces.
In the perspective of a decrease in the urban growth the point of view of people dealing in architecture and the city changes radically. In the meantime, reduction, reuse and recycle seem to be the only sustainable social strategies capable of expressing innovation, generating consensus and producing beauty in the post-crisis city. Reuse and recycling of existing urban materials are coming back to be again the main field of design and construction fields interest, after a long modernist phase in which the construction of new buildings and the conservative restoration seemed to be the most convenient intervention practices. Furthermore, the recent European Directive on the subject of energy efficiency in building clearly sets a highly ambitious innovation horizon. From 2021 all the new public and private interventions will have to have "close-to-zero consumption and emissions [...] but equally important is the fact of creating the conditions for a significant action of requalification and improving the energy and safety performances of the existing real estate assets."[1] The shrinking of the market will thus have to be matched by a reduction in the building output and, above all, in the energy consumption levels.

SF | Why are you interested in studying airports?

MR | I'm interested in the idea of integration between major infrastructure and urban contexts, more than in the study of airports. Precisely, I'm interested in exploring the issue of whether it is true or false, that mega-infrastructures are a vehicle for development in our territories. In other words, I'm interested in understanding if mega-infrastructures are still needed and if they can be a catalyst of enrichment processes for improving the quality and the way of life. The first research began several years ago with the investigation of *Small Airports* that involved the whole Villard research team.[2] In fact, we discovered an enormous endowment of airports in Italy that we did not know about before and that impressed us significantly. Moreover, by studying airports we soon realized that the ways of communication and aviation were changing. The book *Skycar City* by MVRDV argued that in a relatively short time everyone would have their own means of flight, their personal or familiar aircraft [3]. At that time, there were other important researches that created prototypes of airplanes with vertical take-off. So this relatively quick change in the air mobility system brought us to think that this heritage, apparently redundant, could become a molecular network of several heterogeneous points. And that's how we became interested in this topic. We tried to understand what was the consistency of this heritage, in terms of infrastructure and architectural objects. For instance, we analyzed the quality of their flows, the localization of small airports and their relationship with the city. That allowed us to understand if it would be an interesting and useful basis for the reorganization of aviation systems in our country and within the European context. We produced a diagram that showed how with new aircraft, for example the Very Light Jet (VLJ), it could be possible to cover a significant area above the entire Mediterranean, with a molecular network of air transport that was innovative and that could start significant changes in the territorial space and the systems of flows and relationships. All of these ideas were argued in Small Airports research and have also been published in the book *iSpace*.

SF | Which paradigms are envisaged by *ESPON-ADES research*?

MR| Over time, the topic became more defined, in particular with the more recent *ESPON-ADES research*. The opportunity to explicitly investigate the question of whether airport infrastructures lead development in local territories or not, allowed us to understand that at the present time—waiting for a radical change of carriers—we are faced with redundancies: airport infrastructures were built more than the real necessity for development. In fact, economic development is sometimes affected and intersected by the infrastructure development, but generally they have parallel courses. Sometimes the territories least connected by infrastructure have the more interesting and significant development. This was the case in Finland. In one of the Greek cases, we realized that the presence of an airport was not connected to other developmental systems, such as tourism. That significantly affected the urban context. So, we understood that some airports could be improved and used better, while others could be repurposed to begin new life cycles, incorporate other functions or returned to a more natural state as parks. The topic of giving new life cycle to infrastructures is particularly significant for airports but it can easily be transferred to other types of infrastructure.

SF | In what sense is the relationship between city, landscape and infrastructure changed?

MR | The relationship between architecture and the city has changed in two ways. In a first phase, during the 20th century, there was a chase between infrastructure and city. First the infrastructures arrived at the edge of the walled city. Then, the city grew, becoming larger. Airports—like London, Rome Fiumicino and Milan Linate—were built as close as possible to the city. The processes of diffusion and dispersion of the city, but also the increase of land infrastructures, meant that it was possible to concentrate the airport network into a system of large interchanges, with major and minor nodes for spreading local services. However the most significant thing happened later, when the great development of information technologies meant that, once again, we had changed our mobility needs. It is well known that the airport networks have made the rapprochement between remote places possible with improvements—such as increased speed and decreased travel time—but with significant impacts on landscapes and environmental systems. However, today, non-material infrastructures are able to determine the immediate artificial proximity between remote places. This also allows the possibility for reconstructing environments in the network to emulate real physical spaces, sometimes even with a greater efficiency. Together with the revolution in the design of future carriers whose impacts are still unknown—like vehicles with vertical take-off, the possibility of landing on shorter runways and the use of drones to travel and transport by unmanned aircraft—all of these will significantly change the infrastructural airport system. I cannot say what the future transformation will be, but in any case, many airport facilities will become obsolete, others will be used for to others functions and many will start on a new life cycle that will make them more osmotic within the territory. Airports will become territorial aggregation points with multiple functions, like environmental, touristic and leisure. The scenario is bound to change in unexpected ways. As pertains to cities, the issue of infrastructure recycling will be increasingly central in urban planning and design approaches.

SF | What is the specificity of recycling in the reconversion of obsolete airports?

MR | From an architectural and landscape point of view, the specificity in recycling an airport is that the airport is a large, opened and punctual space in time, whereas, the space of highways and railways are linear. Due to their spatial conditions, linear infrastructures have recycling strategies that re-interpret them in segments. In a way, they have fewer levels of complexity and of integration possible. Instead, airport recycling concerns a specific object, isolated in a landscape. So far, airports' recycling concerns its integration within the landscape—the natural as well as the physical, social and cultural landscape. To recycle an airport doesn't just mean giving it back to nature, getting it back to being a park or a cultivated space. The airport can also maintain the aviation functions—the possibility of airplanes take-offing and landing—integrating with other functions and performances in the territory, like environmental monitoring, tourism, business, urban and enterprises facilities. Because of this, I agree with the idea of Francesc Muñoz that airport recycling has to be a multilayered operation. Airports' recycling may be related to different aspects and different functions, but it can also be a continuous mix of all new and former systems.

The recycling rhetoric very often speculates on the ethics of the process. Recycling means putting back into circulation, re-using waste materials which have lost value and/or meaning. Recycling protects the environment. It is a practice that allows to reduce waste, to limit the presence of garbage, to reduce disposal costs and to contain the production of new goods. Recycle means creating new value and new sense, to start a new cycle, another life. The propulsive content of recycling lies in this concept. It is an ecological action that operates on sense and pushes forward the existing into the future by transforming waste into prominent figures. In other words, as architects we do not do research on recycling because it is a good and right action. We study that because today for an architect **to recycle is to design**.

---

[1] Source: *Indagine Conoscitiva del Mercato Immobiliare*, Camera dei Deputati, Commissione VIII, Ambiente, Territorio e Lavori Pubblici, 29 July 2010.
[2] Villard d'Honnecourt is an International Doctoral Programme in Architecture, City and Design. The 3rd cycle was initiated jointly by the following Italian and European Universities: Università IUAV of Venezia (coordinator), Università degli Studi di Camerino (Italy), École Nationale Supérieure d'Architecture de Paris-Belleville (France), Technische Universiteit Delft (The Netherlands), Universidad Politécnica de Madrid (Spain), Lebanese American University (Lebanon). During the three years of the Programme, the Ph.D. candidates met every three months for scientific seminars held every time in a different participating University.
[3] It refers to the report of the research carried out by the Milwaukee University and Harley Davidson. The research was conducted in 2002. So the pre-vision time refers to the range of time from 2020 to 2030.

BIBLIOGRAPHY

Infrastructures
A.A.V.V., *Landscape Infrastructure: Case Studies by SWA*, Birkhäuser, Second Revised Edition, Basel, 2013.
A.A.V.V., *Airports as Drivers of Economic Success in Peripheral Regions (ADES)*, ESPON 2013 Project, Final Report, 2013.
A.A.V.V., *Reinventing A22 Ecoboulevard. Verso Infrastrutture Osmotiche*, ListLab Barcellona/Trento, 2011.
A.A.V.V., *Architect's Journeys*, GSAPP Books, The Graduate School of Architecture, Planning, and Preservation, Columbia University, New York, 6 Edition, 2011.
A.A.V.V., *Machbarkeitsstudie für einen nationalen Innovationspark*, ETH Zürich, Departement Management, Technologie und Ökonomie, Institut für Technologie und Innovationsmanagement: Prof. Dr. Roman Boutellier, Dr. Nadia Jamali, Karin Löffler; ETH Zürich, NSL – Netzwerk Stadt und Landschaft, Institut für Städtebau: Prof. Kees Christiaanse, Nicolas Kretschmann, Christian Salewski, Thomas Kovári, Studierende des städtebaulichen Entwurfsstudios im Sommersemester 2007, September 2007.
A.A.V.V., *La Eenclosión de los Aeropuertos Regionales Españoles*, Documento de Síntesis, University of Lleida and University of Castilla-La Mancha. Research coordinated by Jordi Martí-Henneberg, Francisco J. Tapiador and Angel Pueyo Campos, 2006-2007. Available at: fundacioabertis.org.
Addington M., "Energy Sub-structure, Supra-structure, Infra-structure". In: Mostafavi M., Doherty G. (eds.), *Ecological Urbanism*, Lars Müller Publishers, 2010, pp. 244-251.
Allen S., "Infrastructural Urbanism". In: *Points and Lines: Diagrams and Projects for the City*, Princeton Architectural Press, New York, 1999, pp. 48-57.
Ausubel J. H., Marchetti C., "The Evolution of Transport". In: *The Industrial Physicist*, 2001, pp. 20-24.
Atto di indirizzo per la definizione del Piano Nazionale per lo Sviluppo Aeroportuale, Ministero delle Infrastrutture e dei Trasporti, Roma, 29 gennaio 2013.
Augé M., *Il metrò rivisitato*, Raffaello Cortina Editore, Milano, 2009.
Augé M., *Nonluoghi. Introduzione a una antropologia della surmodernità*, Elèuthera, Milano, 2009.
Augé M., *Dysneyland ed altri nonluoghi*, Bollati Boringhieri, Milano, 1999.
Augé M., *Un etnologo nel metrò*, Elèuthera, Milano, 1992.
Ballard J.G., "Airports: The Cities of the Future". In: *Blueprint: Architecture, Design and Contemporary Culture*, issue: 142, September 1997.
Bélanger P., "Redefining Infrastructure". In: Mostafavi M., Doherty G. (eds.), *Ecological Urbanism*, Lars Müller Publishers, 2010, pp. 332-349.
Bertagna A., "La Città Sublime. Ovvero, dalla Città Sublimata". In: Ciorra P., De Maio F. (eds.), *Piccoli aeroporti. Infrastruttura, città e paesaggio nel territorio italiano*, Marsilio, Venezia, 2008, pp. 84-87.
Binney M., *Airport builders*, Academy Editions, London, 1999.
Candela J., "Airports Dynamics: towards airports system". In: *Airport Regional Conference (ARC)*, 2003.
Cannavò P., with Aebischer P., Cancellieri S. (eds.), *Progettare Paesaggio. Landscape as Infrastructure. A Studio Research Report of the Harvard Graduate School of Design*, Gangemi, 2011.

Ciorra P., De Maio F. (eds.), *Piccoli aeroporti. Infrastruttura, città e paesaggio nel territorio italiano*, Marsilio, Venezia, 2008.
Cipriani L., *Ecological Airport Urbanism. Airports and landscapes in the North East*, Università degli Studi di Trento, Trento, 2012.
Cipriani L., *Airport Urbanism. Aeroporti low cost e nuovi paesaggi*, Aracne, Roma, 2012.
Clementi A., Pavia R., *Territori e spazi delle infrastrutture*, Transeuropa InterSpazi, Ancona, 1998.
Clementi A., Di Venosa M., *Infracity*, List-ActarD, Barcelona, 2007.
Colomina B., "Towards a Posthuman Architect". In: *Design of the In/Human International Symposium*, Akademie Schloss Solitude, November 19-21, 2009.
D'Annuntiis M., "Levitazione. Nuova Frontiera?" In: Ciorra P., De Maio F. (eds.), *Piccoli aeroporti. Infrastruttura, città e paesaggio nel territorio italiano*, Marsilio, Venezia, 2008, pp. 88-91.
De Cesaris A., Infrastrutture e paesaggio urbano, Edilstampa, «I Quaderni di Architettura dell'ANCE», 2004.
Delalex G., *Go with the flow. Architecture, infrastructure and the everyday experience of mobility*, Gummerus Printing, Vaajakoski, Finland, 2006.
Dümpelmann S., *Flights of Imagination: Powered Aviation and the Art and Science of Landscape Design and Planning*, 2014.
Dunlop C., Cortazar J., *Los Autonautas de la Cosmopista. O un viaje atemporal Paris-Marsella*, Muchnik Editores, 1984.
Edwards B., *The modern terminal: new approaches to airport architecture*, E & FN Spon, London, 1998.
Edwards P. N., "Infrastructure and Modernity: Force, Time, and Social Organization in the History of Sociotechnical Systems". In: Misa T. J., Brey P., Feenberg A. (eds.), *Modernity and technology*, Cambridge, Massachusetts, MIT Press, 2003, pp. 185-225.
ENAC, *Studio Sullo Sviluppo Futuro della Rete Aeroportuale Nazionale quale Componente Strategica dell'Organizzazione Infrastrutturale del Territorio*, 2010. Available at: www.enac.gov.it/repository/ContentManagement/information/N234315289/rapporto2010_web110711.pdf
Ferlenga A., Biraghi M., Benno A., (eds.), *L'architettura del mondo. Infrastrutture, mobilità nuovi paesaggi*, Editrice Compositori, Bologna, 2012.
Gastaldi F., "Aeroporto di Albenga: dibattito e prospettive". In: Ricci M., *iSpace*, Meltemi (collana Babele), Roma, 2009, pp. 129-145.
Graham S., Marvin S., *Telecommunication and the city. Electronic spaces, urban places*, Routledge, London and New York, 1996.
Guaralda M., *Le infrastrutture viarie dismesse o declassate ed il progetto di paesaggio*, Libreria CLUP Soc. Coop., Segrate, Milano, 2006.
Güller M., Güller M., *From Airport to Airport City*, Editorial Gustavo Gili, Barcelona, 2003.
Italian Department of Infrastructure and Transport, *Notice of Address for the definition the National Plan for Airport Development* (*Atto di Indirizzo per la Definizione del Piano Nazionale per lo Sviluppo Aeroportuale*), Rome, January 29, 2013.
Kasarda J., Lindsay G., *Aerotropolis. The way we'll live next*, Allen Lane (an imprint of Penguin Book), London, 2011.
Knippenberger U., Wall A., *Airports in Cities and Regions. Research and Practise*, KIT Scientific Publishing, Karlsruhe, 2010.
Rem Koolhaas, "The Generic City". In: OMA, Koolhaan R., Mau B., *S,M,L,XL*, Monacelli Press, New York, 1995, pp. 1248-1264.

Kraffczyk D., *The aeroSCAPE - an Approximation*, Essay, 2011.
Le Corbusier, *Verso una architettura*, Longanesi & C., Milano, 2002.
Le Corbusier, *Aircraft*, Abitare Segesta, Milano,1996.
Le Corbusier, *La mia opera*, Bollati Boringhieri, Torino, 2008.
Le Corbusier, *La mia opera*, Boringhieri, Torino, 1961.
Le Corbusier, *Précisions, On the Present State of Architecture and City Planning*, Edith Schreiber Aujame, trans. The MIT Press, Cambridge, MA, 1991. Originally published in French as *Précisions sur un état present de l'architecture et de l'urbanisme*, Paris, 1930.
Lynch K., *The View from the Road*, The MIT Press, Cambridge, Massachusetts, 1964.
Maas W., La G., (eds.), *Skycar City. A Pre-emptive History*, Actar, Barcelona, New York, 2007.
Marini s., "Spazi del volo e territori. Risonanze europee". In: Ciorra P., De Maio F. (eds.), *Piccoli Aeroporti. Infrastruttura, Città e Paesaggio nel Territorio Italiano*, Marsilio, 2008, pp. 144-145.
Mazzeo G., "Meanings of a territorial infrastructure: the airports. Significati di una infrastruttura territoriale: gli aeroporti". In: *Te.MA*, issue 03.11, Università degli Studi di Napoli, November 2011.
Muñoz F., *Paisatges de la mobilitat: dels espais multiplex als aeroports low cost*, Barcelona, 2008.
Pearman H., *Airports: A Century of Architecture*, Laurence King Publishing, 2004.
Piano Nazionale degli Aeroporti, Ministero delle Infrastrutture e dei Trasporti con ENAC, Roma, Febbraio 2012.
Picon A., "Nature, Infrastructures, and the Urban Condition". In: Mostafavi M., Doherty G. (eds.), *Ecological Urbanism*, Lars Müller Publishers, 2010, pp. 522-541.
Regional Law "*Interventions for the Expansion for Tourism and Sport Airport of Villanova d'Albenga and Luni Sarzana*", n. 26, 1995.
Ricci M., *New Paradigms*, List, Trento, 2012.
Ricci M., *iSpace*, Meltemi (collana Babele), Roma, 2009.
Rispoli F., *Broadacre City: F. LL. Wright tra Mito e Realtà*, Istituto di Architetura e Urbanistica della Facoltà di Ingegneria, Napoli, 1979.
Rizzi C., "Time Table. Evoluzione Spazio-temporale del Trasporto Aereo". In: Mosè Ricci, *iSpace*, Meltemi (collana Babele), Roma, 2009, pp. 23-30.
Roseau N., Aerocity. Quand l'avion fait la ville., Parenthèses, Marseille, 2012.
Scaglione P., Ricci M. (eds.), *A22 New Ecologies for Osmotic Infrastructures,* LISt Lab Barcellona/Trento, 2015.
Schaafsma M., "Accessing Global City Regions. The Airport as a City". In: Thierstein A., Forster A., (eds.), *The Image and the Region - Making Mega-City Region Visible!*, Lars Müller Publishers, Baden, 2008, pp. 68-79.
Schlaack J., *Der Flughafen als Motor für Stadtentwicklung?*, Center for Metropolitan Studies, TU Berlin, 2011.
Shannon K., Smets M., *The landscape of Contemporary Infrastructure*, 2010.
Snyder S. N., Wall A., "Emerging Landscapes of Movement and Logistics". In: *Architectural Design Profile*, issue 134, 1998, pp. 16–21.
Società Geografica Italiana, *Atlante dei trasporti in Italia*, Carocci editore, Roma, 2008.
Sommer R., "Mobility, Infrastructure, and Society". In: Mostafavi M., Doherty G. (eds.), *Ecological Urbanism*, Lars Müller Publishers, 2010, pp. 380-381.
Tchou D., *Villard 4 Piccoli Aeroporti. Progetti del seminario internazionale "Villard4"*, Roma, Edilstampa, 2004.

Territorial Agenda of the European Union 2020. Towards an Inclusive, Smart and Sustainable Europe of Diverse Regions, agreed at the Informal Ministerial Meeting of Ministers responsible for Spatial Planning and Territorial Development, Gödöllő, Hungary, 19th May 2011.
White Paper. The European transport policy for 2010, COM(2001) 370. Reviewed in 2006 by the Council Commission Communication and the European Parliament.
White Paper. Roadmap to a Single European Transport Area – Towards a competitive and resource efficient transport system, COM (2001) 144 final, Council Commission Communication and the European Parliament.
Transport Statistical Pocketbook, European Commission, 2011. Available at:http://ec.europa.eu/transport/facts-fundings/statistics/doc/2011/pocketbook2011.pdf
Tremosa R. , "Importancia de los Aeropuertos Regionales como Complementos de los Grandes Centros Aeroportuarios en el Territorio Arco Latino", research supported by Arco Latino with the sponsorship of Lleida Municipality, 2008-2009.
Urlberger A., (ed.), *Habiter les aéroports. Paradoxes d'une nouvelle urbanité,* MétisPresses, Genève, 2012.

Landscape, City and Territory
Ballard J.G., *Millennium People*, Feltrinelli, Milano, 2012.
Barthes R., "Sulla società di massa". In: *Scritti. Società, testo, comunicazione*, Einaudi, Torino, 1998, pp. 31-59.
Barthes R., *Miti d'oggi*, Einaudi, Torino, 1994.
Bauman Z., *Liquid Modernity*, Polity Press, Cambridge, 2000.
Berger A., *Drosscape: Wasting Land in Urban America*, Princeton Architectural Press, New York 2006.
Boeri S., Lanzani A., Marini E., *Il territorio che cambia. Ambienti, paesaggi e immagini della regione milanese*, Segesta, Milano, 1993.
Bonomi A., Abruzzese A., *La città infinita*, Mondadori, Milano, 2004.
Branzi A., "For a Post-Environmentalism: Seven Suggestions for a New Athens Charter". In: Mostafavi M., Doherty G. (eds.), *Ecological Urbanism*, Lars Müller Publishers, 2010, pp. 110-111.
Butler R., "The Concept of a Tourist Area Cycle of Evolution: Implications for Management of Resources". In: *Canadian Geographer*, issue 24, 1980. pp. 5-12.
Calvino I., *Le città invisibili*, Arnoldo Mondadori ed., Milano, 1993.
Chaslin F., *Architettura della Tabula rasa. Due conversazioni con Rem Koolhaas*, Electa, Milano, 2003.
Ciorra P., De Maio F. (eds.), *(new) european identity,* Marsilio, Venezia, 2011.
Clément G., *Manifesto del terzo paesaggio*, Quodlibet, Macerata, 2004
Clementi A., Ricci A., *Ripensare il progetto urbano*, Meltemi (collana Babele), Roma, 2004.
Corner J., Balfour A., *Recovering Landscape: Essays in Contemporary Landscape Architecture*, New York, NY: Princeton Architectural Press, 1999.
Foucault M., Spazi altri. I luoghi delle eterotopie, Mimesis, Collana: Eterotopie, issue 18, Milano - Udine, 2011.
Foucault M. (author), and Rabinow P. (ed.), "Space Knowledge and Power". In: *The Foucault Reader*, Vintage Books, New York, 2010, (Original: 1984), pp. 239-256.
Gausa M., Devesa R. (eds.), *Otra Mirada. Posiciones Contra Cronicas*, Gustavo Gili, Barcellona, 2010.
Gausa M., *The Metapolis Dictionary of Advanced Architecture*, Actar, Barcellona, 2003.

Gottmann J., *Megalopoli. Funzioni e relazioni di una pluri-città*, Einaudi, Torino, 1970.
Gregotti V., Battisti E., "Periferia di rifiuti". In: *Edilizia moderna*, issue 85, 1965, p. 28.
Guattari F., *Le tre ecologie*, Edizioni Sonda, 1991.
Jakob M., *Paesaggio e tempo*, Meltemi (collana Babele), Roma, 2009.
Koolhaas R., *Junkspace. Per un ripensamento radicale dello spazio urbano*, Quodlibet, Macerata, 2006.
Koolhaas R., "Advancement versus Apocalypse". In: Mostafavi M., Doherty G. (eds.), *Ecological Urbanism*, Lars Müller Publishers, 2010, pp. 56-71.
Koolhaas R., *Delirious New York: A Retroactive Manifesto for Manhattan*, The Monacelli Press, New York, 1994.
Lynch K., *The Image of the City*, The MIT Press, Cambridge, Massachusetts, 1960.
Lynch K., *Progettare la città: la qualità della forma urbana*, Etas Libri, 1996.
Marchigiani E., *Paesaggi urbani e post-urbani*, Meltemi (collana Babele), Roma, 2005.
Mazzeri C. (ed.), *La città europea del XXI secolo*, Skira, Milano, 2002.
Mostafavi M., Doherty G. (eds.), *Ecological Urbanism*, Lars Müller Publishers, 2010.
Mostafavi M., "Why Ecological Urbanism? Why Now?". In: Mostafavi M., Doherty G. (eds.), *Ecological Urbanism*, Lars Müller Publishers, 2010, pp. 12-51.
Muñoz F., *Urbanalización. Paisaje Comunes, Lugares Globales*, Editorial Gustavo Gill, Barcelona, 2008.
Muñoz F., "Geografie low cost. L'Europa dei paesaggi suburbani". In: Agnoletti M., Delpiano A., Guerzoni M. (eds.), *La civiltà dei superluoghi. Notizie dalla metropoli quotidiana*, Damiani Editore, Bologna, 2007, pp. 160-165.
Neumann P., Kentworthy J. R., "The Land Use Transport Connection". In: *Land Use Policy*, Vol. 13, Issue 1, Pergamon, 1996, pp. 1-22.
OMA, Koolhaan R., Mau B., *S,M,L,XL*, Monacelli Press, New York, 1995.
Oswalt P., *Shrinking Cities*, Hatje Cantz, Ostfildern-Ruit, 2006.
Queneau R., *Icaro involato*, Einaudi, Torino, 2006.
Ricci M., *Rischio paesaggio*, Meltemi Editore, Roma, 2003.
Schulz-Dornburg J., *Ruinas Modernas. Una topografia de lucro*, Ambit, Barcelona, 2012.
Sordi J., *Beyond Urbanism*, List, Trento, 2014.
Territorial Agenda of the European Union 2020. Towards an Inclusive, Smart and Sustainable Europe of Diverse Regions, agreed at the Informal Ministerial Meeting of Ministers responsible for Spatial Planning and Territorial Development, Gödöllő, Hungary, 19th May 2011.
The Treaty of Lisbon, Lisbon, 1st December 2009.
Trevelo P. A., Viger-Kohler A., (eds.), *No Limit. Etude Prospective de l'Insertion Urbaine du Périphérique de Paris,* Pavillon de l'Arsenal, Paris, 2008.
Turner L., Ash J., *The golden hordes: international tourism and pleasure periphery*, St. Martin's Press, New York, 1976.
Waldheim C., *The Landscape Urbanism Reader*, Princeton Architectural Press, New York, 2006.
Waldheim C., Dümpelmann S., (eds.), *Airport Landscape: Urban Ecologies in the Aerial Age*, Harvard Graduate School of Design, Cambridge, 2016.
Waldheim C., *Landscape as Urbanism: a general theory*, Princeton University Press, Princeton, New Jersey, 2016.
Zardini M. (ed.), *Paesaggi ibridi*, Skira, Milano, 1999.

Life Cycle

A.A.V.V., *Economic Crisis: Resilience of Regions (ECR2)*, ESPON 2013 Project, (Draft) Final Report, 2014.
A.A.V.V., *Reduce, Reuse, Recycle*, Book of 13th International Architecture Exhibition Venezia, German Pavillion, 2012.
A.A.V.V., *Tunnel REvision*, Book of 12th International Architecture Exhibition Venezia, 2010.
A.A.V.V., *Convertible City*, Book of 10th International Architecture Exhibition Venezia, German Pavillion, 2006.
a+t, *Reclaim. Remediate, Reuse, Recycle*, a+t architecture publishers, issue 39-40, Vitoria-Gasteiz, 2012.
Augè M., *Rovine e macerie. Il senso del tempo*, Bollati Boringhieri, Torino, 2004.
Bertola P., ManziniE., (eds.), *Design Multiverso. Appunti di fenomenologia del design*, Edizioni POLI.design, Milano, 2006.
Boeri S., "Five Ecological Challenges for the Contemporary City". In: Mostafavi M., Doherty G. (eds.), *Ecological Urbanism*, Lars Müller Publishers, 2010, pp. 444-453.
Bunschoten R., "Urban Prototypes". In: Mostafavi M., Doherty G. (eds.), *Ecological Urbanism*, Lars Müller Publishers, 2010, pp. 616-621.
Ciorra P., *Senza architettura. Le ragioni di una crisi*, Laterza, Bari, 2011.
Ciorra P., Marini S. (eds.), *Recycle. Strategies for Architecture, City and Planet*, Electa, Milano, 2011.
Cyrulnik B., Malaguti E. (eds.), *Costruire la resilienza: la riorganizzazione positiva della vita e la creazione di legami significativi*, Gardolo, Trento, 2005 (print in 2006).
Forster K. W., "The light at the end..." In: *Tunnel REvision*, pp.54-59.
Latouche S., *Usa e getta. Le follie dell'obsolescenza programmata*, Bollati Boringhieri, Torino, 2013.
Lister N.M., "Insurgent Ecologies: (Re)Claiming Ground in Landscape and Urbanism". In: Mostafavi M., Doherty G. (eds.), *Ecological Urbanism*, Lars Müller Publishers, 2010, pp. 536-547.
Marini S., Roselli C. (eds.), *Re-cycle Op_positions*, vol. I-II, Aracne, 2014.
Marini S., Santangelo V. (eds.), *New Life Cycles for Architecture and Infrastructure of City and Landscape*, Aracne, 2013.
Marini S., Santangelo V. (eds.), *VIaggio in Italia*, Aracne, 2013.
Marini S., Santangelo V. (eds.), *Recycland*, Aracne, 2013.
Marini S., *Architettura parassita. Strategie di riciclaggio per la città*, Quodlibet, Macerata, 2009.
Manzini E., "Il design in un mondo fluido". In: Bertola P., Manzini E. (eds.), *Design multiverso. Appunti di fenomenologia del design*, Edizioni POLI.design, Milano, 2006, p. 17.
McDonough W., Braungart M., *Cradle to cradle: remaking the way we make things*, North Point Press, 2002.
Mozas J., "Remediate, Reuse, Recycle. Re-processes as atonement". In: *Reclaim. Remediate, Reuse, Recycle*, a+t architecture publishers, issue 39-40, 2012, pp. 4-25.
Oswalt P., *Urban Catalyst: Strategies for Temporary Use*, Actar, 2009.
Reed C, Lister N.M. (eds.), *Projective Ecologies*, Actar Publishers, New York, 2014.
Reed C, "The Agency of Ecology". In: Mostafavi M., Doherty G. (eds.), *Ecological Urbanism*, Lars Müller Publishers, 2010, pp. 324-329.
Sommariva E., *Cr(eat)ing City*, List, Trento, 2014
Spyropoulos T., *Adaptive Ecologies: Correlated Systems of Living*, AA Publications, London, 2013.

Tamborrini P., Tartaro G., *Design Sostenibile*, Essay, 2013.
Thackara J., *In the bubble. Designing in a complex world*, Cambridge, Massachusetts, 2005 (trad. it. Torino 2008).

Press
Bartoloni M., "Come cambia la mappa degli aeroporti italiani". In: *Il sole 24 Ore*, January 29, 2013.
Brownlee J., "What It Was Really Like To Fly During The Golden Age Of Travel". In: *fastcodesign.com*, December 5, 2013.
De Cesare C., "Tutti i voli portano a Londra". In: *Corriere della Sera*, November 3, 2013.
Efe, "Alguaire Multiplica su Capacidad para Recibir a Pasajeros Internacionales". In: *El Mundo*, July 29, 2011.
Govan F., "Spain's White Elephants – How Country's Airports Lie Empty", In: *The Telegraph*, October 5, 2011.
Livini E., "Aero Flop Italia. La Sprecopoli dei Mini Aeroporti: 150 Milioni Bruciati in Tre Anni", March 1, 2013.
Morel S., "Aéroports Fantômes". In: *Le Monde*, January 17, 2012.
Paleari S., Redondi R., "Piccoli Aeroporti Perché non sono Troppi". In: *LaRepubblica.it*, December 6, 2010.
Page D., "España llena aeropuertos con dinero público: las aerolíneas reciben 250 millones en ayudas durante la crisis". In: *Expancion.com*, October 25, 2010.
Petroni M., "Re-Cycle at Maxxi". In: *Abitare*, December 5, 2011.
Rosenfield K., "Venice Biennale 2012: Reduce/Reuse/Recycle. German Pavilion". In: *ArchDaily*, August 27, 2012.
Unioncamere, *A rischio 15 aeroporti al servizio dei territori*, comunicato stampa di Unioncamere, Rome, April 18, 2013
Vanuzzo A., "L'insostenibile Lusso Italiano di un Aeroporto Ogni 50 km". In: *Linkiesta*, January 9, 2013.

Audio and Video
A.A.V.V., *Landscape Infrastructure Conference*, Graduate School of Design, 2012, http://www.youtube.com/watch?v=BLQkslziVEY
A.A.V.V., *Air Transportation (1947): workings of a commercial airline before air travel became a mass phenomenon.*
This movie is part of the collection: Prelinger Archives, https://archive.org/details/AirTrans1947
A.A.V.V., *Fifty Years of Aviation - The Big Picture*, http://www.youtube.com/watch?v=mFtUb29Ga2o
Almodovar P., *Los amantes pasajeros*, El Deso S.A., Renn Productions, France 2 Cinema, 2013.
Anderson M., *Logan's Run*, 1976.
Belanger P., *Landscape Infrastructure*, Graduate School of Design, 2013, http://www.youtube.com/watch?v=X69sSSegiDk
Boursier G., "Chi non vola è perduto". In: *Report*, episode of April 27, 2008.
Eno B., *Ambient 1: Music for Airports*, Polydor Records, Recorded in London/Cologne, 1978.
Eno B., *Music For Airports Interview*, http://www.youtube.com/watch?v=ykJg-vE3k-E
Jonze S., *Her*, 2013.

Lang F., *Metropolis*, 1927.
Melega M., "Perchè...gli aeroporti?". In: *Report*, episode of March 24, 2002.
Monteleone A., "Piano aeroporto". In: *Off the Report*, episode of May 26, 2013
Otomo K., *Akira*, 1988.
Reirman J., *Up in the Air*, Universal Picture, 2009.
Scott R., *Blade Runner*, 1982.
Spielberg S., *Minority Report*, 2002.
Spielberg S., *The Terminal*, 2004.
Studio Azzurro, *Il giardino delle cose*, Video installation for Infra-Red Images, 1992, http://www.youtube.com/watch?v=fgdSzBnP-0M

Website
http://www.enac.gov.it
http://www.enav.it
http://www.istat.it
http://www.aena-aeropuertos.es
http://www.forgottenairfields.com
http://www.airfields-freeman.com
http://www.ferrovieabbandonate.it
http://www.espon.eu
http://www.ecpitalia.uniroma2.it
http://www.eu-territorial-agenda.eu/Pages/Default.aspx
http://europa.eu/lisbon_treaty/index_en.htm
http://www.resilientcity.org
http://urbanresiliencenetwork.blogspot.it
http://www.dübenholz.ch
http://www.denkallmend.ch
http://www.skavsta.se
http://www.liegeairport.com
http://www.nosoloaviones.com
http://www.vintageadbrowser.com
http://www.fastcodesign.com
http://www.fundacioabertis.org
http://www.rtve.es/alacarta/videos/repor/repor-aterriza-donde- quieras/1648370

Published by
LISt Lab
info@listlab.eu
listlab.eu

Produzione
GreenTrenDesign Factory
Piazza Manifattura, 1
38068 Rovereto (TN) - Italy
T: +39 0464 443427
info@greentrendesign.it

Author
Sara Favargiotti

Editorial Director
Pino Scaglione

Editorial Assistant
Gioia Marana

**Art Director &
Graphic Design**
Blacklist Creative Studio, Barcelona
based on an idea by Sara Favargiotti

Digital Production
Arianna Scaglione

Printed and bound in the European Union
September 2016

ISBN 9788898774944

All rights reserved
© of the edition LISt Lab
© of the texts the author
© of the images, the author

Illustrations on pages 54-59, 64-67 and 72-75: Maps and data elaboration by Sara Favargiotti | 2014

Illustrations on pages 116-137: Maps and drawings by Sara Favargiotti, Romina Ghezzi and Beatrice Moretti
ESPON-ADES Research | 2012-2013

Promotion and distribution in Italy
Messaggerie Libri, Spa, Milano,
Numero verde 800.804.900
assistenza.ordini@meli.it

International promotion and distribution
ACC, London

Scientific Board of the List Edition
Eve Blau (Harvard GSD), Maurizio Carta (Università di Palermo), Alfredo Ramirez (Architectural Association London) Alberto Clementi (Università di Chieti), Alberto Cecchetto (Università di Venezia), Stefano De Martino (Università di Innsbruck), Corrado Diamantini (Università di Trento), Antonio De Rossi (Università di Torino), Franco Farinelli (Università di Bologna), Carlo Gasparrini (Università di Napoli), Manuel Gausa (Università di Genova), Giovanni Maciocco (Università di Sassari/Alghero), Antonio Paris (Università di Roma), Mosè Ricci (Università di Trento), Roger Riewe (Università di Graz), Pino Scaglione (Università di Trento).

LISt Lab is an editorial workshop, based in Europe, that works on the contemporary issues. LISt Lab not only publishes, but also researches, proposes, promotes, LISt Lab produces, creates networks.

LISt Lab is a green company committed to respect the environment. Paper, ink, glues and all processings come from short supply chains and aim at limiting pollution. The print run of books and magazines is based on consumption patterns, thus preventing waste of paper and surpluses. LISt Lab aims at the responsibility of the authors and markets, towards the knowledge of a new publishing culture based on an intelligent resource management.

GreenTrenDesign Factory, member of Progetto Manifattura, is a multiplatform structure, that provides advanced design services. In the balance between sustainability and quality, craftsmanship and digital experimentation, the company operates in partnership with LISt Lab.

Cover: Sheep at Lleida-Alguaire Airport, Catalonia, Spain. Courtesy of Enric Seres

Sara Favargiotti profile picture: photo by Paolo Bernardotti | 2016